"This volume illumines the multiple biblical metaphors t[...] of baptism, offers a lucid and richly attested account of [...] practices, and awakens the imagination of readers to engag[...] ebrations of baptism with renewed vitality. The book demo[...] architecture, visualization, and liturgy are not mere applic[...] rather help constitute theology, and it does so in a way that is both accessible to students and instructive for veteran pastors and theological educators."

—**John D. Witvliet**, Calvin Institute of Christian Worship, Calvin College and Calvin Theological Seminary

"True to our social-human natures, we Christians have an insatiable desire to dig into the treasures of our past to discover the world of ancient beliefs and practices behind the images, names, texts, and symbols composing the biblical-traditional faith we practice today. Robin Jensen has taken the vast and varied array of treasures from early Christian baptism and organized them into a theologically enlightening exhibit, leading the reader through a series of 'rooms' through which one may marvel at the rich and varied elements composing the sacramental whole."

—**Bruce T. Morrill, SJ**, Vanderbilt University

"Robin Jensen's attention to art and architecture is an important addition to existing scholarship that focuses primarily on texts. This fresh approach to the topic is carefully researched and amply illustrated. Christians concerned with a renewal of baptismal practice today will find a rich trove of biblical stories and metaphors that inspired and informed early Christian communities."

—**Ruth A. Meyers**, Church Divinity School of the Pacific

"This new study of baptism may be unique in exploring the early history of Christian initiation not through authors or ideas but symbols. Drawing material and literary evidence together in a deft and unprecedented way, Jensen reveals how early Christians themselves experienced their rite of initiation. The book, like the rite, is rich and diverse; it demonstrates the variety of baptismal images and understandings that could coexist and catalyze one another. Washing, community membership, illumination, rebirth, and new creation are all vividly drawn in word and image. This array of fundamental images and their ritualization provides new insight not only into baptism but also into the ways Christian identity itself was created and expressed."

—**Andrew McGowan**, Trinity College, The University of Melbourne

"Those who are designing baptisteries and fonts and those involved in preparing the elect for baptism will be grateful for this book. It is a brilliant synchronization of rich resources: Scripture, early Christian documents, poetry, and initiatory customs. Its many illustrations show how the languages of art, architecture, and ritual behavior complement and sustain one another. The people who may have experienced these ancient places and liturgies come to life. The book will kindle your senses."

—**Richard S. Vosko**, PhD, Hon. AIA, designer and consultant for sacred spaces; author, *God's House Is Our House: Re-imagining the Environment for Worship*

BAPTISMAL IMAGERY IN EARLY CHRISTIANITY

*Ritual, Visual,
and Theological Dimensions*

ROBIN M. JENSEN

B
Baker Academic
a division of Baker Publishing Group
Grand Rapids, Michigan

Published by Baker Academic
a division of Baker Publishing Group
P.O. Box 6287, Grand Rapids, MI 49516-6287
www.bakeracademic.com

Printed in the United States of America

Library of Congress Cataloging-in-Publication Data

Jensen, Robin Margaret, 1952–
    Baptismal imagery in early Christianity : ritual, visual, and theological dimensions / Robin M. Jensen.
        pages cm
    Includes bibliographical references and index.
    ISBN 978-0-8010-4832-6 (pbk.)
    1. Baptism—History—Early church, ca. 30–600. 2. Baptism in art. 3. Liturgy and art. 4. Christian art and symbolism—To 500. I. Title.
BV803.J45 2012
234′.161—dc23   2012004913

In keeping with biblical principles of creation stewardship, Baker Publishing Group advocates the responsible use of our natural resources. As a member of the Green Press Initiative, our company uses recycled paper when possible. The text paper of this book is composed in part of post-consumer waste.

green press INITIATIVE

For Michael and Andrea,
who included me on their catechetical journeys

Contents

Illustrations

Acknowledgments

This manuscript began many years ago. First drafts were filed away, then moved to a new home, and gradually revised during alternate summers. Originally intended to serve a catechetical purpose, its function has changed slightly through these stages. It now aims both to provide a visual and textual resource for students of early Christian liturgy and to show the symbolic and sensual dimensions of ancient rituals. This is not meant to be a history of Christian baptism. Fine examples of such works have been produced in recent years, many by valued and learned colleagues, whom I have to thank for their erudition.[1] I am also grateful to many others for their encouragement, able editorial and bibliographical assistance, proofreading of final drafts, and indexing help. Among them are my husband, J. Patout Burns; my former students Michael Domeracki, Lauren Griffin, and Andrea Thornton; my current student, John Burnam; and my editors at Baker Academic, James Ernest and Brian Bolger. If I were the one to award them, they would all be wearing starry crowns.

1. Among these are Everett Ferguson, author of *Baptism in the Early Church*; Bryan Spinks, author of *Early and Medieval Rituals and Theologies of Baptism*; Maxwell Johnson, author of *The Rites of Christian Initiation*; and Thomas Finn, author of *Early Christian Baptism and the Catechumenate*. Many others are listed in the bibliography at the end of this book.

Abbreviations

Old Testament

Gen.	Genesis	Song	Song of Songs
Exod.	Exodus	Isa.	Isaiah
Lev.	Leviticus	Jer.	Jeremiah
Num.	Numbers	Lam.	Lamentations
Deut.	Deuteronomy	Ezek.	Ezekiel
Josh.	Joshua	Dan.	Daniel
Judg.	Judges	Hos.	Hosea
Ruth	Ruth	Joel	Joel
1–2 Sam.	1–2 Samuel	Amos	Amos
1–2 Kings	1–2 Kings	Obad.	Obadiah
1–2 Chron.	1–2 Chronicles	Jon.	Jonah
Ezra	Ezra	Mic.	Micah
Neh.	Nehemiah	Nah.	Nahum
Esth.	Esther	Hab.	Habakkuk
Job	Job	Zeph.	Zephaniah
Ps/Pss.	Psalms	Hag.	Haggai
Prov.	Proverbs	Zech.	Zechariah
Eccles.	Ecclesiastes	Mal.	Malachi

New Testament

Matt.	Matthew	1–2 Thess.	1–2 Thessalonians
Mark	Mark	1–2 Tim.	1–2 Timothy
Luke	Luke	Titus	Titus
John	John	Phlm.	Philemon
Acts	Acts	Heb.	Hebrews
Rom.	Romans	Jas.	James
1–2 Cor.	1–2 Corinthians	1–2 Pet.	1–2 Peter
Gal.	Galatians	1–3 John	1–3 John
Eph.	Ephesians	Jude	Jude
Phil.	Philippians	Rev.	Revelation
Col.	Colossians		

Old Testament Pseudepigrapha

Odes Sol.   *Odes of Solomon*   *Sib. Or.*   *Sibylline Oracles*

Mishnah and Talmud

b.   *Babylonian Talmud*   *Miqw.*   *Miqwa'ot*
m.   *Mishnah*   *Pesah.*   *Pesaḥim*
                                              Yebam.   *Yebamot*

Apostolic Fathers

Barn.   *Barnabas*   *Herm. Vis.*   *Shepherd of Hermas,*
1–2 Clem.   *1–2 Clement*   *Vision(s)*
Did.   *Didache*   *Ign. Eph.*   *Ignatius, To the Ephesians*
Herm. Sim.   *Shepherd of Hermas,*   *Ign. Smyrn.*   *Ignatius, To the*
               Similitude(s)   *Smyrnaeans*
                                              Mart. Pol.   *Martyrdom of Polycarp*

Nag Hammadi

Trim. Prot. XIII.1 *Trimorphic*
               Protennoia

New Testament Apocrypha and Pseudepigrapha

Acts Thom.   *Acts of Thomas*   *Gos. Thom.*   *Gospel of Thomas*
Ap. John   *Apocryphon of John*   *Prot. Jas.*   *Protevangelium of James*
Gos. Phil.   *Gospel of Philip*

Ancient Authors and Works

Adv.   *Adversus Novatianum*   **Athanasius**
Novatian.   *Vit. Ant.*   *Vita Antonii*
Ambrose   **Augustine**
Exp. Luc.   *Expositio Evangelii secun-*   *Bapt.*   *De baptismo contra*
               dum Lucam   *Donatistas*
Hel.   *De Helia et Jejunio*   *Catech.*   *De catechizandis rudibus*
Isaac   *De Isaac vel anima*   *Civ.*   *De civitate Dei*
Myst.   *De mysteriis*   *Conf.*   *Confessionum libri XIII*
Paen.   *De paenitentia*   *Cur.*   *De cura pro mortuis*
Psal.   *Ennarationes in psalmos*   *gerenda*
Sacr.   *De sacramentis*   *Div. Quaest.* *De diversis quaestionibus*
Virg.   *De virginibus*   *octoginta tribus*
Ambrosiaster   *Enarrat. Ps.* *Enarrationes in Psalmos*
Comm. Rom.   *Commentarii in Romanos*   *Ep.*   *Epistulae*
                                              Haer.   *De haeresibus*
Anonymous   *C. Jul. op.*   *Contra secundam Juliani*
Rebapt.   *De rebaptismo*   *imp.*   *responsionem*
Ant. Lat.   **Latin Anthology**   *C. litt. Petil.* *Contra litteras Petiliani*
Aphrahat   *Nat. orig.*   *De natura et origine animae*
Dem.   *Demonstrationes*   *Parm.*   *Contra epistulam*
Apuleius   *Parmeniani*
Metam.   *Metamorphoses*   *Serm.*   *Sermones*

Tract. ep. Jo.	*In epistulam Johannis ad Parthos tractatus*
Tract. Ev. Jo.	*In Evangelium Johannis tractatus*
Trin.	*De Trinitate*

Augustine (attrib.)

Mir. sanct.	*De miraculis Sancti*
Steph.	*Stephani Protomartyris*

Basil of Caesarea

Bapt.	*De baptismo*
Spir. Sanct.	*De Spiritu Sancto*

Brev. Hipp.	*Breviarium Hipponense*

Clement of Alexandria

Paed.	*Paedagogus*
Paed. Hymn	*Hymnus*
Protr.	*Protrepticus*
Strom.	*Stromata*
Con. Carth.	*Concilium Carthaginensis,*
coll. Hisp.	*collectio Hispana*
Const. ap.	*Constitutiones apostolicae*

Cyprian

Dom. orat.	*De dominica oratione*
Ep.	*Epistulae*
Hab. virg.	*De habitu virginum*
Laps.	*De lapsis*
Unit. eccl.	*De catholicae ecclesiae unitate*

Cyril of Alexandria

Dial. Trin.	*De sancta et vivifica Trinitate*

Cyril of Jerusalem

Cat.	*Catecheses illuminandorum*
Hom. para.	*Homilia de paralytico*
Myst.	*Catecheses mystagogiae*
Procat.	*Procatechesis*
Did. Apos.	*Didascalia Apostolorum*

Didymus the Blind

Trin.	*De Trinitate*

Egeria

Itin.	*Itinerarium*

Ennodius

Carm.	*Carmina*

Ephrem

Eccl.	*Hymni de ecclesia*
Epiph.	*De Epiphania*
Virg.	*Hymnos de virginitate*

Epictetus

Diatr.	*Diatribai (Dissertationes)*

Epiphanius

Pan.	*Panarion (Adversus haereses)*

Eusebius

Coet. sanct.	*Ad coetum sanctorum*
Hist. eccl.	*Historia ecclesiastica*
Vit. Const.	*Vita Constantini*

Fortunatus

Carm.	*Carmina*
Gel. Sac.	*Sacramentarium Gelasianum*

Gregory of Nazianzus

Carm. th.	*Carmina theologica*
Or.	*Orationes*

Gregory of Nyssa

Diem lum.	*In diem luminum sive in baptismum Christi*
Diff. bapt.	*Adversus eos qui differunt baptismum*
Hom. op.	*De hominis opificio*
Orat.	*Orationes*
Vit. Mos.	*De vita Moysis*

Herodotus

Hist.	*Historiae*

Hesiod

Frag.	*Fragmenta*

Hippolytus

Comm. Dan.	*Commentarium in Danielem*
Haer.	*Refutatio omnium haeresium*

Hippolytus (attrib.)

Serm. Epiph.	*Sermon in Epiphania Domini*
Trad. ap.	*Traditio apostolica*

Ildephonsus

Cognit.	*De cognitione baptismi*
Ecc. off.	*De ecclesia officiis*

Irenaeus

Epid.	*Epideixis tou apostolikou kērygmatos*
Frag.	*Fragmenta*
Haer.	*Adversus haereses*

Isidore of Seville

Eccl. off.	*De ecclesiasticis officiis*

Jerome

Comm. Dan.	*Commentariorum in Daniel liber*
Ep.	*Epistulae*
Hom.	*Homiliae*

| Pelag. | Adversus Pelagianos dialogi III |
| Vigil. | Adversus Vigilantium |

John Chrysostom

Catech.	Catecheses ad illuminandos
Cont. eb.	Contra ebriosos et de resurrectione
Ep. Innoc.	Ad Innocentium papam epistula
Hom. Act.	Homiliae in principium Actorum Apostolorum
Hom. 1 Cor.	Homiliae in epistulam i ad Corinthios
Hom. Gen.	Homiliae in Genesim
Hom. Jo.	Homiliae in Joannem
Hom. Rom.	Homiliae in epistulam ad Romanos
Laz.	De Lazaro

John Moschus

| Prat. spir. | Pratum spirituale |

John the Deacon

| Ep. Sen. | Epistula ad Senarius |

Josephus

| A.J. | Antiquitates judaicae |
| Vita | Vita |

Justin Martyr

| 1 Apol. | Apologia i |
| Dial. | Dialogus cum Tryphone |

Lactantius

| Ave phoen. | Ave phoenice |
| Inst. | Divinarum institutionum libri VII |

Leo I

| Ep. | Epistulae |
| Serm. | Sermones |

Leo I (attrib.)

| Verona Sac. | Verona Sacramentary |

Lib. Pont. **Liber Pontificalis**

Macrobius

| Som. Scip. | Somnium Scipionis |

Maximus of Turin

| Contra pag. trac. | Tractatus contra paganos |
| Serm. | Sermones |

Maximus the Confessor

| Ep. | Epistulae |

Minucius Felix

| Oct. | Octavius |

Narsai

| Hom. Epiph. | Homily on the Epiphany |

Optatus of Milevis

| Parm. | Contra epistula Parmeniani |

Origen

Cels.	Contra Celsum
Comm. Jo.	Commentarii in evangelium Joannis
Comm. Matt.	Commentarii in evangelium Matthaei
Comm. Rom.	Commentarii in Romanos
Hom. Exod.	Homiliae in Exodum
Hom. Gen.	Homiliae in Genesim
Hom. Jos.	Homiliae in Joshuam
Hom. Lev.	Homiliae in Leviticum
Hom. Luc.	Homiliae in Lucam
Mart.	Exhortatio ad martyrium

Ovid

| Am. | Amores |
| Metam. | Metamorphoses |

Pacian of Barcelona

| Bapt. | De baptismo |

Palladius

| Hist. Laus. | Historia Lausiaca |

Passio Perp. et Fel. | **Passio Perpetuae et Felicitatis**

Paulinus of Nola

| Carm. | Carmina |
| Ep. | Epistulae |

Peter Chrysologus

| Serm. | Sermones |

Philo

| QG | Quaestiones et solutiones in Genesin |

Pliny the Elder

| Nat. | Naturalis historia |

Pliny the Younger

| Ep. | Epistulae |

Plutarch

| Caes. | Caesar |

Prudentius

| Carm. | Carmina |
| Perist. | Peristephanon |

Ps. Ambrose

| Trin. | De Trinitate |

Ps. Dionysius

| Ecc. hier. | De ecclesiastica hierarchia |

Quodvultdeus

| Symb. | De symbolo |

Sidonius Apollinaris
 Ep.   *Epistulae*
Suetonius
 Jul.   *Divus Julius*
Tacitus
 Ann.   *Annales*
Tertullian
 An.   *De anima*
 Apol.   *Apologeticus*
 Bapt.   *De baptismo*
 Cor.   *De corona militis*
 Exh. cast. *De exhortatione castitatis*
 Idol.   *De idololatria*
 Marc.   *Adversus Marcionem*

 Or.   *De oratione*
 Pud.   *De pudicitia*
 Res.   *De resurrectione carnis*
 Scap.   *Ad Scapulam*
 Scorp.   *Scorpiace*
Theodore of Mopsuestia
 Bapt. hom. *Homiliae de baptismo*
Theodotus
 Excerpt. *Excerpta ex Theodoto*
Theon of Smyrna
 Exp. math. *Expositio rerum*
       mathematicarum
Zeno of Verona
 Tract.   *Tractatus*

Modern Sources

ABR	*Australian Biblical Review*
AC	*Antike und Christentum*
ACIAC	*Congresso Internazionale di Archeologia Cristiana—Atti*
ACW	Ancient Christian Writers
AM	*Arte medievale*
ANF	*Ante-Nicene Fathers*
ANRW	*Aufstieg und Niedergang der römischen Welt: Geschichte und Kultur Roms im Spiegel der neueren Forschung.* Edited by H. Temporini and W. Haase. Berlin, 1972–
ANT	*Apocryphal New Testament.* Edited by J. K. Elliott. Oxford, 1993
Apoc. Anec.	*Apocrypha anecdota.* Edited by M. R. James. Cambridge, 1893
AugStud	*Augustinian Studies*
BRev	*Bible Review*
CahArch	*Cahiers archéologiques*
CCSL	Corpus Christianorum: Series Latina
CH	*Church History*
CIL	*Corpus inscriptionum latinarum*
CSEL	Corpus scriptorum ecclesiasticorum latinorum
DACL	*Dictionnaire d'archéologie chrétienne et de liturgie.* Edited by F. Cabrol. 15 vols. Paris, 1907–53

DOP	*Dumbarton Oaks Papers*
ECA	*Eastern Christian Art*
ECR	*Eastern Churches Review*
EphLit	*Ephemerides Liturgicae*
GCS	*Die griechïschen christlichen Schriftsteller*
FC	Fathers of the Church
HR	*History of Religions*
HTR	*Harvard Theological Review*
ICUR	*Inscriptiones christianae urbis Romae.* Edited by J. B. de Rossi. Rome, 1857–88
JAC	Jahrbuch für Antike und Christentum
JECS	*Journal of Early Christian Studies*
JRH	*Journal of Roman History*
JWCI	*Journal of the Warburg and Courtauld Institutes*
MGH.AA	Monumenta Germaniae historica: Auctores antiquissimi
Misc. Agos.	*Miscellanea Agostiniani*
NHL	*Nag Hammadi Library in English.* Edited by J. M. Robinson. 4th rev. ed. Leiden, 1996
NHS	Nag Hammadi Studies
NPNF[1]	*Nicene and Post-Nicene Fathers,* series 1
NPNF[2]	*Nicene and Post-Nicene Fathers,* series 2
NTS	*New Testament Studies*

OCD	*Oxford Classical Dictionary*. Edited by S. Hornblower and A. Spawforth. 3rd ed. Oxford, 1996
OTP	*Old Testament Pseudepigrapha*. Edited by J. H. Charlesworth. 2 vols. New York, 1983, 1985
PG	Patrologiae cursus completus: Series graeca
PL	Patrologiae cursus completus: Series latina
PTR	*Princeton Theological Review*

RAC	*Reallexikon für Antike und Christentum*. Edited by T. Kluser et al. Stuttgart, 1950–
RivAC	*Rivista di archeologia cristiana*
RQ	*Römische Quartalschrift für christliche Altertumskunde und Kirchengeschichte*
SC	Sources chrétiennes
StLit	Studia liturgica
StPatr	Studia patristica
VC	*Vigiliae christianae*

Introduction

In the 1930s, archaeologists uncovered a long-buried Christian house church in the ancient Syrian city of Dura Europos. This building housed a mid-third-century congregation; it had a room for meetings of the assembly and a chamber apparently dedicated to baptism. Its deep, rectangular font would have served for the immersion of new adherents to the faith. Although other parts of the building were likely decorated, most of the remaining wall paintings were found in the baptismal chamber. There the decorative scheme includes the figure of the Good Shepherd with his flock along with Adam and Eve, painted in the arch just behind the font. On the adjacent walls are representations of the Samaritan woman at the well, Jesus healing the paralytic, Jesus stilling the storm, David slaying Goliath, and a procession of women bearing vessels and torches to a gabled structure (see figs. 2.8, 3.6, 5.6).

Various scholars have proposed one or all of these scenes as especially appropriate for a baptismal context. Although scholars debate the identity of individual figures, most agree that the images were selected because of their bearing on the baptismal ritual and its meaning for that particular time and place.[1] That is, the program's liturgical, geographic, and chronological context is relevant to their interpretation. Yet the figures or scenes were not only selected and composed for their specific setting; they also shaped, relayed, and reinforced the values that were otherwise conveyed through written texts, physical space, and ritual actions. Thus, while the following study is an elaboration of how visual images both express and transmit certain theological and sacramental values or themes, it also attends to how the design and decoration

---

1. Most recently, Peppard, *New Testament Imagery*; Dirven, "Paradise Lost, Paradise Regained"; and Serra, "Baptistery at Dura-Europos." See discussion below, esp. chap. 5 under the heading "Genesis Themes in Baptismal Iconography."

of ritual space corresponds to the baptismal rite itself, both as it might have been enacted and as it was described or explained to those who experienced it.

This synthesis is requisite because early Christian baptism was itself a synthetic ritual; it comprised multiple purposes and manifold meanings. Although historians of Christian liturgy acknowledge the rite's ancient and enduring complexity, the fullness of its meaning may not be evident to those whose experience of baptism is limited to a brief ceremonial sprinkling of water on an infant's forehead, or even to those who have observed (or undergone) full-body dunkings in a significant tub or body of water. In the early church, the application of water was essential, but it was only one aspect of an elaborate ceremony that had several stages and benefits. The following analysis of baptism's effects by Didymus, an early fourth-century Alexandrian catechist, provides a preliminary summary:

> The Holy Spirit as God renovates us in baptism, and in union with the Father and the Son, brings us back from a state of deformity to our pristine beauty and so fills us with his grace that we can no longer make room for anything that is unworthy of our love; he frees us from sin and death and from the things of this earth; makes us spiritual persons, sharers in the divine glory, children and heirs of God and of the Father. . . . He gives us heaven in exchange for earth, and bestows paradise with a bounteous hand, and makes us more honorable than the angels; and in the divine waters of baptism extinguishes the inextinguishable fire of hell.[2]

Didymus continues, explaining that by baptismal immersion recipients wash away their old selves as well as their sins. They are reborn, sealed, and signed by the Holy Spirit. They put on Christ as an incorruptible garment and find themselves as they were originally created—free from sin and in the perfect image of God.

Didymus's synopsis conforms to a several-stage ritual pattern that characterized most early Christian baptismal rites. Initially those who wished to join the community were enrolled, catechized, exorcised, scrutinized, and given sponsors. Their sincerity of purpose was judged as they fasted, refrained from bathing, kept vigils, and gave alms. When their baptismal day arrived, they were required formally and publicly to renounce Satan and to declare their allegiance to Christ. They were stripped, anointed over their whole bodies, and then dunked three times in cold, fresh water as they affirmed faith in the trinitarian God.

Once they emerged from the font, they were given new white garments, and received certain concluding (or confirming) gestures from the bishop: the imposition of hands, the sign of the cross, and a final anointing with scented chrism. In some places, the bishop also washed their feet. Finally, they joined

---

2. Didymus, *Trin.* 2.13, trans. Quasten, *Patrology*, 3:98, slightly adapted by author.

the community for their first eucharistic meal, which consisted of milk and honey as well as bread and wine.

Each act had a distinct purpose and significance. Recipients were corporally bathed and spiritually cleansed by the water. In their renunciations and affirmations, they were liberated from bondage to Satan and allied with Christ. The exorcism, the signing, and the imposition of hands marked them as belonging to the Christian family. Thereafter, they were part of the Good Shepherd's flock, athletes competing for crowns, and warriors against the forces of evil. Their initial nudity indicated their lack of shame; the white garments their restored innocence. The scented chrism imparted the gift of the Holy Spirit. The lights they carried represented their newly enlightened minds and souls.

When candidates entered the baptistery, they were ready to shed their old lives along with their clothing. The font into which they stepped was, simultaneously, a watery tomb and a watery womb. When they emerged, they were newborn children, only now free from the stain of original sin. Gathering with their new siblings, they celebrated their new identity. They had become a people set apart, citizens of a holy nation, members of a priestly caste, and heirs to a kingdom. Finally, as new Adams and Eves, they found themselves standing before the reopened gates of paradise. Once swept through those gates by the River Jordan, they would exchange their old garments of dead skins for wedding raiment and sit down to a splendid banquet in honor of the divine bridegroom.

These transformations can be coordinated with ritual acts, visual art, ancient stories, and symbols that were themselves vehicles that either delivered the benefits or conveyed their significance. Wherever, whenever, and however baptism was administered, its purpose and effects were explained or expressed through gestures, pictures, settings, or spoken words, which were delivered to catechumens, candidates, and recipients alike. Added to these were the indispensable material elements of the ritual: water, oil, breath, and light. The ritual was as bodily as it was intellectual or spiritual in nature. It left an indelible memory and mark.

This study does not try to reconstruct the details of actual baptismal practices in different places and times; rather, it elucidates its effects and meaning for those who received and administered the ritual. Baptism not only inaugurated Jesus's ministry on earth, but as it developed into the inauguration of the Christian life, it also effected certain social, spiritual, and ontological changes in the lives of those who received it. Thus this book seeks to explicate the sensory as well as the spiritual experience by showing how symbols and figures emerged, merged, and took precedence at various points in the ritual process. It wishes to demonstrate how visible images and actions, along with verbal recitation of ancient stories, prayers, hymns, all contributed to making an invisible presence more palpably sensed. Every aspect of the sacrament aimed at bringing a transcendent reality to earth, where it could be apprehended through the bodily senses. To accomplish this required created matter (i.e., water, oil), human agents, ritual actions, a special spatial context, a set of stories and symbols that could be reinforced both verbally and visually.

Ritual acts and their order were not the same everywhere and always; consequently, the following chapters do not intend to suggest great consistency in the use and application of different symbols or ceremonies through the centuries and across space. Rituals are by nature local and adaptable even though they are, ideally, timeless and changeless. Thus this study does not try to re-create a single, actual experience of baptism. This would be impossible in any case, since a written text, no matter how richly illustrated and descriptive one might try to make it, is as unlike a lived ritual as a written script is unlike a play when it is performed. Added to this is the enormity of the distance in time from antiquity to the present. To step back into the past and to experience such a ritual would require more than a time machine; one would need to become a different person altogether. The aim of this book, therefore, is to appeal to the reader's imagination by offering a collection of both textual and material data that both informs and inspires it.

The following five chapters try to do this by presenting Christian baptism according to five core motifs. Although they do not represent the only way to sort and present the data, they are reasonably coherent and comprehensive and follow a somewhat chronological trajectory. Thus, the first chapter discusses baptism as a ritual of cleansing, perhaps its most ancient understanding. In time it became a rite of initiation into the Christian community, a means to impart sacred knowledge, and a way to participate in Christ's death and resurrection through personal rebirth. Chapters 2 through 4 correspond to each of these sacramental purposes. The final chapter attends to the eschatological themes in baptism and the ecological hope for the restoration of creation itself, which seems a fitting conclusion. And although this study presents five different baptismal effects and shows how each was typified in Scripture, instantiated through ritual, expressed in visual art, or explained by theologians, the effects themselves are not meant to be discrete. Each one in some way overlaps with some or all the others. Similarly, the study does not make a point of regional or chronological differences and allows that the significance of any of these effects would have varied according to place and time. The goal, rather, is to demonstrate the complexity of this sacrament by considering its textual and nontextual illustrations, ritual processes, and ritual spaces.

Among the richest sources of information about early Christian baptism are the catechetical lectures of early Christian writers. These documents not only provide data about the actual ritual but also explain the significance of its many components, often by reference to a story or event in Scripture, which the authors interpreted as a figure or "type" of baptism. They searched the Bible for images, events, or patterns that pointed toward future realities. These figures could be known only retrospectively; types are apparent only after their antypes appear. Moreover, the figures never represent simple one-to-one correspondences, nor are they sufficient by themselves. Multiple and different aspects of the same reality are indicated through different types. The reality is presaged by far more than one or two figures. Only through the collection of various images does one comprehend the whole.

Typological exegesis does not unfold analytically. It is synthetic and therefore depends on retrieval and reevaluation of past events, signs, or symbols. It inserts the past into the present as a potent source of meaning and validates the symbolic or prophetic value of past events. Such validation happens when the type is completed—fulfilled—by its antitype. Nothing comes into being that was not foretold or foreshadowed, and the truth of the present is realized through a nuanced interpretation of the past. Yet the antitype's emergence never relativizes the type. Typological interpretation depends on the types' continuing to have independent validity. For example, the story of Israel's crossing the Red Sea must continue to be true on its own terms, even as it points to the conquest of Satan in the baptismal font.

Such an approach is fundamental to the sacramental theology of the early church, partly because the efficacy of any ritual is certified by its antiquity, and partly because rituals are symbols themselves. They can be understood only through other symbols. An ancient explanation of this principle occurs in the Valentinian *Gospel of Philip*:

> Truth did not come into the world naked, but it came in types and images. One will not receive truth in any other way. There is a rebirth and an image of rebirth. It is certainly necessary that they should be born again through the image. What is the resurrection? The image must rise again through the image. The bridegroom and the image must enter through the image into the truth; this is the restoration. . . . The Lord did everything in a mystery, a baptism and a chrism and a eucharist and a redemption and a bridal chamber.[3]

Gregory of Nyssa, a more traditionally orthodox writer, elaborated the same idea, saying that baptism was prophesied long before Jesus came to John in the Jordan. Before he begins to enumerate its types, he offers this preamble: "I find that not only do the Gospels, written after the crucifixion, proclaim the grace of baptism, but, even before the incarnation of our Lord, the ancient scripture everywhere prefigured the likeness of our regeneration; not clearly manifesting its form, but foreshowing, in dark sayings, the love of God to humanity. And as the Lamb was proclaimed by anticipation, and the cross was foretold by anticipation, so, too, was baptism shown forth by action and by word."[4] Thus ancient, pre-Christian figures (e.g., shepherd, bridegroom, lamb) are incorporated into the art, architecture, and ritual elaboration of the

---

3. *Gos. Phil.* 67.9–30, *NHL*, 140.
4. Gregory of Nyssa, *Diem lum.*, NPNF², 5:521.

baptismal rite. Because the stories of Noah's flood and the Israelites crossing the Red Sea, for example, verify the links between the sacred past and the present moment, they are indispensable symbols and therefore vital to visual and verbal elucidations of the sacrament. Baptism thus becomes the ritually realized symbol of God's first covenant with humanity, the liberation of captives, the coming of Jesus, and the restoration of creation at the end of time. That is to say, while baptism was prefigured in ancient events, its effects and its promise are known only in practice. The signs, symbols, and types are necessary to understand the meaning or purpose of the rite, but they do not substitute for the ritual process itself. And yet the ritual process is not the final reality. It is itself a figure of something that is yet to come.

The necessary union of type and antitype, prophecy and fulfillment, figure and reality is paralleled by the practical need to see the baptismal ritual in its multilayered fullness as spiritual and bodily, intellectual and physical, heavenly and earthly. It takes place within space and time, is apprehended through the senses, is understood with the mind analytically, and comprehended with the imagination artistically. Thus, the following chapters strive to elaborate its effects in these ways.

1

Baptism as Cleansing from Sin and Sickness

The story of Christian baptism begins with John the Baptist's baptizing Jesus in the Jordan River (Matt. 3; Mark 1; Luke 3). Although the accounts of the three Synoptic Gospels differ in certain respects, their descriptions of this event are more consistent than divergent. John goes about Judea preaching baptism for repentance from sin, yet he also tells those who receive his baptism that someone mightier than he is coming after him: someone who will baptize with the Holy Spirit (and with fire, according to Matthew and Luke). Jesus comes to be baptized and, according to Matthew, John consents to administer it. After Jesus comes up from the water, the Holy Spirit descends like a dove, and a voice from heaven announces, "This is my Son."

This event is the source, authorization, and paradigm for Christian baptism. The following discussion does not try to re-create its historical context or origins; rather, it attends to the ways early Christian exegetes interpreted the story of Jesus's baptism, how those interpretations shaped the developing theology and practice of Christian baptism, and the material expressions of that theology and practice in visual art and architecture. Specifically, this first chapter focuses on an aspect of the rite that was proclaimed by John: repentance and sin forgiveness. It assesses the paradigmatic baptism of Jesus as a cleansing ritual and then considers the ways that other biblical stories were construed as types or prefigurations of baptismal purification. Following the presentation of those stories, the chapter attends to how they appeared in early Christian visual art. The chapter concludes with a summary of specifically purificatory ritual acts in order to examine the ways the actual ritual contained or conveyed this cleansing benefit.

New Testament Baptisms as Cleansing Rites

All four canonical Gospels present John the Baptist as a prophet, warning sinners of imminent crisis, preaching repentance, baptizing (*baptizein* = "to dip in water"), and proclaiming the one who was to come after him.[1] The baptism that John offered appears to have been a symbolic, bodily cleansing that signified the recipient's repentance and desire for forgiveness of his or her sins. Although the rite appears to be unprecedented, the texts do not imply that John's audience found his words or actions inexplicable. Certain other passages from the Synoptic Gospels suggest that witnesses were confused about the authority by which John acted, asking whether it was "from heaven" or of "human origin" (cf. Matt. 21:25; Mark 11:30; Luke 20:4).[2] Yet, since the initial accounts of Jesus's baptism offer neither explanation for the ritual nor defense of John's role, it seems the Baptist rite was understood in his own milieu (or at least retrospectively to the authors or redactors of the narratives).

The Synoptic Gospels each claim that the central purpose of John's baptism was for the sake of repentance. Luke and Mark add that such repentance led to forgiveness. The Baptist issued warnings that divine wrath was imminent. His exhortations have the ring of the prophets' admonitions, for example, "Wash yourselves, make yourselves clean; remove the evil of your doings from before my eyes; cease to do evil, learn to do good" (Isa. 1:16–17a). In Luke's narrative, John admonishes his listeners to perform charitable acts, to abstain from extortion and false accusations, and to be satisfied with their wages.

John also announces that his baptism is preparatory: someone to come after him would surpass him. This one, whose sandals he was unworthy to untie, would baptize not with water but with the Holy Spirit. Matthew and Luke add that he would also baptize with fire. John likens this baptism of fire to the fire that burns chaff off wheat before it can be gathered into the granary (Matt. 3:11–12; Luke 3:17–18). John's Gospel lacks an account of Jesus's baptism but reports that when the Pharisees interrogate John about his authority to baptize, John testifies that he baptized with water in order to reveal another one (a man who was already standing among them)—the Son of God, who would baptize with the Holy Spirit (John 1:24–31). Without saying that he

---

1. Matt. 3; Mark 1:1–12; Luke 3:1–21; John 1:19–34.
2. Studies of New Testament baptism abound, but a recent and extensive study can be found in several chapters of Ferguson, *Baptism in the Early Church*. Ferguson's study contains an extensive bibliography. A few classic studies include Cullmann, *Baptism in the New Testament*; Beasley-Murray, *Baptism in the New Testament*; and A. Y. Collins, "Origins of Christian Baptism."

baptized Jesus, John identified him as the Lamb of God, who would take away the sins of the world, the one who ranked before him (because he came before him), and upon whom John himself saw the Spirit descend in the form of a dove. Based on these different narratives, early Christian readers would have interpreted John's baptism, on one hand, as cleansing or expiatory or, on the other, as transitional and eschatological. The baptism of the coming one would be purificatory, sanctifying, ethical, and apocalyptic.

All four Gospels refer to the Holy Spirit's descent upon Jesus. In the Synoptic Gospels this distinguishes Jesus's baptism from the other baptisms that John administers, even though they are ambiguous about whether anyone apart from Jesus could see the dove or hear the voice from heaven say, "You are my Son, the Beloved" (Luke 3:22). Thus, while John's baptism was offered to ordinary folk as a sign of their repentance, Jesus's baptism included something that John could not give: the gift of the Holy Spirit. Eventually, both elements in Jesus's paradigmatic baptism (immersion in water and the descent of the Spirit) became incorporated into the ritual of Christian initiation. In this respect, Jesus's baptism did inaugurate baptism with the Holy Spirit, as prophesied by John, even as water baptism continued to be practiced as the primary symbol of repentance and cleansing from sin.

In summary, before Jesus came to be baptized, John's proffered baptism in water was essentially penitential and signaled an individual's repentance and desire for forgiveness. The Gospels do not present John as performing an initiatory rite that granted membership in an exclusive community, a permanent spiritual (or bodily) transformation, or a one-time, nonrepeatable act. Moreover, John foretells a future baptism given by one mightier than he, which would substantially differ from what he offers: a baptism in the Holy Spirit (and fire). Thus, while John's baptism serves as a prototype for later Christian baptism, it does so only in respect to its offering reconciliation to sinners.

Other New Testament passages emphasize the importance of being cleansed and sanctified through ritual washing. For example, 1 Corinthians 6:11 starkly contrasts sinners (fornicators, idolaters, thieves, etc.) with those who have been "washed," "sanctified," and "justified in the name of the Lord Jesus Christ and in the Spirit of our God." Readers of Ephesians are asked to recall the purifying bath given to the bride prior to marriage—a sign that the church (also called a "bride") has been cleansed and consecrated "with the washing of water by the word" (5:25–26). The Epistle to the Hebrews invites the faithful to approach the house of God, having "hearts sprinkled clean from an evil conscience and . . . bodies washed with pure water" (10:22). All these texts, but especially the last, echo the lines from the book of Ezekiel where the Lord says, "I will sprinkle clean water upon you, and you shall be clean from all your uncleanness, and from all your idols I will cleanse you" (36:25).

Despite this emphasis on washing as sanctifying in the New Testament Epistles, only three of the eight baptism accounts in the Acts of the Apostles specifically mention the necessity of repentance and imply that the rite's primary purpose was to wash away sin. The first of these three, the story of the baptism of the three thousand in Acts 2, followed a call to repentance. When the crowd asked Peter, "What shall we do?" he answered, "Repent, and be baptized every one of you in the name of Jesus Christ so that your sins may be forgiven; and you will receive the gift of the Holy Spirit" (2:38). Although Acts' first report of Ananias's baptizing Saul (Paul) is vague regarding the rite's purpose (9:17–18), in Paul's retelling (22:16), it was clearly a rite of sin remission. The baptism of Cornelius and his household (10:42–48) brought about the forgiveness of sins as well.

By contrast, the effects of Philip's baptism of Simon and the Samaritans (8:9–14) or his baptism of the Ethiopian court official (8:26–29) are unspecified. This is also the case in the baptisms of Lydia (16:15), Paul and Silas's jailers (16:30–33), and the household of Crispus (18:8). Those accounts suggest that the rite's foremost purpose is to demonstrate the candidate's belief in the good news of the kingdom of God and allegiance to the name of Jesus.

Jesus's Baptism as a Cleansing Rite in Early Christian Writings

Despite John the Baptist's proclamation that his baptism would be superseded, early Christian writers understood John's baptism as more than a provisional or preparatory rite. This is primarily because he baptized Jesus. For example, although Basil of Caesarea describes John's baptism of others as a preliminary ritual, he judges Jesus's baptism as the fulfilled and paradigmatic act. John's baptisms signified simple repudiation of sin; Jesus's baptism effected union with God.[3] And while such a view could have justified supplanting water (cleansing) baptism for some kind of Spirit baptism, most early theologians and catechists continued to emphasize water immersion as a means—and demonstration—of sin forgiveness.[4] Understanding the rite as retaining this original purpose raised a particular question, however: If baptism was the means by which sinners could be cleansed of sin, then was Jesus a sinner who similarly required cleansing and forgiveness? If not, what other purpose did Jesus's baptism serve?

Did Jesus Need Baptism?

If baptism was for sinners, why did Jesus seek it? This awkward question appears implicitly, even prior to the final stages of textual redaction in the

---

3. Basil of Caesarea, *Bapt.* 1.

4. Although some Christians do seem to have believed that water baptism was no longer necessary. See discussion of waterless baptism in chap. 3, under the heading "Early Controversies about Water and Spirit Baptism."

Gospel of Matthew, where John is resistant to baptizing Jesus: "I need to be baptized by you, and do you come to me?" (Matt. 3:14). Jesus answers enigmatically that he should receive baptism because "it is proper in this way to fulfill all righteousness" (Matt. 3:15). This was apparently not a completely satisfactory clarification, for the question surfaced again in early Christian documents, as well as in fragments of two apocryphal gospels, the *Gospel of the Hebrews* and the *Gospel of the Ebionites* (both are found in later orthodox polemics against various heresies).[5] While the latter is a gloss on the above-cited passage in Matthew, the former elaborates. It describes Jesus as initially resisting the suggestion of Mary and his brothers that they should go to be baptized by John for the remission of sins. He asks, rather, what sin he has committed that he should need it.[6]

Early theologians also recognized the problem and tried to resolve it. The troubling implication (that Jesus was a repentant sinner) needed to be addressed, especially at a time when critics of the Jesus movement were raising questions about the origins and character of its savior figure. For example, Ignatius of Antioch cites Jesus's explanation that he sought baptism "so that all righteousness might be fulfilled" and adds a new idea: that Jesus submitted to baptism in order to cleanse the water.[7] This assertion, that Jesus was baptized in order to sanctify the water of the Jordan and thereby all future baptismal water, became standard.[8]

Justin Martyr proposes a different solution. He asserts that Jesus's baptism was not for his own sake (i.e., to be cleansed of personal transgression) but so that he might be revealed to the world and publicly identified as the Messiah (as opposed to being merely Jesus, son of the carpenter Joseph). This revelation was accomplished through the descent of the Spirit and the divine proclamation, "This is my Son" (Matt. 3:17). Justin thereby repudiates any suggestion that Jesus became the Messiah only at his baptism, when God adopted him as his Son and (by God's spoken words and the dove's descent) was endowed with divine power. Instead, Justin points out that the magi had already recognized Jesus's divinity at his nativity. Just as he condescended to birth and suffered crucifixion, Jesus submitted to baptism in order to enter, transform, and redeem the human race from the power of sin and death. By his baptism he proved that he was the Christ who had come to save humankind.[9]

Irenaeus similarly argues that the Spirit descended upon Jesus at his baptism and, against the gnostics, not on some other divine being or the so-called

5. *Gos. Heb.* as quoted by Jerome, *Pelag.* 3.2; *Gos. Eb.* as cited in Epiphanius, *Pan.* 30.13.

6. As cited by Jerome, *Pelag.* 3.2; the relevant fragment from the *Gos. Eb.* was quoted by Epiphanius, *Pan.* 30.13.7–8. For the texts, see *ANT*, 13, 15.

7. Ign., *Eph.* 18.2; Ign., *Smyrn.* 1.

8. See, e.g., Ambrose, *Sacr.* 1.18; Gregory of Nazianzus, *Or.* 38.16, 39.15; Ephrem, *Epiph.* 6.3; and the *Odes Sol.* 24.7.

9. Justin Martyr, *Dial.* 88.

superior savior. Thus, like Justin, Irenaeus sees this event not as the inception of Jesus's messianic identity but as the inauguration of his public ministry. The Spirit's descent upon the Son in his human incarnation declared his identity. Jesus's baptism further signaled his willingness to be fully human and his desire to renew humanity through his becoming one with it.[10]

By contrast with Irenaeus's emphasis on—and explanation for—the Spirit's descent, Tertullian simply asserts that Jesus was baptized even though he had nothing to repent of.[11] Tertullian may have intended to refute a troublesome teaching in Carthage. The third-century *Treatise on Rebaptism*, written by an anonymous African, cites a heretical book titled *The Preaching of Paul*, in which, contrary to Scripture, Christ confesses personal sin and is unwillingly compelled by his mother to accept John's baptism.[12] This apocryphal text has been lost, but it bears similarities to the above-mentioned *Gospel of the Hebrews*.[13]

Jesus's Baptism as Cleansing and Sanctifying Water

Fourth-century writers tend to repeat the older explanations for why Jesus was baptized. Like Ignatius, Cyril of Jerusalem explains that Christ did not receive baptism for remission of sins (since he was without sin), but he received it so that he could cleanse and sanctify water for the sake of those who would follow him.[14] Citing Luke 10:18–19, Cyril says that when Jesus descended into the water, he trod on Satan. This foreshadowed his later giving his disciples a similar power over snakes, scorpions, and all evil powers.[15] Cyril also claims, citing Psalm 114:3 and Joshua 3:13–17, that the Jordan received Jesus "without fear," although when he entered, the river turned back and stopped flowing, rising up in a heap.[16] Ambrose, remarking on these same biblical texts, explains that this river alone, among bodies of water, rises and turns back. Likewise, the person descending into it rises and turns back to God, the source of all life.[17]

Both Jerome and Peter Chrysologus refer to this claim that the Jordan rose up and turned back. In a homily, apparently inspired by his visit to the actual

---

10. Irenaeus, *Haer.* 3.17.1

11. Tertullian, *Bapt.* 12. Within a longer discussion on whether John's baptism was from heaven or was only preparatory, Tertullian argues that John's baptism was made complete and salvific in Christ's death, resurrection, and ascension.

12. Anon., *Rebapt.* 17

13. Clement of Alexandria mentions a book titled *The Preaching of Peter* (*Periodoi Petrou*) in four places, in his *Strom.* 1.29.182; 6.5.39–44; 6.6.48; 6.15.128—possibly the same lost document.

14. Cyril of Jerusalem, *Cat.* 3.1–5; 11, "Jesus sanctified baptism when he himself was baptized."

15. Cyril of Jerusalem, *Cat.* 3.11 cont.

16. Cyril of Jerusalem, *Cat.* 10.11; 12.15.

17. "*Solus Iordanis retrorsum conversus est*," according to Ambrose, *Psal.* 61.32 (CSEL 64:396). See also Gregory of Nyssa, *Diem lum.*

site of Jesus's baptism in the Jordan, Jerome expounds, "The Jordan River that dried up when Joshua led the Israelites into the Land of Promise now longed to gather together all its waters in one place, if it could, to bathe the body of the Lord."[18] Peter Chrysologus, preaching on the Feast of Epiphany, explains why the Jordan, which fled at the presence of the ark of the covenant, did not similarly flee at the presence of the whole Trinity at Jesus's baptism. He says the one who shows true homage and deference ceases to be fearful.[19] Peter's imagery may have inspired the iconography of the Jordan as witness to Christ's baptism in the Orthodox Baptistery of Ravenna, built by his predecessor, Neon, but decorated during the tenure of his successor, Ursus.

The question of why Jesus was baptized was central to the early fifth-century controversies surrounding the person and work of Jesus as Savior. Theodore of Mopsuestia asserts that Jesus received John's baptism not as a sign of repentance (he did not need it since he was free of sin) but rather in anticipation of "our baptism," which confers the Spirit, establishes righteousness, and leads to the transformation of the human state.[20] Differing from Theodore's christological emphasis on Jesus as a model of obedience, Cyril of Alexandria argues that Christ received baptism in order to begin the sanctification of all of human nature in and through his personal, physical descent into the water.[21]

However they resolved the issue of why Jesus was baptized, early Christian writers never doubted that the sacrament of baptism cleansed the recipient of sin—a benefit primarily conveyed by the liturgical action of immersion in water. The cleansing was not merely a washing away of inherited or personal sin; it also brought healing, both to individuals and to humanity as a whole. Thus, as an act of solidarity with humanity, Jesus's baptism modeled submission to God. At the same time, by assuming the fallen and sinful human race through his incarnation, Christ inaugurated its redemptive healing.

Eastern theology understood this divine condescension to be essential to humanity's salvation. Narsai, a fifth-century Syrian poet, wrote several baptismal homilies, one of them titled "On the Epiphany of Our Lord." Here he provides Jesus with an eloquent reply to the question of why he must bathe his majestic glory in ordinary water:

> Let it be so! I am being baptized as one deficient and in need of mercy,
> so that I may fill up in my person what is lacking to the human race.

18. Jerome, *Hom.* 89, trans. Ewald, *Homilies of St. Jerome*, 2:230. The mentions of the Jordan turning back or rising up in the Hebrew Scriptures (Ps. 114:3 and Josh. 3:13–17) led to a tradition that the Jordan "stopped" at John's command while Jesus was being baptized.

19. Peter Chrysologus, *Serm.* 160.4.

20. Theodore of Mopsuestia, *Bapt. hom.* 3.22–24.

21. Cyril of Alexandria, *Dial. Trin.* 5.591, and parallel arguments in Lactantius, *Inst.* 4.15. For an important discussion of the problem of Jesus's being baptized for sin, see Wilken, "Interpretation of the Baptism of Jesus"; Vigne, *Christ au Jourdain*, 161; and McDonnell, *Baptism of Jesus*, 19–25.

From the same race that has succumbed to sin I am also.
Let it be so! I am paying for the bond that Adam wrote in Eden.
From the same clay that passions have overwhelmed is my structure.
Let it be so! I am heating our weak clay in the water of the Spirit.
I am from the same lineage that death has swallowed and defrauded of
    its life.
Let it be so! I am descending in mystery into the water and raising it
    up.
I am a member of the race that is captive to the evil one of its own
    accord.
I will go forth to bring back our captive race from the rebel.
A bond of death my forefathers wrote out and succumbed to sin;
and I have made an agreement that I will pay for it in mystery first of
    all. . . .
If I do not scour away bodily filth in my own person, the body will not
    be purified;
and if it does not descend with me to baptism, it will not receive
    pardon.[22]

Here Narsai offers the reason for Jesus's baptism and moreover explains how it initiated human redemption and established both the element and the ritual that instantiates it.

Jesus's Baptism in Early Christian Art

Baptism scenes, dated from the third through the sixth centuries, have been found among wall paintings, carved in relief on sarcophagi and ivories, and depicted in mosaics (figs. 1.1, 1.2, 2.1, 3.8, 5.1). Most of these depictions appear to show Christ's baptism by John the Baptist, although certain details vary from the presentation of the story in the Gospel narratives. For example, Christ ordinarily is shown as a small, naked youth standing up to his ankles in running water. John is adult sized by comparison. In many of these images John wears a garment made from an animal skin (see figs. 1.7, 2.1, 3.8); in others he wears a short, one-shouldered tunic, and in a few he wears a long tunic and pallium or only the pallium, following the style of the Stoic philosopher (see figs. 1.1, 1.2, 2.4, 3.7). In almost every instance, John places his right hand on the top of Jesus's head, a gesture that suggests either the baptizer's pushing the candidate under the water or the imposition of hands—a postbaptismal act performed by the bishop and usually associated with the giving of the Holy Spirit (cf. 2 Tim. 1:6). A dove usually appears in the composition as well, a detail taken from the biblical narrative that also

22. Narsai, *Hom. Epiph.* 2.245–62, trans. McLeod, *Narsai's Metrical Homilies*, 85–87, slightly adapted by author.

Figure 1.1. Detail of Jesus being baptized by John. Sarcophagus, Sta. Maria Antiqua, Rome. Late third century. (Photo by author.)

Figure 1.2. Jesus baptized by John. Painting, catacomb of Peter and Marcellinus, Rome. Early fourth century. (Photo © Estelle Brettmann, The International Catacomb Society.)

strengthens the connection of the placement of John's hand with the post-immersion descent of the Spirit.

The discontinuities between the biblical narrative and the iconography have caused problems for interpreters. Although the text says nothing about whether Jesus was baptized in the nude, he almost certainly was not a small child (cf. Luke 3:23). John the Baptist was neither a bishop nor the mediator of the Holy Spirit in the narratives. Because of these divergences, scholars have argued that some of these images portray an ordinary Christian baptism (the characters are then a neophyte and a bishop), while others (those in which John wears an animal skin) represent Jesus's baptism.[23] This explanation fails, however, because in some of the former cases the baptizer is clearly not a bishop but John, and in some of the latter cases the baptizer is wearing a knee-length tunic and thus not garbed like a bishop. The outdoor setting and the appearance of the dove make little sense in a depiction of an "ordinary" Christian baptism, unless the imagery conflates the baptism of Jesus with the baptism of a neophyte, thus alluding to both. Jesus's baptism by John was, after all, the prototype for all subsequent Christian baptisms. In this respect,

23. See Fausone, *Die Taufe in der frühchristlicher Sepulkralkunst*; and Masseron, *Saint Jean Baptiste dans l'art.*

depicting the recipient as a child is not a departure from narrative tradition but rather shows the newly baptized as having regained a childlike innocence through the remission of sins.[24]

The funerary context of many of these images (catacombs and sarcophagi) also bears upon their interpretation. The iconography implies that the deceased had received baptism and, now released from the consequences of sin, looks forward to a blessed afterlife in heaven. The dual image of Jesus's and a neophyte's baptism links sacred narrative with ritual practice and transmits the essential idea that in baptism the reborn Christian is forgiven, purified, and joined symbolically to Jesus, who is the prototypical recipient and model.

Other Biblical Figures of Baptismal Cleansing and Healing

Early Christian exegetes believed that certain biblical narratives (from both the Old and the New Testaments) signified the church's developed baptismal practice. The widely-practiced form of typological interpretation viewed Scripture as having embedded symbols or types prefiguring future events, individuals, or rituals. For example, Abraham's binding of Isaac foreshadowed Christ's self-offering on the cross, and Melchizedek's offering of bread and wine signified the eucharistic meal. Basil of Caesarea explains how this kind of interpretation worked: "The nature of the divine is very frequently represented by the rough and shadowy outlines of the types; but because divine things are prefigured by small and human things, it is obvious that we must not therefore conclude the divine nature to be small. The type is an exhibition of things expected, and gives an imitative anticipation of the future."[25]

In practice, almost any narrative that involved water could be a type of baptism. Tertullian, for example, regards the account of creation (Gen. 1), the flood (Gen. 7), Moses's making the water sweet and striking the rock in the wilderness (Exod. 15, 17), the wedding at Cana (John 2), Jesus meeting the Samaritan woman (John 4:14), Jesus walking on the water (Matt. 14:25), Jesus crossing the Jordan (Matt. 14:32), Jesus washing the disciples' feet (John 13:5), Pilate washing his hands (Matt. 27:24), and the water spilling from the crucified Jesus's side (John 19:34) as allusions to baptism.[26] Cyprian makes the straightforward assertion that every reference to water in the Holy Scriptures is a prophetic allusion to baptism.[27]

---

24. On this point, see the discussion in chap. 4 under the heading "Nudes and Small Figures in Early Christian Art."

25. Basil, *Spir. Sanct.* 14, NPNF[2], 7:19.

26. Tertullian, *Bapt.* 4, 9.

27. Cyprian, *Ep.* 63.8.1. On specific texts as prefiguring baptism, see Dassmann, *Sünden-vergebung durch Taufe*, 76–103; Daniélou, *Bible and the Liturgy*; Daniélou, *From Shadows to Reality*; and Lundberg, *La typologie baptismale*.

More than general references, these different figures refer to particular benefits or aspects of the rite. Among all the baptismal figures, the ones that were most often interpreted as exemplifying baptism's cleansing benefit were the stories of the flood (Gen. 7) and of Moses and the Israelites crossing the Red Sea (Exod. 14). Likewise, three healing stories—Naaman (2 Kings 5), the healing of the paralytic (John 5), and the man born blind (John 9)—attest not only to baptismal purification but also to its healing power.

While much of this exegetical tradition appears in early Christian written documents (theological treatises, catechetical lectures, homilies, and even poetry), it also appears in visual art. This is especially clear when apparently distinct narrative images are brought together in one composition. They are juxtaposed because of their symbolic rather than their illustrative purpose. The selections and arrangements of different scenes are neither random nor meaningless. Similarly, visual and textual exegesis are striking and mutually illuminating when juxtaposed with each other.[28] Viewed together, they reinforce each other and provide a more complex view of what baptism meant to early Christians.

Noah and the Flood

One of the most popular Old Testament narratives, the story of Noah, appears as a baptismal figure in the New Testament Petrine Epistles (1 Pet. 3:20–21; 2 Pet. 2:5). In these letters, Noah and the seven others saved from the flood signify the righteous souls who receive baptism (not as a removal of dirt from the body but as a sign of their good conscience). The flood signifies the means of purification (a water bath). In 2 Peter 2:5–7, the world is both formed from water and, when found unrighteous, purified by means of water.

This interpretation of the flood continued in early Christian documents. In his *Dialogue with Trypho*, Justin Martyr argues that only those who had been prepared by water, faith, and wood, as forecast in the story of the deluge, would be spared God's judgment. According to Justin, the waters of the flood represent waters of baptism, the righteousness of Noah symbolizes the faith of the candidates, and the wood of the ark signifies the wood of the cross.[29]

Perceiving the water of Noah's flood both as a means of judgment (drowning sinners) and as a medium for purifying the righteous shows the power and danger of baptismal water. Since water is both death dealing and life giving, an unworthy person who enters the font puts himself or herself in danger. Unrepentant sinners would drown in a spiritual sense. The symbol of the ark is only positive. The ark represents the church; it is the place where sinners are converted, faith is delivered, and the righteous (once inside) are safe. This idea

---

28. See Jensen, "Earliest Christian Images and Exegesis."
29. Justin, *Dial.* 138.2–3. See also *1 Clem.* 9.4.

appears initially in Tertullian's *Treatise on Baptism* and then, a few decades later, in the writings of his fellow North African, Cyprian.[30]

Tertullian's treatise also explicitly connects the condemnation of the unrighteous in the flood story with John the Baptist's warnings against trying to flee God's impending wrath (cf. Matt. 3:7). The dove's appearance in both stories signifies their unity: "But even this [the dove] beyond doubt has a preceding figure—since as after the waters of the flood, by which ancient sins were washed away (so, it is said, after the baptism of the world), the dove that was sent from the ark and returned with an olive branch, announced to the earth the peace of heaven."[31] Tertullian warns, however, that the salvation won in baptismal water could be lost. Like the cities of Sodom and Gomorrah (cf. 2 Pet. 2:6), the one who sins after baptism will be condemned to the fire.[32]

Fourth-century exegetes similarly read the story of Noah as a symbol and figure of baptism. John Chrysostom interprets the ark as a type of the church, given by God to protect those who stay safely inside and do not stray.[33] In two treatises (one addressed to candidates and one addressed to neophytes), Ambrose cites Noah's story as an ancient testimony to the meaning of baptism and asks whether any could doubt its meaning: human depravity required salvific cleansing. As the floodwaters dispersed, Noah first sent out a raven (the symbol of sin) that did not return. The dove, by contrast, returned with an olive twig in its mouth (a sign of God's forgiveness and gift of the Spirit).[34] Augustine likewise sees the ark as typifying the church, and, like many before him, linked the wood of the ark with the wood of the cross. Both the ark and the cross promise salvation from the purifying flood, destroying the iniquity of the world.[35]

Beyond textual exegesis, the Noah story is one of the most popular in early Christian painting and sculpture. The oldest extant example is seen in the Catacomb of Domitilla (the hypogeum of the Flavii), and the motif appears frequently in other Roman catacombs and on many third- and fourth-century sarcophagus reliefs (figs. 1.3, 1.4, 4.4). Nearly all the examples from this period show Noah standing with his arms outstretched as in prayer in a small boxlike ark, its lid at his back (rather like a modern jack-in-the-box).[36] His typological function is apparent even in the art, since the Genesis narrative had little

30. Tertullian, *Idol.* 24; Cyprian, *Unit. eccl.* 6 and *Ep.* 67.2; 73; and 75. See also Origen, *Hom. Gen.* 2, in which he describes Christ as the spiritual ark, which frees the human race from destruction, as his church.

31. Tertullian, *Bapt.* 8.4 (CCSL 1:283), trans. author.

32. Tertullian, *Bapt.* 8.4.

33. John Chrysostom., *Laz.* 6.7.

34. Ambrose, *Myst.* 3.10–11. See also idem, *Sacr.* 1.23; 2.1.

35. Augustine, *Catech.* 20.32, 34.

36. This iconography may have been derived from classical Roman depictions of Deucalion and Pyrrha, who were cast into the sea in a chest. Some variations occur infrequently. In the Velletri sarcophagus, for instance, the ark is shown with feet, and in one fresco in the Cemetery

Figure 1.3. Noah in the ark with dove. Painting, catacomb of Peter and Marcellinus, Rome. Early fourth century. (Photo © Estelle Brettman, The International Catacomb Society.)

Figure 1.4. Noah with Daniel. Sarcophagus (end), Museo Pio Cristiano, Vatican. Early fourth century. (Photo by author with permission from the Vatican Museum.)

obvious influence on the composition. Images predating the fifth century do not include Noah's wife, his family, or paired animals.[37] The dove is the only additional narrative detail; it flies into the scene, bearing an olive branch in its beak. As in Ambrose's text, the water, wood, and dove are enough for viewers

of Panfilo, the ark is closed; see Hooyman, "Die Noe-Darstellung in der frühchristlichen Kunst"; and Franke, "Bemerkungen zur frühchristlichen Noe-ikonographie," 171.

37. The most famous of these examples are the Cotton Genesis, Ashburnham Pentateuch, and Vienna Genesis images, which show the ark with several floors floating in the water surrounded by fish and drowning figures.

to make the association and perceive the image's significance. Noah floating in his boxlike ark—perhaps meant to symbolize the ark of the covenant—(to which the dove flies) symbolizes the justification of sinners through the ritual of baptism.

This image of Noah frequently appears adjacent to the scene of the book of Daniel's three youths in the fiery furnace. Such a composition may be an iconographic expression of the two ways the world was, and will be, purified—by flood or flame. Viewers would be reminded that John the Baptist announced impending judgment and that, according to 2 Peter 3:5–7, just as the unrighteous world was once deluged with water, future sinners would be burned by fire. The otherwise enigmatic pairing of these two images can be explained by the traditional typological emphasis on Noah as a symbol of righteousness and a reminder of God's judgment and rescue from flood and from flame.

The Red Sea Crossing

Paul's First Epistle to the Corinthians provides the earliest example of a baptismal typology. Here, the Israelites' crossing of the Red Sea (Exod. 14) signifies their baptism: "I do not want you to be unaware, brothers and sisters, that our ancestors were all under the cloud, and all passed through the sea; and all were baptized into Moses in the cloud and in the sea" (1 Cor. 10:1–2). Third- and fourth-century documents, however, offer a different interpretation. They tend to see the destruction of Pharaoh and his armies as symbolizing the annihilation of sins and a victory over Satan and the powers of evil. Each reading, however, compares the Israelites' crossing the sea with Christian neophytes' entering and exiting the font's water. Both groups escaped from slavery (in Egypt or to sin) and crossed safely into the promised land (Canaan or the church). Tertullian's work offers a clear instance of this: "The first [testimony to the use of water as a means of grace] was when the people were liberated from Egypt and, by passing through the water, escaped the Egyptian king's power, the king himself with all his forces, having been destroyed by water. How is this figure manifest in the sacrament of baptism? Plainly that, in this age, the gentiles are (also) liberated through water and forsake their original oppressor, the devil, who is drowned in that water."[38]

Cyprian also views the Egyptians (especially the pharaoh) as personifications of the evil that holds humans captive to wickedness and sin. For Cyprian, baptismal water alone was adequate to remove that evil's poisonous power. Even by affusion (offered to the mortally ill), it served this purpose. Moreover, while Cyprian acknowledges that exorcising the candidates before their entry

---

38. Tertullian, *Bapt.* 9.1 (CCSL 1:284), trans. author. On the Red Sea as baptismal type, see Dölger, "Der Durchzug durch das Rote Meer"; Daniélou, *Bible and the Liturgy*, chap. 5, 86–98; Daniélou, *From Shadows to Reality*, chap. IV.III, 175–201; and Lundberg, *La typologie baptismale*, 116–46.

to the font begins the process of release from bondage to the demonic power, only the actual reception of the waters of salvation could overpower the devil's grasp. The wicked spirits are, for Cyprian, like scorpions and serpents that live on dry land and lose their venom when cast into water and crushed underfoot in the font (cf. Ps. 74:13–14).[39]

Origen similarly compares the pursuing Egyptians to wicked spirits and worldly tyrants. Like Moses and the Israelites (Exod. 15), Christians who pass safely through baptismal water emerge safe and free: singing a new song in a new land. Origen allegorizes most other aspects of the Exodus story as an internal battle with evil. Egypt represents the darkness of ignorance; Moses's rod, the word of the Law; and the path through the sea, the "right way of faith." The one who avoids works of darkness destroys the Egyptians by living spiritually rather than carnally.[40] Origen's comparison of neophytes' singing as they leave the font with the Israelites' singing as they enter the promised land was echoed a century later in Zeno of Verona's interpretation of Miriam as a type of the church; she beats her timbrel and leads the people through the water into heaven itself.[41]

In the fourth century other writers, like Zeno, understood the Red Sea crossing as a figure both of the baptismal destruction of personal evil and of cleansing from sin. Gregory of Nyssa's *Life of Moses* allegorizes the Egyptians as various base human passions (covetousness, rapaciousness, conceit, arrogance, malice, deceit, etc.) that are overcome in the font's water. No trace of that malicious company could survive the cleansing water; all would be destroyed and drowned.[42] Similarly, in his sermon for the Day of Lights (Epiphany), Gregory declares that candidates entering the font are symbolically escaping Egypt (their burden of sin).[43] Basil of Caesarea reminds the unbaptized that if the Israelites had not gone through the sea, they would not have escaped Pharaoh and entered the promised land and then asks how they expect to be rescued or enter paradise if they do not enter the water to escape Satan's tyranny.[44] Augustine, too, understands the Red Sea crossing as prefiguring the drowning of sins in the baptismal font: "and while you escape, not one of those that oppress you survives."[45]

In his catechetical lectures, Cyril of Jerusalem provides an overall summary of the Exodus story (including the Passover) and shows how it was mystically

39. Cyprian, *Ep.* 69.15.1–2. See a parallel statement by Jerome, *Ep.* 69.6.

40. Origen, *Hom. Exod.* 5.5, trans. Heine, *Origen*, 283–84.

41. Zeno of Verona, *Tract.* 1.54 (*De Exodo*) (PL 11:509–10).

42. Gregory of Nyssa, *Vit. Mos.* 2.125, trans. Malherbe and Ferguson, *Gregory of Nyssa*, 83–84. See also Ambrose, *Sacr.* 1.20; *Myst.* 3.12; Didymus, *Trin.* 2.14; Ephrem, *Epiph.* 1.6; and Aphrahat, *Dem.* 12.8.

43. Gregory of Nyssa, *Diem lum.*

44. Basil of Caesarea, *Bapt.* 2.

45. Augustine, *Enarrat. Ps.* 106.3 (CCSL 40:1571), trans. author.

related, first, to the rites that take place in a room adjacent to the baptismal chamber where the candidate renounces Satan and professes faith in Christ and, second, to the ways it symbolizes the candidate's subsequent plunge into the font:

> This moment, you should know, is prefigured in ancient history. When that tyrannous and cruel despot, Pharaoh, was oppressing the noble, free-spirited Hebrew nation, God sent Moses to deliver them from the hard slavery imposed upon them by the Egyptians. The doorposts were anointed with the blood of a lamb that the destroyer might pass over the houses signed with the blood; so the Jews were miraculously liberated. After their liberation, the enemy gave chase, and on seeing the sea part miraculously before them, still continued in hot pursuit, only to be instantaneously overwhelmed and engulfed in the Red Sea. Pass, pray, from the old to the new, from the figure to the reality. There Moses [was] sent by God to Egypt; here Christ [was] sent from the Father into the world. . . . There the blood of a lamb was the charm against the destroyer; here, the blood of the unspotted Lamb, Jesus Christ, is appointed your inviolable sanctuary against demons. Pharaoh pursued that people of old right into the sea; this outrageous spirit, the impudent author of all evil, followed you, each one, up to the very verge of the saving streams. That other tyrant is engulfed and drowned in the Red Sea; this one is destroyed in the saving water.[46]

This kind of typological exegesis, orally delivered in sermons and catechetical lessons and literarily expounded in theological treatises, would have influenced the way early Christians viewed pictorial images of the Israelites crossing the Red Sea and of the chariots of the Egyptians being dashed and destroyed by the closing waters. Observers would have been predisposed to associate this story of both destruction and rescue with the purification and promise of baptism. Such salvific implications make this image particularly appropriate for a funerary context as well as a baptismal one. Considering Paul's early citation of this as a baptismal type, its appearance in visual art is surprisingly late; surviving examples are no earlier than the mid- to late fourth century. Two wall paintings in the Via Latina Catacomb in Rome, nearly two dozen sarcophagus reliefs, and a fresco from El-Bagawit in Egypt depict the scene (figs. 1.5, 1.6).

Two Via Latina Catacomb paintings, each appearing on the back wall of a burial niche (cubicula C and O), are quite similar in composition. They show the Egyptians (dressed as Roman soldiers) riding their horses into the sea while the unarmed Israelites stand safely on the other side. The Israelites

---

46. Cyril of Jerusalem, *Myst.* 1.1–3, trans. McCauley and Stephenson, *Works of Saint Cyril of Jerusalem*, 2:153–54. Compare Basil of Caesarea, *Spir. Sanct.* 14. For similar use of the blood and the Passover themes, see John Chrysostom, *Catech.* 3.23–24 (Stav. 3, Pk. 4); Ambrose, *Sacr.* 1.12, 20 and 4.18 and *Myst.* 3.12; and Augustine, *Catech.* 20.34.

Figure 1.5. Moses and the Israelites crossing the Red Sea. Painting, Via Latina Catacomb, Rome. Mid-fourth century. (Photo © Estelle Brettman, The International Catacomb Society.)

Figure 1.6. Exodus from Egypt. Sarcophagus, Museo Pio Cristiano, Vatican. Early fourth century. (Photo by author with permission from the Vatican Museum.)

are barefoot and dressed in simple short tunics. Moses, the exception, wears a long tunic and sandals and holds his wonder-working staff (fig. 1.5).[47]

Fourth-century sarcophagi also depict the crossing of the Red Sea, and, like the catacomb paintings, show the Egyptians in Roman military dress. They charge out of a city gate at the left, only to plunge into the sea as the waves drown the leading charioteers at the composition's center (fig. 1.6). Sometimes personifications of the sea as reclining figures making a gesture of awe appear beneath the hooves of the horses. The weaponless men standing on the right bank are the Israelites, carrying bundles, leading their children by the hand, and looking back at the destruction of the enemy armies. Miriam appears in one of the relief carvings, playing her timbrel. The placement of these images within a funerary context suggests that they refer to the Christian's escape from evil power and its consequences, namely, mortality. This, the effect of baptism, is realized in the next world.

Biblical Healing Stories

Typological interpretations of Noah's flood and the Israelites crossing the Red Sea focus on the destruction of sin through the agency of water. A second

---

47. Compare this with the frescoes from the Dura Europos synagogue. Four scenes, which read from right to left, show the Israelites as armed rather than weaponless. See discussion in Tronzo, *Via Latina Catacomb*, 42–47.

cleansing theme concentrates more on physical as well as spiritual healing through the water of baptism. A connection between sin purification and bodily healing was especially strong in a culture that regarded sin or demon possession as a source of physical illness. Christians tended to believe that cures, such as they were, were gifts from God that were meant to apply as much to the soul as to the body.[48]

Embedded in a long discussion of sickbed (clinical) baptism, Cyprian of Carthage asserts that baptismal water also has the power to exorcise the demons that cause bodily infirmities or illnesses. Nevertheless, he remarks that some sickbed baptisms fail to bring about physical healing. In these cases, Cyprian insists, those afflicted should be nonetheless assured that the baptized are set free. Although the devil may continue his torments, they will have no effect. Cyprian also acknowledges that Satan may return if faith falters, and any who fall into sin might see the return of those unclean spirits.[49]

Bodily cure is also a prominent theme in some early Christian baptistery inscriptions. One of Pope Damasus's epigrams attached to his own house church (the Titulus Damasi) describes baptismal water as washing off pestilence and restoring health:

> This glorious spring contains the waters of health,
> and is able to cleanse human pestilence.
> Should you wish to know the benefits of these holy waters—
> the holy rivers grant a royal faith.
> Wash off the contagion of the old life in the sacred font.
> O most happy one, living reborn through the water;
> whoever seeks this spring relinquishes earthly matters,
> and tramples evil deeds underfoot.[50]

The relationship of sin and sickness in addition to the associations between curing illness and casting out demons is particularly evident in two New Testament accounts of healing: the cases of the paralytic and of the man born blind as recounted in the Gospel of John (John 5 and 9). Although the Synoptic Gospels describe parallel events, early Christian writers (and artists) referred more frequently to the Johannine pericopes as baptismal typologies, in part because John's narratives were more elaborated but even more because both of the Johannine versions incorporated the element of water (cf. Matt. 9:1–8; Mark 2:1–12; and Luke 5:17–21 with John 5:2–12 and cf. Matt. 20:27–34; Mark 10:46–52; and Luke 18:35–43 with John 9). For example, the Synoptic Gospels place the story of the paralytic within the context of a dispute about whether

---

48. See Amundsen, *Medicine, Society, and Faith*, 127–57; Bruyne, "L'imposition des mains."
49. Cyprian, *Ep.* 69.15.1–16.1. On the work of unclean spirits, see Minucius Felix, *Oct.* 27.2.
50. Inscription found in De Rossi, *ICUR* 2.135.6 (*Sylloge Virdunensis*), trans. author. See Jensen, "Inscriptions in Early Roman Baptisteries."

Jesus may forgive sins, especially when his forgiveness has a by-product of bodily healing, but never mention the function or place of water in the healing. By contrast, in the Gospel of John, Jesus meets the paralytic at the pool of Beth-zatha, waiting to be placed into the water. Jesus only later meets the former paralytic and urges him, "Do not sin any more, so that nothing worse happens to you" (John 5:14).

Similarly, the narrative of the healings of the blind men in Matthew (20:29–34) and, especially, of Bartimaeus in Mark (10:46–52; cf. Luke 18:35–43) credit the men's faith as the basis for their cure. By comparison, at the beginning of John's version of Jesus's healing the blind man, Jesus refutes the accusation that sin was the cause of the man's infirmity (John 9:1–3).[51] Moreover, in John's account, Jesus makes a healing poultice with spittle and clay and tells the man to wash it off in the pool of Siloam, where he gains his sight (John 9:6–7). These stories assert that the action of purification or cleansing from sin can have a secondary benefit: healing from illness or bodily impairment. In John's telling, the cure involves washing in water.[52]

Naaman the Syrian

The clearest Old Testament prefiguration of baptismal healing is the episode of Naaman the Syrian. According to the account in 2 Kings 5, Naaman, a commander of the army of the king of Aram, suffered from leprosy but was cured by seven immersions in the Jordan River at the suggestion of Elisha (2 Kings 5:1–14; cf. Luke 4:27). After his healing bath, Naaman's flesh was restored like that of a young boy. In his commentary on Luke, Origen interprets the disease of leprosy as a symbol of sin and Elijah as a figure of Christ. According to Origen, because the cleansing of Naaman's flesh was both healing and restorative it foreshadowed the efficacy of baptism: "Realize that those who are covered with the filth of leprosy are cleansed in the mystery of Baptism by the spiritual Elijah, our Lord and Savior. To you he says, 'Get up and go into the Jordan and wash, and your flesh will be restored to you.' . . . When he [Namaan] washed, he fulfilled the mystery of baptism, and his flesh became like the flesh of a child. Which child? The one that is born in the washing of rebirth."[53]

Nearly two centuries later, Ambrose of Milan offered a similar interpretation.[54] In his prebaptismal lectures to catechumens, Ambrose points out that

---

51. See also Luke 7:21 and 9:1, in which healing the sick and casting out demons are combined.

52. See Cyprian's discussion on the relationship between baptism and healing, regarding the problem of the *clinicus* who recovered, and the differences between ordinary healing and cleansing and baptism, *Ep.* 69.12.1–15.1.

53. Origen, *Hom. Luc.* 33.5, trans. Lienhard, *Origen*, 136; and cf. Origen, *Comm. Jo.* 6.28. Compare Irenaeus, *Frag.* 34.

54. Ambrose, *Sacr.* 1.13–14.

Naaman (like Jesus) had been dipped in the Jordan, thus granting the water of baptism both curative and expiatory powers:

> What then does this [Naaman's cure in the Jordan] mean? You have seen water. Not all water cures but only the water that has the grace of Christ cures. Its substance is different by virtue of its consecration; its work is different from its effect. The work belongs to the water, the effect to the Holy Spirit. The water does not heal unless the Holy Spirit descends into it and consecrates it. Just as you read: when our Lord Jesus instituted the rite of baptism, he came to John and John said to him, "I need to be baptized by you, and do you then come to me?" Christ answered him, "Let it be, it is thus fitting for us to fulfill all righteousness." See how all righteousness is constituted in baptism. Why then did Christ descend, except that that flesh of yours might be cleansed, the flesh that he took over from our condition? For no washing away of his sins was necessary for Christ, "who did no sin," but it was necessary for us who remain subject to sin.[55]

Although Namaan's story provides both precedent and prototype for the consecration of the water, the figure must be adapted to fit the specific baptismal context that Ambrose addresses. In a later sermon to the newly baptized, Ambrose elsewhere explains that while Naaman was dipped seven times (under the law), those who are baptized are dipped three times (in the name of the Trinity).[56]

In his Epiphany sermon on the baptism of Christ, Gregory of Nyssa evokes a number of baptism types from the Old Testament, including the crossing of the Red Sea and the story of Naaman, in which he emphasizes the element of cleansing and the Jordan as signifying the font. He urges the unbaptized to enter into it as Naaman, washing themselves clean, body and soul.[57] Likewise, the fourth-century Syrian poet Ephrem sees Naaman as representing the one seeking baptismal cleansing. One of his hymns for Epiphany (a baptismal day in Ephrem's Edessa) cites a number of types but opens with a comparison between the candidates and Naaman:

> Gather together, you lepers, and come to receive cleansing without any toil, for there is no need, as in Naaman's case, to be baptized in the river seven times over; nor again is there the weariness, which the priests imposed with all their sprinklings. Seven times over did Elisha cleanse Naaman, symbolizing seven evil spirits. The hyssop and blood serve as a powerful type: there is no place now for being kept apart, for the Lord of All's son is not kept apart from the Lord of All.[58]

55. Ambrose, *Sacr.* 1.15 (SC 25:68), trans. author.

56. Ambrose, *Myst.* 4.21.

57. Gregory of Nyssa, *Diem lum.*, NPNF², 5:522. See also Gregory of Nazianzus, *Or.* 40, 34, where he parallels baptism with the cleansing of the ten lepers in Luke 17:12.

58. Ephrem, *Epiph.* 1.2–3, trans. Sebastian Brock, in Finn, *Early Christian Baptism*, 165. See also *Epiph.* 6.12. Daniélou cites Ethiopic and Coptic prayers for the consecration of the water that mention Naaman; see *Bible and the Liturgy*, 110.

THE PARALYTIC AND THE MAN BORN BLIND

As noted above, the stories of the healing of the paralytic and the blind man are baptismal types primarily because of their use of healing pools. Unlike Naaman, however, neither of these characters is cured through immersion. In John's Gospel, Jesus instructs the man born blind to wash in the pool of Siloam to remove the saliva-based mud that Jesus had spread over his eyes (John 9:6–7). Earlier in the Gospel, Jesus encountered an invalid (not actually specified as a paralytic but traditionally identified as such) waiting next to a pool by the Sheep Gate in Jerusalem (John 5:5–9). This pool, known for its miraculous healing properties, had been a gathering place for the sick. In an ancient variant of the latter text, an angel of the Lord mysteriously stirred up this water at certain seasons, and the first person to step into this water would be cured. Unfortunately for this particular man, the instant the water was stirred, someone always got in front of him.

Tertullian cites the paralytic's story in order to compare the therapeutic benefits of baptism with ordinary healing of the body. Such bodily cure, he says, signifies the water's spiritual healing and the restoration of the divine image that had been lost through sin. This, Tertullian explains, conforms to the general principle that carnal matters precede and point to higher spiritual truths. As God's grace makes headway, the water that previously healed only bodies now also heals spirits. That which used to give earthly health now offers a spiritual remedy.[59] In a more practical context, and defending the efficacy of sickbed baptism, Cyprian remarks that the invalid's frailty was no obstacle to his obtaining both strength and salvation. Not only did he get up and walk, he carried his bed away with him.[60]

Ambrose also refers to the paralytic's story (specifically the variant version in John) in his catechetical sermons. According to Ambrose, the angel who normally stirred the water foreshadowed Jesus. However, in this instance Jesus himself appeared and chose to heal this single individual because Jesus alone recognized that the man needed someone to help him into the water:

> See the mystery here. Our Lord Jesus Christ came to the pool: many sick people were lying there. Yes, certainly there were many sick lying there, and only one was cured. Then he said to the man who was paralyzed, "Go down into the water." He replied, "I have no man to take me down." See where you are baptized, see the source of your baptism. It is none other than the cross of Christ, the death of Christ. Here is the whole mystery: he suffered for you. In him you are redeemed, in him you are saved. [61]

Ambrose points out that both the water of the font and the water of this pool were miraculously consecrated for their purposes. But the invalid needed the

---

59. Tertullian, *Bapt.* 5.
60. Cyprian, *Ep.* 69.13.1.
61. Ambrose, *Sacr.* 2.6, trans. Yarnold, *Awe-Inspiring Rites of Initiation,* 112.

arrival of the man, Jesus, to make the water efficacious.[62] Other fourth-century writers concur. Among them, Gregory of Nazianzus who compares those who are not yet baptized with the paralytic who had no one to put him into the pool. And, perhaps seeing himself as an agent of Christ, he asserts that baptism itself brings help—in the form of a person both human and divine.[63] Cyril of Jerusalem's sermon on the pericope is perhaps the most extensive ancient treatment of the paralytic story. Although focused more on the thera-peutic ministry of Jesus (including the healing of the two blind men in Matt. 20:30–34) than on the story as a figure of baptism, Cyril compares the pool to the fountain of everlasting life. Jesus, the physician of both souls and bod-ies, chose a chronic sufferer to be the first one to receive his gift of healing.[64]

Of these two healing stories, Jesus's cure of the blind man (John 9:1–7) is less frequently cited in the extant documents as a baptismal type. Irenaeus views the story as a symbol of God's continuing care for the creation (against the gnostics); Tertullian regards it as a sign to Marcion that the power of Christ was manifest in the man's bodily healing.[65] A passage from Augustine's *Commentary on John* points to this story as a demonstration of baptismal enlightenment more than a washing from sin.[66]

Despite the lack of literary evidence for interpretations of the story in a baptismal context, the story's details themselves offer some interesting paral-lels to the actual ritual of baptism. Jesus's use of spit to heal the man's eyes precisely parallels his healing of the deaf-mute in the Gospel of Mark (7:32), and both miraculous cures are symbolically incorporated into a Western rite known as the *ephphetha* (or *apertio*), in which the bishop touches the nostrils and ears of the candidate (with either oil or spittle), commanding them to "be opened."[67] This ritual action offers a liturgical link between biblical story and visual image, underscoring the idea that baptism offered both bodily and spiritual healing.

Healing Stories in Early Christian Visual Art

The visual art of early Christianity has a few representations of Naaman, but they are vastly outnumbered by images of the healing of the paralytic and the blind man. Although the two paralytic stories are quite different (cf. Mark 2:12 and parallels with John 5:2–15), the art depicts the common thread

---

62. Ambrose, *Myst.* 4.24.

63. Gregory of Nazianzus, *Or.* 40.33.

64. Cyril of Jerusalem, *Hom. para.* 7, trans. McCauley and Stephenson, *Works of Saint Cyril of Jerusalem*, 2:214–25.

65. Irenaeus, *Haer.* 5.12.2; Tertullian, *Marc.* 4.36.

66. Augustine, *Tract. Ev. Jo.* 44.2.

67. See Ambrose, *Sacr.* 1.2 and compare with John the Deacon, *Ep. Sen.* 5, which suggests that the rite actually closes the senses following the exorcism; see discussion below under the heading "Exsufflation." The word *ephphetha* comes from Jesus's command in Aramaic, "Eph-phatha" (see Mark 7:34).

Figure 1.7. Baptism and Jesus raising Jairus's daughter. Sarcophagus fragment, Museo Pio Cristiano, Vatican. Early fourth century. (Photo by author with permission from the Vatican Museum.)

Figure 1.8. Peter striking the rock, Peter's arrest, Jesus healing the paralytic, Jesus healing the blind man, the Cana miracle, and the multiplication of loaves and fish. Sarcophagus, Museo Pio Cristiano, Vatican. Early fourth century. (Photo by author with permission from the Vatican Museum.)

between the versions, showing the paralytic seated on his bed (fig. 1.8) or carrying it off at Jesus's command (fig. 1.8, 1.9). Representations of Jesus healing the blind man are equally popular in funerary art (figs. 1.8, 1.9), and often the two images appear together or near each other.[68] In most of these images, the healed one is shown as smaller than the other figures in the composition. Additionally, Jesus normally accomplishes the miraculous cure by his touch (a "laying on of hands"). The diminutive stature of the healed persons, just as the small stature of Jesus at his baptism, may allude to their status as newly baptized "children" (a name often used to designate the neophytes in the first week following their baptism), and the imposition of hands might refer not only to healing but to the gift of the Holy Spirit in the baptismal rite.[69]

The baptismal significance of the paralytic's healing is reinforced when it appears in a baptismal room, as it does in the third-century Dura Europos house church. At least one art historian has speculated that it also appears among the now-missing figures in the mosaic decoration of the fourth-century

68. These images also are juxtaposed with representations of the raising of the dead and the resurrection of Lazarus.

69. See Bruyne, "L'imposition des mains," 113–266. On the use of the term "children" for the newly baptized, see below, chap. 2, under the heading "Church as Mother and God as Father."

Figure 1.9. Adam and Eve, Cana miracle, Jesus raising the dead, Jesus healing the paralytic, and Peter striking the rock. Sarcophagus, Museo Pio Cristiano, Vatican. Mid-fourth century. (Photo by author with permission from the Vatican Museum.)

baptistery of San Giovanni in Fonte, along with the healing of the blind man, and the baptism of Jesus.[70]

All these types are linked in that they share some aspect of cleansing, purification, and healing. Ambrose effectively summarizes it: "Now behold the incidents one by one. We said that a figure had preceded on the Jordan, when the leprous Naaman was cleansed. . . . We have another in the flood; you have a third kind, when the ancestors were baptized in the Red Sea; you have a fourth kind in the pond, when the water was moved."[71]

Ritual Actions Signifying Cleansing and Healing

Several parts of the early baptismal ritual were specifically purificatory and therapeutic. Although the ritual itself varied according to time and place, most early baptisms incorporated some action that removed sin, drove away evil, or imparted health and strength to recipients. These actions aimed to help them remain steadfastly faithful and armored against backsliding into sin, idolatry, or other bad habits. Tertullian declares that any water that has been sanctified by the invocation of God has the power to wash both body and spirit. Because sin resides in both, the water simultaneously washes the soul corporally and the flesh spiritually.[72]

Preliminary Rites

Immersion in water (or a thorough soaking by pouring) is the basis for cleansing in the baptismal ritual. However, prior to that are several preliminary

70. See the argument of Bruyne, "La décoration des baptistères paléochrétiens," esp. 344. Bruyne bases his argument partly on the parallels with Dura and also surmises that one of the scenes could have depicted John baptizing Jesus, based on the remains of some bare feet in the iconography.

71. Ambrose, *Sacr.* 2.8–9, trans. author (SC 25:78).

72. Tertullian, *Bapt.* 4.20–30; cf. idem, *Res.* 8.

acts that also serve a cleansing purpose, even to prepare the body to enter the bath. These prebath rites included exorcism, offering salt to catechumens, blowing on them (exsufflation), and then a series of ascetical practices taken on by the candidates themselves: fasting; almsgiving; abstaining from sex, sleep, and baths; and a spoken renunciation of Satan while (in some places) standing on a goatskin or haircloth shirt. Once inside the baptistery, candidates disrobed and (in some instances) were anointed with the oil of exorcism before entering the font. In addition to these individually administered rites, the baptismal water itself might be exorcised prior to being consecrated.

Scrutinies and Exorcism

Demons were a widely perceived reality in the ancient world. Polytheists and Jews, like Christians, practiced exorcism of various kinds. The book of Acts notes Jewish exorcists (Acts 19:13), and according to the Talmud, R. Simon ben Yohai even drove a demon out of the Roman emperor's daughter.[73] The Greek word *daimōn* does not necessarily denote a malevolent power but, rather, some kind of divine, intermediary, or quasi-divine being. It might also refer to an individual's guiding spirit (*genius*) or to a departed person's soul (akin to the Latin *manes* or *lemur*).[74] When such beings are malignant they tempt, deceive, and—most commonly—overtake and possess their victims, causing frenzy or madness. These kinds of demons need to be appeased or forcibly expelled through magic or exorcistic rituals. Jesus also casts out demons and empowers his disciples to do so as well (cf. Matt. 10:1; Mark 1:21–28; 3:15; Luke 8:26–39; 9:1, 49; Acts 5:16).

Forms of the verb *exorkizō*, "to exorcise," rarely appear in the New Testament (cf. the exception in Acts 19:13); rather the verb *exerchomai*, "to come out," refers to the action of Jesus and the disciples when they "cast out" demons (e.g., Mark 1:25). The practice of prebaptismal exorcism may have been associated with Jesus's having been led by the Spirit into the wilderness to be tempted by Satan immediately after his baptism (cf. Matt. 4:1 and parallels). Sinners were also assumed to be demon-possessed, servants of the devil. As noted above, some New Testament healing stories suggest that sin was the cause of certain illnesses. For example, Jesus instructs the paralytic not to sin any longer, "so that nothing worse happens to you" (John 5:14). The disciples ask Jesus whether the blind man's disability was caused by his own sin or by his parents' sins (John 9:2).

A repentant sinner therefore needed exorcism in order to be freed from possession, and sick persons were admonished to refrain from sin. For this reason, baptismal rites began with exorcism, which initially delivered candidates from their bondage to Satan and sin and made their bodies and souls

---

73. *Me'ilah* 17b. See Bowman, "Exorcism and Baptism."
74. See Ferguson, *Demonology of the Early Christian World*.

ready to receive the Holy Spirit. A long section of Minucius Felix's dialogue between Octavius and Caecilius discusses the activities of demons, which include deceiving (instilling errors in the mind), alienating their victims from God, stirring up lust, causing insomnia, fomenting mania, contriving diseases, terrifying minds, and wrenching limbs. Minucius Felix also mentions that they lurk in religious statues (idols), haunt shrines, and suggest prophecies to seers and diviners.[75]

The *Apostolic Tradition* lays out the final preparation of candidates for baptism, and includes actions that are exorcistic in nature. Once the candidates had been enrolled and separated from the other catechumens, their regimen included daily exorcism. As the day for baptism drew close, the bishop performed this rite so that he personally could be assured of their purity. On the day before their baptism (Friday or Saturday), the bishop performed a final exorcism over each individual, commanding all the evil spirits to flee and not to return. After this act, the bishop breathed in each candidate's face and then sealed his or her forehead, ears, and nostrils.[76] Those coming for baptism were thus freed from demonic powers and servitude to sin.

Generally, exorcism was a process and not a single event. From the moment candidates presented themselves for baptism, regular exorcisms were performed on them. According to many of the early liturgical writings, exorcisms prior to baptism were especially important, since Satan, suddenly aware of the potential loss of one of his own, worked especially hard to retain the catechumen for his own. Tertullian claims that the devil even practiced baptism himself, as if unclean things could make clean or the damned offer absolution. Furthermore, he warns, impure spirits frequent watery places such as streams, springs, baths, and wells, hoping to snatch souls and bring them to ruin.[77]

Such pressing danger meant that catechumens being readied for baptism needed as much support as they could get in escaping the wiles of Satan and his minions. Tertullian does not mention a ritual of exorcism as such but implies that it happens within the water bath. By the action of the angel, the water cleanses and prepares the neophytes for the reception of the Holy Spirit.[78] In the mid-third century, Cyprian alluded to a special category of clerics who exorcised prior to baptism.[79]

By the mid-fourth century, rituals of prebaptismal exorcism were practiced in most parts of the Christian world. In her account of her visit to Jerusalem, the pilgrim Egeria likewise describes the clergy performing daily exorcism of candidates for baptism during the Lenten season.[80] Also from the fourth

---

75. Minucius Felix, *Oct.* 26–27.
76. Hippolytus, *Trad. ap.* 20
77. Tertullian, *Bapt.* 5.
78. Tertullian, *Bapt.* 6.
79. Cyprian, *Ep.* 69.15.2.
80. Egeria, *Itin.* 46.1; cf. Cyril of Jerusalem, *Cat.* 1.5.

century, John Chrysostom's baptismal instructions show that prebaptismal exorcism of catechumens was also practiced in Antioch. According to John, the candidates were sent to exorcists on a daily basis after their catechetical instructors had finished with them.[81] In his catechetical lectures, Cyril compares such exorcisms to the work of a metallurgist removing the impurities from gold: "The soul cannot be purified without exorcisms, which, since they are culled from the divine Scriptures, possess divine power."[82] He also compares the progress of the catechumen toward baptism to that of a hero on a journey toward a prize. The prize is wonderful—ransom for captives, remission of sins, a shining new garment, a heaven-bound chariot, and all the delights of paradise. The journey was perilous, however. Somewhere along the road a dragon lay waiting in ambush. "Seeing this numerous company winning salvation, he selects and stalks his prey."[83]

Gregory of Nazianzus describes that demon in more detail. Chased away by water baptism, the demon retreats, but soon resumes his assault:

He will not submit to the expulsion, he will not resign himself to be houseless and homeless. He goes through waterless places, dry of the divine stream, and there he desires to abide. He wanders, seeking rest; he finds none. He lights on baptized souls, whose sins the font has washed away. He fears the water; he is choked with the cleansing, as the Legion were in the sea. Again he returns to the house whence he came out. He is shameless, he is contentious, he makes a fresh assault upon it, he makes a new attempt. If he finds that Christ has taken up his abode there, and has filled the place which he had vacated, he is driven back again, and goes off without success and becomes an object of pity in his wandering state. But if he finds in you a place, swept and garnished, but also empty and idle, equally ready to take in this or that which shall first occupy it, he makes a leap into it; he takes up his abode there with a larger train; and the last state is worse than the first.[84]

By contrast to Cyril's use of heroic metaphors, Theodore of Mopsuestia describes the work of exorcism in forensic terminology. For Theodore, the candidate is the defendant, the devil the plaintiff, and the exorcist acts as the advocate for the defense.[85] John Chrysostom and Augustine employ more personal images: John's operative metaphor is house cleaning. The candidates should view their bodies as if being readied for a royal visit.[86] Augustine's similarly domestic analogy compares the acts of threshing and milling wheat,

81. John Chrysostom, *Catech.* 2.12 (Stav. 2).
82. Cyril of Jerusalem, *Procat.* 9. It appears, from this text, that those being exorcised had their faces veiled. Compare John Chrysostom, *Catech.* 9.21–22 (Montf. 1, Pk. 1).
83. Cyril of Jerusalem, *Procat.* 16.
84. Gregory of Nazianzus, *Or.* 40.30, NPNF², 7:373, slightly adapted by author.
85. Theodore of Mopsuestia, *Bapt. hom.* 2.1.
86. John Chrysostom, *Catech.* 2.12 (Stav. 2).

mixing dough, and baking bread to the preparation of catechumens: "Where or when was your threshing? It consisted in the fasts, the Lenten observances, the exorcisms. You were being ground when you were being exorcised."[87]

The font's water needed to be exorcised as well as consecrated; it was both cleansed and sanctified. The earliest evidence for this comes from Cyprian, who, citing a line from Ezekiel 36 ("I will sprinkle clean water upon you, and you shall be clean from all your uncleannesses, and from all your idols I will cleanse you," v. 25), argues that only a bishop may perform both actions: "It is absolutely necessary that the water be first cleansed and sanctified by the bishop, so that it may wash away by its baptism the sins of the person baptized."[88]

More than a century later, Ambrose asserted that this cleansing and consecration of the font water gives it curative powers; not all water has the power to heal, only water into which the Spirit has descended. According to Ambrose, this was initially accomplished when the Holy Spirit descended upon Christ in the Jordan. For this reason, the presider first exorcises the font as if the water were a creature. After the candidates have been exorcised, he offers an invocation of the Holy Spirit and prayer for the water's consecration.[89] Ambrose explains this order of actions by referring to Scripture. Jesus entered the water first (thus exorcising it), and subsequently the Holy Spirit sanctified it:

> Christ descended; the Holy Spirit also descended. Why did Christ descend first and the Holy Spirit afterwards, since in ordinary baptismal practice the font is consecrated before the one to be baptized descends into it? For this reason: when the priest first enters, he performs the exorcism according to the creation of water. Afterwards he delivers an invocation and prayer, that the font may be sanctified and that the presence of the eternal Trinity may be at hand. Christ, however, descended first, and the Spirit followed. For what reason? Not that the Lord Jesus himself might seem to be in need of the mystery of sanctification, but that he himself might sanctify and that the Spirit might also sanctify.[90]

Thus the font's water became an agent of healing as well as sanctification. The priest's invocation of the Holy Spirit is the means for this. The *Apostolic Constitutions* records such a prayer for the blessing of the water. After thanking God for sending Christ as savior and briefly rehearsing the history of salvation, beginning with Adam, the bishop then says, "Look down from heaven, and sanctify this water, and give it grace and power, so that the one to be baptized, according to the command of your Christ, may be crucified with him, may die with him, may be buried with him, and may rise with him

---

87. Augustine, *Serm.* 229A, trans. Hill, *Works of Saint Augustine*, 270.
88. Cyprian, *Ep.* 70.1.3 (CCSL 3C:503), trans. author.
89. Ambrose, *Sacr.* 1.18.
90. Ambrose, *Sacr.* 1.18 (SC 25:70), trans. author.

to the adoption which he offers and so that he may be dead to sin and live to righteousness."[91]

Giving of Salt

Salt given to catechumens is attested in North Africa, Italy, and Spain. Usually blessed or exorcised before it was offered, it was either given with bread or placed directly on the tongue of the candidate. In some sense the salt was a substitute sacramental sign, given to those not yet eligible to receive the Eucharist. John the Deacon refers to the catechumen being "signed with salt." Salt also had the particular benefits of warding off demons and strengthening the purpose of those who received it, perhaps in the same way that salt serves to preserve and flavor food. Although it is not directly cited in surviving documents, presumably the practice also recalled the Gospel expression "salt of the earth" (Matt. 5:13). John the Deacon adds that the salt preserves the flesh while also strengthening the mind by adding the salt of wisdom.[92] Regarding the African practice, Augustine claims that by the very words of blessing pronounced over it, salt acquires the property of seasoning along with its purificatory and preservative properties. The flavoring benefits of sacramental salt were even noted by the sixth-century Spanish bishop Isidore of Seville who explained that giving salt to catechumens seasons them with wisdom, it also deterred them from straying in folly from the flavor of Christ or, like Lot's wife, turning and looking backward.[93]

Exsufflation

Exsufflation (blowing on the face of the candidate) was another exorcistic rite. Like signing with salt, it was practiced in North Africa, Italy, and Spain and literally blew the devil out of the person. Based on the story of Jesus breathing on his disciples to give them the power to forgive sins (John 20:22–23), or the text from 2 Thessalonians that says that Jesus will destroy the lawless with the breath of his mouth (2:8), the action was like the ancient Christian practice of spitting at pagan idols.[94] Tertullian's treatise against idolatry uses the term *exsufflabit* to describe the Christian practice of spitting or blowing on the smoking incense on pagan altars.[95] The *Apostolic Tradition* describes

91. *Const. ap.* 7.43, ANF, 7:477, slightly adapted by author.
92. John the Deacon, *Ep. Sen.* 3; *Con. Carth. III coll. Hisp.* can. 5; Augustine, *Catech.* 26.50 (which some interpreters take to mention salt as a sacrament); and Augustine, *Conf.* 1.11.17; also *Gel. Sac.* 31. On the history and significance of the giving of salt to catechumens, see Botte, "Sacramentum catechumenorum"; and De Latte, "Saint Augustin et le baptême."
93. Isidore of Seville, *Eccl. off.* 2.21.1–3; on Lot's wife, see also Cyril of Jerusalem, *Myst.* 1.8.
94. See Tertullian, *Idol.* 11.7; *Scap.* 2; cf. Minucius Felix, *Oct.* 8.4. Athanasius described Anthony hissing at a demon (*Vit. Ant.* 40). Cf. Origen, *Cels.* 8.38; 8.41, which speaks of mocking and reviling statues of the gods; and an article by Dölger, "Heidnische Begrüssung."
95. Tertullian, *Apol.* 23.16.

a Holy Saturday rite in which the bishop exorcises the candidates, breathes on their faces, and then seals their foreheads, ears, and noses.[96]

John the Deacon's epistle to Senarius describes the action and its meaning: "[A catechumen] therefore is exorcised by exsufflation that, with the devil put to flight, entry may be prepared for Christ our Lord. . . . And Satan is exorcised because the ancient deserted merits such disgrace. He is exorcised—that is, he is commanded to get out and depart."[97] The letter also mentions a subsequent action, anointing the candidates' ears and nostrils with the oil of sanctification. This ritual strengthens and fortifies those organs, creating a kind of protection against worldly temptations that could bring them harm.[98]

Similarly, Augustine cites the practice of exsufflation at baptism as evidence of the bondage of the unbaptized to Satan: In his unfinished refutation of Julian of Eclanum, he remarks on this ritual. Referring to the Christian practice of hissing (*exsufflare*) at images of the emperor as a kind of apotropaic or exorcistic act, he notes that the same is done to "little ones" (*parvuli*) preparing for baptism so that the devil, who binds the candidates through the infection of sin, would be blown out of them.[99] Cyril of Jerusalem similarly connects the ritual of breathing on the candidates as related to exorcism, describing it like a flame scorching and burning away sin.[100] Finally, the seventh canon of the Council of Constantinople (381) advises that the baptism of certain kinds of heretics (e.g., Montanists and Sabellians) include an exorcism by three breaths expelled into their face and ears.[101]

This breathing ritual is related to the *ephphetha*, when the bishop touches the ears and nostrils of the candidates. This slightly different ritual, mentioned by Ambrose, is inspired by Jesus's actions when healing the deaf-mute and the man born blind. Ambrose describes it as "the opening," which makes it possible for candidates to hear the word and smell (and then emit) the sweet fragrance of eternal goodness—the aroma of Christ. Ambrose also explains that, for propriety's sake, the mouth is not touched. Moreover, opening the nostrils has the added effect of allowing candidates to speak of the heavenly mysteries.[102] While Ambrose interprets this act as an opening of the senses,

96. Hippolytus, *Trad. ap.* 20.8.

97. John the Deacon, *Ep. Sen.* 3, trans. author; cf. text in Wilmart, *Analecta reginensia*, 172. See also Isidore of Seville, *Eccl. off.* 2.21.3; and a useful article, Botte, "La sputation, antique rite baptismal?"

98. John the Deacon, *Ep. Sen.* 4–5.

99. Augustine, *C. Jul. op. imp.* 3.199 (CSEL 85.1, 498). Compare Augustine, *Ep.* 194.46, in which he equates exorcism with exsufflation and claims that this is done also to infants at baptism.

100. Cyril of Jerusalem, *Procat.* 9; *Cat.* 16.19; *Myst.* 2.3.

101. Council of Constantinople, *Canon* 7.

102. Ambrose, *Sacr.* 1.2–3. Ambrose's rite appears to be unique, and he mentions no use of oil, but he merely touches the candidate. Later on, this ritual used spittle; see *Gel. Sac.* 42.

John the Deacon understands a slightly different rite, that of anointing the ears and nostrils in order to close the sensory organs. This, he says, builds a fortification against external evil.[103]

RENUNCIATION OF SATAN

The candidates' renunciation of Satan was another rite that ordinarily took place at the threshold of the baptismal chamber. In some places candidates performed this by turning to the west, the direction of the diminishing light and, therefore, symbolically the region of sin. Cyril of Jerusalem recounts the words of their declaration: "I renounce you, Satan, you wicked and cruel tyrant; I no longer fear your power. . . . I renounce you, crafty scoundrel of a serpent; I renounce you, traitor, perpetrator of every crime, who inspired our first parents to revolt. I renounce you, Satan, agent and abettor of all wickedness . . . and all your works."[104] After this abjuring of Satan, the candidate turned east, toward the place of paradise, promise, and the light of the rising sun. There he or she swore allegiance to Christ.

John Chrysostom offers a vivid description of this ritual of renunciation. The candidates look like submissive captives kneeling and begging mercy: "See the external attitude of captivity; the priests bring you in. First they bid you to pray on bent knees, with your hands outstretched to heaven, and to remind yourselves by your posture from what evil you are delivered and to what good you will dedicate yourselves. Then, the priest comes to you one by one, asks for your contract and confession, and prepares you to utter those awesome and frightening words, 'I renounce you, Satan.'"[105]

The candidates' renouncing Satan and professing loyalty to Christ outside the baptismal chamber incorporated several other actions that were exorcistic in nature. In one of these they stood on sackcloth or a goatskin that symbolized their penitence while they renounced Satan and the demons (cf. Ps. 69:10–11). Theodore of Mopsuestia's mystagogical catecheses attest to this tradition. In one of his homilies on baptism, Theodore explains that while the words of exorcism are being pronounced, the frightened candidates stand with outstretched arms, outer garments removed, and barefoot on garments of sackcloth. The rough cloth pricks and stings their feet in order to remind them

---

103. John the Deacon, *Ep. Sen.* 4. Cyril of Jerusalem also mentions the anointing of nostrils and ears, *Cat.* 3.4, as one of the postbaptismal anointing rites. See below, chap. 3, under the heading "Anointing in the Eastern Churches."

104. Cyril of Jerusalem, *Myst.* 1.4–5; see also 6–11, which outlines the rest of the renunciation and profession, including the turning toward the east. Compare Ambrose, *Myst.* 2.7 (which tells the candidate to face toward the east for the renunciation, rather than the west); and idem, *Sacr.* 2.5. See also Hippolytus, *Trad. ap.* 21; and *Const. ap.* 7.41. Tertullian, *Cor.* 3, simply says that this happens before the washing and in the presence of the congregation.

105. John Chrysostom, *Catech.* 2.18 (Stav. 2), trans. Harkins, *St. John Chrysostom,* 50. See also John Chrysostom, *Catech.* 11.19–26 (Pk. 3) and 12.48–52 (Montf. 2).

of their sins and the sins of their original parents.[106] One of Narsai's homilies on baptism also attests to this practice in the East. The candidates, naked and wretched, with bent knees and bowed head, stand on spread sackcloth and beg forgiveness for their former service to the evil one.[107]

A similar ritual was practiced in North Africa. Augustine, speaking to those about to be baptized, admonishes them to be humble and wary of the last-minute urgings of the tempter:

> So amid all these gangs of people vexing and troubling you, put on sackcloth and humble your soul with fasting. Humility is rewarded with what pride has been denied. And you, indeed, while you were being scrutinized, and that persuader of flight and desertion was being properly rebuked by the terrifying omnipotence of the Trinity, were not actually clothed in sackcloth, but yet your feet were symbolically standing on it. The vices and the fleeces of the she-goats must be trampled on; the ragged garments of the he-goats on the left hand side must be torn.[108]

Augustine's contemporary Quodvultdeus of Carthage reports a similar practice in his church. He describes the candidates as being brought in front of the entire congregation with once-proud heads bowed, standing barefoot on goatskin, and having the devil driven out of them.[109]

Spiritual and Bodily Disciplines

Preparing candidates for baptism also involved rigorous ascetical practices for the purpose of both purifying and strengthening, not only for the rite but also for the life candidates would be expected to live once they were full members of the church. Catechumens would undertake several disciplines, including fasting (especially from meat and wine), refraining from sexual intercourse, keeping all-night vigils, and ceasing to bathe for the period of their training.

For example, the *Apostolic Constitutions* argues that just as Jesus had fasted forty days and nights after his baptism (even though he had no need to purify himself), the candidate for baptism should fast beforehand. Fasting afterward would be inappropriate, since the newly baptized ought to appear joyous and not dejected.[110] Similarly, Gregory of Nazianzus's *Oration on Holy Baptism* lists several preparatory practices, including candidates' observing vigils,

106. Theodore of Mopsuestia, *Bapt. hom.* 2.2. See Mingana, *Commentary of Theodore of Mopsuestia*, 17–44, which also gives the text of the renunciation. See also the article by Quasten, "Theodore of Mopsuestia"; and Hermann, "Cilicium."

107. Narsai, *Hom. Epiph.* 22. See Connolly, *Liturgical Homilies of Narsai*, 39.

108. Augustine, *Serm.* 216.10–11, trans. Hill, *Works of Saint Augustine*, 173.

109. Quodvultdeus, *Symb.* 1.1.5; cf. 2.1.2–6 on the renunciation of the devil, his pomps, and all his angels. See Ildephonsus, *Cognit.* 54.1, for later evidence from Spain. Cyril of Jerusalem mentions trampling Satan underfoot but is not specific about an animal skin (*Myst.* 1.9).

110. *Const. ap.* 7.22.

keeping fasts, sleeping on the ground, weeping for their sinfulness, and giving alms to the needy. They are to consider poor Lazarus and be like charitable Zacchaeus—feeding the hungry, clothing the naked, and forgiving debtors in order to honor their own approach to the sacramental table.[111]

Such training prepared candidates for a lifetime of striving for holiness once they were admitted to the communion of the church. John Chrysostom declares that the newly baptized would be rigorously disciplined. They would henceforth refrain from luxuries, personal vanity, and careless or abusive speech (swearing, slander, blasphemy, and perjury). For this reason, he says, the days prior to baptism are like wrestlers' training exercises. However, instead of defeating ordinary opponents, they are preparing to fight the ultimate enemy, Satan.[112] And John urges them not to forget the value of self-denial once the Lenten discipline was relaxed: "Even if the time of holy quarantine has gone by, let us not put aside the memory of it. . . . I used to hear many people say that they found it difficult to endure the burden of want of food and blame the weakness of their bodies upon it and utter many other bitter laments, saying that their health was being ruined because they had to go without a bath and had to confine their drinking to water."[113] Ambrose also compares catechumens to athletes in training and, like John, chose the analogy of wrestlers, whose regimen included refraining from rich foods and sexual intercourse.[114]

Giving up baths from the beginning of Lent until Holy Thursday caused a certain amount of suffering because bodies would begin to itch and develop sores.[115] The candidates' preparatory bath on Holy Thursday was therefore as aesthetic and hygienic as it was purificatory for a group of naked bodies that had been unwashed for six weeks.[116] Augustine confirms this, saying candidates' bodies had become foul and would be offensive if they came to the font without bathing. The day chosen for the purpose—when the Lord's Supper was annually commemorated—was especially appropriate because that was the day when Jesus washed the apostles' feet. Augustine allows others to join with them in bathing and relaxing their fast on this day.[117] Perhaps in respect for their bodies' having been immersed in consecrated water, the newly baptized were admonished to refrain from bathing again for one full week after

111. Gregory of Nazianzus, Or. 40.31. The candidates weeping and confessing sins are described by Cyril of Jerusalem, Cat. 2.15, 19–20; and Cat. 3.7.

112. John Chrysostom, Catech. 9.27–47 (Montf. 1); 10.1–4 (Pk. 2).

113. John Chrysostom, Catech. 5.1–3 (Stav. 5), trans. Harkins, St. John Chrysostom, 80–82. On baptismal anointing (a complex and much-debated series of actions), see Winkler, "Original Meaning of the Prebaptismal Anointing"; and L. L. Mitchell, Baptismal Anointing.

114. Ambrose, Hel. 21.79.

115. On the sores and itching that probably came with it, see John Chrysostom, Cont. eb. (PL 50:433b).

116. See Hippolytus, Trad. ap. 20 on the Thursday bath.

117. Augustine, Ep. 54.

baptism.[118] Augustine tells the newly baptized on Easter that, like the wheat of newly baked bread, they have been threshed by the fasts and vigils, ground by the exorcisms, mixed with water to become dough, and baked in the trials and tribulations of life.[119]

Augustine, too, saw the training of catechumens during Lent as a kind of moral indoctrination and also recognized the value of extending these practices of self-denial to the entire congregation. All of them together were expected to fast, to be more than usually generous with alms, and to refrain from sexual intercourse with their spouses.[120]

STRIPPING AND PRELIMINARY ANOINTING

The complex baptismal rite usually incorporated the practice of anointing, although the type, placement, and numbers of anointings varied according to time and place. At least three different kinds of baptismal anointing were practiced in antiquity: a prebaptismal anointing of the body or head only, for the purpose of exorcism and strengthening; a second anointing, either before or after the bath, whose purpose varied; and a third anointing, usually with scented oil (chrism) on the head or forehead, to signify the conferring of the gift of the Holy Spirit.[121]

The first of these types, the anointing meant for exorcism over the entire nude body, usually took place after the renunciation of Satan. The act of stripping symbolized the removal of the "old self" and the transition to the new. The most relevant biblical text here is Colossians 3:9–10: "Do not lie to one another, seeing that you have stripped off the old self with its practices and have clothed yourselves with the new self, which is being renewed in knowledge according to the image of its creator."

Cyril of Jerusalem directly cites this text as well as two others in his explanation of this step in the baptismal rite:

> Immediately, then, upon entering, you removed your tunics. This was a figure of the "stripping off of the old self with its deeds" [Col. 3:9]. Having stripped, you were naked, in this also imitating Christ who was naked on the cross, by his nakedness "throwing off the cosmic powers and authorities like a garment and publicly upon the cross leading them in his triumphal procession" [Col. 2:15]. For as the forces of the enemy made their lair in our members, you may no longer wear the old garment. I do not, of course, refer to this visible

---

118. Tertullian, *Cor.* 3.

119. Augustine, *Serm.* 219A.2.

120. Augustine, *Serm.* 210. 2 (establishes the catechumens as fasting and the congregation as following). On Lenten fasts in general, see idem, *Serm.* 205.2; 206.3; 207.2; 208.1; 209.3; 210.4–9. See also Quodvultdeus, *Symb.* 1 on the vigil kept on the night before baptism.

121. See discussion below, chap. 3, under the heading "Anionting and the Spirit's Gift in the Fourth Century."

garment, but to "the old man which, deluded by its lusts, is sinking towards death" [Eph. 4:22].[122]

In the *Apostolic Tradition* this first apotropaic anointing immediately follows the renunciation of Satan. The bishop first exorcises the oil, which a deacon then brings to the presbyter, who performs the anointing on candidates who have been stripped of all clothing and any ornaments (lest anyone take any "alien thing" down into the water with him). Just before he administers the anointing, the presbyter commands the candidate to declare, "I renounce thee, Satan, and all thy servants, and all thy works." After the candidate has said this, the presbyter anoints the candidate's entire body, saying, "Let all spirits depart from thee."[123]

John Chrysostom vividly describes this rite as it took place in Antioch, explaining its strengthening and apotropaic purposes. Here, too, the anointing occurs after the candidate's renunciation of Satan, which, in this instance is after an initial anointing on the forehead with the "oil of the Spirit" and the sign of the cross. Only then, according to John, "in the full darkness of the night, [the presbyter] strips off your robe, and, as if he were going to lead you into heaven itself by this ritual, he causes your whole body to be anointed with that olive oil of the Spirit, so that all your limbs may be fortified and unconquered by the darts which the adversary aims at you."[124]

Cyril of Jerusalem also administered the anointing after the renunciation of Satan, although, at this point, the candidate had moved from the outer to the inner baptismal chamber and had already disrobed. As the *Apostolic Tradition* also describes it, this was the last ritual action before the candidate was brought to the water. Citing the Colossians text (3:9–10), Cyril describes the rite of anointing in dramatic detail:

> Then, when stripped, you were anointed with exorcised olive oil from the topmost hairs of your head to the soles of your feet, and became partakers on the good olive tree, Jesus Christ. . . . The exorcised olive oil, therefore, symbolized the partaking of the richness of Christ; its effect is to disperse every concentration of the cosmic forces arrayed against us. For as the breath of the saints upon you, with the invocation of the name of God, burns the devils like fierce fire and expels them, so this exorcised olive oil receives, through prayer and the invocation of God, power so great as not only to burn and purge away the traces of sin, but also to put to rout all the invisible forces of the Evil One.[125]

122. Cyril of Jerusalem, *Myst.* 2.2, trans. McCauley and Stephenson, *Works of Saint Cyril of Jerusalem*, 2:161–62.

123. Hippolytus, *Trad. ap.* 21. See also *Const. ap.* 7.42.

124. John Chrysostom, *Catech.* 2.22–24 (Stav. 2), trans. Harkins, *St. John Chrysostom*, 51–52.

125. Cyril of Jerusalem, *Myst.* 2.3, trans. McCauley and Stephenson, *Works of Saint Cyril of Jerusalem*, 2:162–63.

Ambrose places the first anointing before the renunciation of Satan, rather than after, and likens the process to athletes rubbing oil over their bodies.[126] In Mopsuestia, candidates first removed their outer garments for the renunciation, received an initial anointing on the forehead afterward (as in Antioch), and then were stripped completely and anointed over their entire bodies. According to Theodore, the stripping of candidates symbolizes their returning to the state of Adam and Eve in paradise (and naked) prior to the fall, while their anointing and baptism signify their recovered "garments of immortality."[127] Thus the exorcistic or baptismal anointing of the nude body came to signify a step in the recovery of the prelapsarian state.

The Water Bath

Water is essential to the plain sense of washing. The Latin word *baptisterium* referred to a large basin, or *piscina*, in the *frigidarium* of a Roman bath.[128] In a homily on Christ's baptism, Gregory of Nyssa emphasizes this basic association: "But water serves to express the cleansing. For since we customarily wash in water to render our body clean when it is soiled by dirt or mud, we therefore apply it also in sacramental action, and display the spiritual brightness by that which is subject to our senses. . . . Do not despise the divine laver, nor think lightly of it, as a common thing, on account of the use of water."[129] Thus, among other things, baptism is, simply, a bath.

Baptism's cleansing effect links Jesus's baptism by John (and thus all subsequent baptisms) to other bathing/purification/ablution practices in the ancient world (whether or not they were derived from them). For although John's practice has no exact parallels in earlier or contemporary religious rituals, neither does an explanation of the term "baptism" appear in the canonical Gospels. Presumably, readers (or hearers) understood what was meant. For example, the Epistle to the Hebrews' reference to instructions about baptisms (6:1–2) presumes some knowledge but offers no details.

The symbolism of full bodily immersion in water and the usual practice of performing this three times is discussed elsewhere in this volume.[130] For now, it is enough to point out that early Christian baptism required a full drenching of the body. Only in cases of sickbed (clinical) baptism, when an exception

126. Ambrose, *Sacr.* 1.4. On the anointing compared to that of an athlete, see also Ps. Dionysius, *Ecc. hier.* 2.3, 7.3.

127. Theodore of Mopsuestia, *Bapt. hom.* 3.8. See discussion on the restoration of Adam and Eve in chap. 5, under the heading "Adam and Eve's Nudity as Symbolizing Innocence."

128. See Pliny the Younger, *Ep.* 2.17.11, and discussion below, under the heading "Roman Bathing Practices as Background to Christian Baptism."

129. Gregory of Nyssa, *Diem lum.*, NPNF[2], 5:518–24, slightly adapted by author.

130. See chap. 4, under the headings "Triple Immersion" and "Stripping and Nude Immersion."

was made for the sake of the invalid, was sprinkling allowed.[131] Cyprian of Carthage, however, refuses to say that sprinkling is any less efficacious than immersion. In his view, the water is inherently redemptive however it is applied: whether by sprinkling, by pouring, or by full immersion. He even adds that baptism differs from ordinary bathing because it washes away sin, while a bath washes away only external impurities.[132]

Some fourth-century authors explain how bodily immersion would have been accomplished. Theodore of Mopsuestia, for example, provides the following instructions:

> Then the bishop lays his hand on your head with the words "In the name of the Father" and while pronouncing them pushes you down into the water. You obediently follow the signal he gives you by word and gesture and bow down under the water. . . . You bow your head when you immerse yourself to show your sincere agreement with the bishop's words. You bow down under the water, then lift your head again. Meanwhile the bishop says "And of the Son," and guides you with his hand as you bend down into the water as before. . . . You raise your head, and again the bishop says, "And of the Holy Spirit," pressing you down into the water again with his hand. You bend beneath the water again, humbly acknowledging by the same sign that you hope for the blessings of baptism from the Holy Spirit.[133]

In like manner, John Chrysostom instructs the priest to use his right hand to push the candidate's head down into the water three times and lift it out again three times.[134]

ROMAN BATHING PRACTICES AS BACKGROUND TO CHRISTIAN BAPTISM

Roman secular bathing practices may have had a role in the construction of baptism's meaning as much as the religious ablutions of Jews or pagans. Zeno of Verona vividly describes the scene inside a baptistery, using an analogy that a Roman bather would understand: "Already the girded bath attendant awaits you, ready to furnish the necessary anointing and drying, and a golden denarius sealed with triple effigy."[135] Here the bath attendant is the bishop. The coin's three faces probably refer to the Trinity, invoked over each of the

---

131. For example, see the discussion of Novatian's baptism in Cyprian, *Ep.* 69; and Eusebius, *Hist. eccl.* 6.43.13–15. See also *Did.* 7, which allows affusion when water is insufficient for immersion.

132. Cyprian, *Ep.* 69.12.3.

133. Theodore of Mopsuestia, *Bapt. hom.* 3.18–19, trans. Yarnold, *Awe-Inspiring Rites of Initiation*, 191–92.

134. John Chrysostom, *Catech.* 2.26 (Stav. 2).

135. Zeno of Verona, *Tract.* 1.23 (CCSL 22:70), trans. author.

candidate's three immersions in the font; its precious metal (gold) reflects the value of the faith.

Certain Roman bathing practices have parallels in Christian baptismal rites, including the use of oil as a cleansing agent and, in some instances, the structures and pools that accommodated the rite. In some instances, baptisteries were built over earlier bath complexes and could have exploited existing pipes and drains. And even though some church authorities disapproved of public bathing because of the possibility of immodest behavior, a general prohibition would have been extremely unpopular with most Roman Christians.[136] Cyril of Jerusalem points out that even Jesus visited the baths in Jerusalem and, moreover, healed the paralytic at a public bath. Aware of traditional civic pride in bath structures and noting that John 5:2 describes a pool with five porticoes, Cyril adds, "When, as now, he [Jesus] visits the public baths, it is not out of interest in the architecture, but to heal the sick."[137] Thus bathing also was considered a part of good health practice. For example, Tertullian attended the baths and believed them hygienic.[138] Clement of Alexandria, while condemning excesses, had given guidelines for Christians who wished to attend the baths. The baths might even give comfort to the mourning. Augustine mentions going to the bath after the death of his mother as a balm for his grief.[139]

However church officials judged the baths, the combination of water and oil in baptism shows its superficial parallels with ordinary bathing. Like bathers, the baptized removed their clothing. They applied oil to their bodies as a cleansing and healing substance. Moreover, certain key words, borrowed from Latin bathing terminology, make the parallel more striking. For example, the Latin word *baptisterium* referred to a large pool in the *frigidarium* and only from the mid- to late fourth century referred to a ritual bathing chamber or font.[140] *Lavacrum* (an ordinary bath) was another Latin word for (Christian) baptism.[141]

Most suggestive of all is the word *piscina*, which literally meant "fishpond" but could also mean a pool large enough for swimming. The mosaics that adorned many of the pools of Roman houses also were lavishly decorated with fish and sea creatures, creating a virtual (if not actual) fishpond, or

---

136. For cautioning against the baths, see Clement of Alexandria, *Paed.* 3.5, and Cyprian, *Hab. virg.* 19, admonishing consecrated virgins to avoid baths where they might be seen by men.

137. Cyril of Jerusalem, *Hom. para.* 1. Although see his passing comment on the public baths in *Procat.* 16.

138. Tertullian, *Apol.* 42.

139. Clement of Alexandria, *Paed.* 3.9; Augustine, *Conf.* 9.7.32.

140. In a letter to a friend describing his villa in Tuscany, Pliny the Younger describes the baths in some detail, using the terms *baptisterium* and *piscina*, *Ep.* 5.6.25–26; also *Ep.* 2.17.11. The first recorded use of *baptisterium* in a Christian context comes from Sidonius Apollinaris, *Ep.* 2.2; 4.15.

141. See, for example, Tertullian, *Cor.* 3 and *Bapt.* 2.2; 7.1; 11.4.

piscina (cf. fig. 5.4). Christians, adapting the image to fit their understanding of themselves as "little fish" when in the font, also could call their baptistery pools *piscinae*. Optatus, bishop of Milevis, speaks of the consecration of the font in these terms: "This is the fish, who through invocation is joined to the waters of the font in baptism so that due to the fish's presence in the water it [the font] is called *piscina*; the fish whose name in Greek contains in one word all that is sacred in its individual letters: *ichthys,* which means Jesus Christ, Son of God, Savior."[142]

GRECO-ROMAN PARALLELS TO CHRISTIAN BAPTISM

Concern with external (bodily) as well as internal (spiritual) purity was paramount in the religious practices of the first-century Mediterranean world.[143] Various ancient cults administered a bath prior to performing certain rituals (e.g., sacrifice, marriage, initiation), and such practices may have been familiar to gentile Christian converts. For example, the initiates to the mysteries of Demeter and Persephone at Eleusis immersed themselves in the Aegean (followed by the ritual sacrifice of a pig) prior to their full initiation into the cult.[144] Apuleius's Lucius underwent a ritual bath prior to his initiation into the cult of Isis. At this purification, a priest of Isis specifically prayed that Lucius receive divine forgiveness.[145] In Lucius's case, the bath was given prior to initiation, not as a part of his induction. Just as in other mystery cults, entrance rites included several secret ceremonies that were often sequentially graded, allowing initiates to gain higher ranks of membership.[146]

Several early Christian writers refer to bodily purifications in contemporary pagan practice, remarking on their similarities to baptism. Justin Martyr, for example, claims that demons deliberately imitated Christian rites for the purpose of leading people astray. Among these imitative rites, he says, were ablutions performed before entering and leaving temples.[147] Tertullian similarly warns his readers against being confused by the purificatory practices of their non-Christian neighbors:

---

142. Optatus of Milevis, *Parm.* 3.2.8–12 (CSEL 26:68–69), trans. author. See discussion of this acrostic and the fish as a metaphor for the community below, chap. 2, under the heading "Fish."

143. See Ferguson, *Baptism in the Early Church*, chap. 2, 25–37. Among earlier essays on the parallels between Christian ritual and the practices of Greco-Roman mystery cults is a key study by Yarnold, "Baptism and the Pagan Mysteries."

144. See Mylonas, *Eleusis and the Eleusinian Mysteries*, 237–85. An interesting fifth-century BCE relief from Eleusis shows a naked initiate about to be affused with water from a dish held by a female figure (the goddess? a priestess?). Compare with images of Jesus's baptism by John (figs. 1.1, 1.2, 2.7) and the discussion above, under the heading "Jesus's Baptism in Early Christian Art."

145. Apuleius, *Metam.* 11.22.

146. See Finn, *From Death to Rebirth*, 68–69, as well as source texts, notes, and bibliography.

147. Justin Martyr, *1 Apol.* 62.

In certain sacred rites they [the gentiles] are initiated by means of a bath, some so as to belong to Isis, others to belong to Mithras. They even carry their gods out for washings. Elsewhere they purify their villas, homes, temples, and entire cities by walking around sprinkling water. Certainly at the Apollinarian and Pelusian games they are bathed indiscriminately, and presume this renews and releases them from false oaths. Among the ancients, one who had infected himself with homicide sought purifying waters. Thus if they seek the favors of purification from an idol because cleansing is a natural property of water, how much more truly would waters exhibit that benefit through the authority of God, by whom their nature has been constituted? If they suppose water has a medicinal use through religion, what more potent religion is there than knowing the living God? Here too we recognize the devil's wish to rival the things of God, he practices baptism among his own. How could it be similar? Should the unclean cleanse, the profligate liberate, the condemned absolve? It is evident that this would destroy his own work, washing away the sins he himself inspires.[148]

Like Justin, Tertullian recognizes the similarities between pagan ablutions and Christian baptism. He also credits Satan with intentionally misleading and ensnaring the unwary or the confused, those who fail to differentiate the true and beneficial rites from the demonic ones.

Jewish Ablutions

In its multiform and complex manifestations, first-century Judaism continued an ancient practice of purification, including ritual ablutions, washings, and—based on New Testament evidence—baptisms. Purificatory ablutions were particularly characteristic of the Qumran community and certain other ascetical sectarian groups (e.g., the Essenes). The Qumran community may have practiced a two-stage initiation process: an initial ablution that cleansed candidates of sin-caused ritual impurity and allowed them to be provisionally accepted into the community, and a second initiation that confirmed their inner purity and symbolized the holiness of those who received it.[149] In any case, observant Jews of the first century would have sought the benefits of purificatory baths. Some of them, apparently, became followers of John the Baptist (cf. John 4:1).[150]

Josephus is the sole nonscriptural witness to John the Baptist. He asserts that John's mission was to exhort the Jews to lead righteous lives, practice justice toward their fellows, and show piety toward God. According to Josephus, John's baptisms were not for repentance for sin but for consecrating the body, since the soul was purified through performing virtuous deeds.[151] Josephus's

---

148. Tertullian, *Bapt.* 5.1–3 (CCSL 1:280–81), trans. author. See also Tertullian, *Marc.* 1.14.
149. See Cansdale, *Qumran and the Essenes*, 38; Thiering, "Inner and Outer Cleansing."
150. See Ferguson, *Baptism in the Early Church*, chap. 4, 60–82; Gavin, *Jewish Antecedents*. On the Essenes, see Josephus, *Vita* 2; Robinson, "Baptism of John"; Pryke, "John the Baptist"; and Thiering, "Inner and Outer Cleansing."
151. Josephus, *A.J.* 116–19.

description more closely parallels the practice of Jewish ritual bathing, which aimed at external rather than internal cleansing and at reinforcing the pious obligation to keep God's laws.

Even though baptism was rooted in—or at least related to—Jewish water-purification rites, these rituals of cleansing of external pollution could be repeated as often as necessary. The need arose when an individual had physical contact with something defiling, including corpses, blood, bodily emissions, or other bodies or objects regarded as unclean. This kind of defilement could be removed by ritual bathing.[152]

Thus such pollution was temporary, external, and had a defined remedy. By contrast, although the inner character was related to bodily purity, moral pollution (sin) was a more complex matter. Groups like the Essenes appear to have regarded their lustrations as internal (ethical and spiritual) cleansing as well as external washing. They also may have practiced a staged rite of initiation, the first for removal of outward impurities and the second for perfecting the candidates, allowing them to be brought into the community of the pure elect.[153]

At some point, probably in the late first or early second century (the date is disputed), a practice of initiatory bathing emerged within Judaism.[154] Men and women who converted were given a bath (*tebilah*) prior to their entry into the community (signified by the offering of a sacrifice). Although this seems to have been originally a purificatory bath following rituals of conversion and entry into the community (e.g., circumcision for males), it may have replaced those rites in certain places, causing a debate among rabbis about the continuing role of circumcision for male proselytes. The bath itself was like other Jewish ritual baths (*mikvaoth*). The recipients were naked and fully immersed in the water (all parts of the body were washed).

This new ritual practice seems to contain aspects of purification that go beyond washing of external, bodily impurity and instead suggest a total conversion of life (akin to John's preaching of repentance). Conversion became a precondition for entrance into a new community and was therefore parallel in nature to Christian baptism (although not necessarily its source or model). As the ritual for Jewish proselytes developed, it came to include instruction in Torah and an elaborate grading of the water that could be used for the purpose

152. The laws on impurity are mostly found in Lev. 11–16. See also Num. 19:17–21. A. Y. Collins, "Origins of Christian Baptism," argues that both Jewish and Christian baptism are derived from these instructions for purificatory washing.

153. See Thiering, "Inner and Outer Cleansing."

154. See Ferguson, *Baptism in the Early Church*, 76–82; Bamberger, *Proselytism in the Talmudic Period*; Cohen, "Is Proselyte Baptism Mentioned in the Mishnah?" The main (and oldest) reference to this tradition comes from the Babylonian Talmud, *Yebam.* 47a–b, but the *Midrash Sifré Numbers* is the first to enumerate the three basic elements of a proselyte conversion ritual (circumcision, immersion, and sacrifice), according to Porton, *Stranger within Your Gates*, 51, 60–61.

(the most acceptable being living water, i.e., cold, fresh running water such as that from a spring or spring-fed river).[155] Such concern for the properties of appropriate water for immersion finds a parallel in the *Didache*, which states a preference for cold, fresh water for baptism: "If you have no running water, then baptize in some other water; and if you are not able to baptize in cold water then do so in warm."[156]

Some Christian writers appear to be aware of the parallels between Jewish cleansing rites and Christian baptism. Justin Martyr argued that Jewish ablutions were inferior to Christian baptism because they could not cleanse the soul as well as the body.[157] Ambrose, for instance, insists that only Christian baptism heals and purifies and that the baptism of unbelievers polluted rather than cleansed. Moreover, he asserts that the Christian sacraments are earlier, more divine, and more efficacious than those of the Jews, whose baptisms were either superfluous or prefiguration of Christian rites. He draws the contrast further, the Jews who passed through the sea died in the desert, while the one who passes through the baptismal font does not die but rises to eternal life.[158]

Foot Washing

John's Gospel alone mentions Jesus washing his disciples' feet (13:3–16). In this story, Jesus insists that Peter's feet must be washed if the apostle is to have any share in him, and adds, "One who has bathed does not need to wash, except for the feet, but is entirely clean" (John 13:10). Although this event is now more commonly taken to be a sign of discipleship, humility, or charity and not practiced as a cleansing or baptismal rite, some ancient authorities believed that it represents the disciples' baptism, which is otherwise not specified in the biblical narratives.[159] This was proposed in a now-lost writing of Clement of Alexandria, as well as in the *Demonstrations* of the Syrian father Aphrahat, who deemed Jesus's washing of the disciples' feet to be the true circumcision and thus the true baptism.[160] Similarly, within a homily on Isaiah, Origen addressed Jesus as the divine foot-washer. In his prayer, Origen invites Jesus to come to wash his dirty feet, because he, like Peter, even though

---

155. *Miqw.* 9. See the helpful article on the various arguments about Jewish proselyte baptism as a source for Christian baptism by A. Y. Collins, "Origins of Christian Baptism," 41–46.

156. *Did.* 7.2, trans. Holmes, *Apostolic Fathers*, 355. Note Tertullian's disagreement—any water is appropriate, *Bapt.* 4.3. See also Hippolytus, *Trad. ap.* 21, which requires that the water be moving through the tank, or (in case of scarcity) that it be poured from above—and that any water will suffice in a situation of scarcity.

157. Justin Martyr, *Dial.* 14.

158. Ambrose, *Myst.* 4.23; idem, *Sacr.* 1.12; 2.2; 4.10–11.

159. See Kantorowicz, "Baptism of the Apostles."

160. Clement's text is included in John Moschus, *Prat. spir.* 5.176. Aphrahat's mention is in *Dem.* 12.9. See Echle, "Baptism of the Apostles."

washed, still lacks the baptism that the Lord predicted he would receive (cf. Mark 10:38–39; Luke 12:50).[161]

Consequently, the Johannine text justifies an ancient practice of washing the neophytes' feet, and it was practiced in several places (northern Italy, Gaul, Spain, Syria, North Africa, and the British Isles).[162] Ambrose describes the rite as happening immediately after their postbaptismal chrismation, before the newly baptized were re-robed. Presumably their feet were washed while they were still naked. In fourth-century Milan, after the neophytes heard the reading of John's text, the bishop girded himself (*succinctos sacerdos*) and led the group over to a small side basin where he washed their feet. Ambrose reasons that this was necessary to remove the last of the serpent's poison (cf. Gen. 3:15): "The one who is washed need not wash again, but only the feet. Why? In baptism all fault is washed away. But when Adam was overthrown by the Devil the venom (of the serpent) was poured out upon his feet. Thus the feet must be washed—the part of the body where the serpent yet lies in wait."[163]

Augustine refers to variations of the rite and indicates that it was somewhat controversial (perhaps being associated with Donatist rebaptisms). Nevertheless, in some North African churches (though perhaps not in Augustine's Hippo), a ritual washing of the feet of the newly baptized was performed during or at the end of the week following the baptism so that it would not be confused with the baptismal washing.[164] In his commentary on the Gospel of John, Augustine explains the postbaptismal foot washing as the symbolic removal of those sins that occur in daily Christian living: sins that normally (and subsequently) would be forgiven through private penance, the recitation of the Lord's Prayer, the forgiving of others, and acts of kindness toward the poor.[165] In this sense, the washing of feet was appropriately celebrated on the day the neophytes took off their special garments and shoes, returned to their normal clothing, and joined the congregation for the communal Eucharist.

A depiction of Jesus washing the disciples' feet appears on some early Christian sarcophagi (fig. 1.10), occasionally juxtaposed with the scene of

161. See a recent translation and discussion of this prayer by Christman, "Origen's Prayer." It is not certain that Origen's prayer was prompted by an actual baptismal practice.

162. The evidence from Spain includes *Can.* 48 of the Council of Elvira (ca. 305), which forbids the practice. This canon was probably added to the acta of the council at a later date. See Brandt, "Strutture del IV secolo per la lavanda."

163. Ambrose, *Sacr.* 3.1.7 (SC 25:94–97), trans. author. Augustine testifies to its practice but chooses to hold it off until the third day of the octave of Easter, in order that it not be confused with baptism. See Augustine, *Ep.* 55.18.33. On foot washing in general, see Beatrice, *La lavanda dei piedi.*

164. Augustine, *Ep.* 55.18.33.

165. Augustine, *Tract. Ev. Jo.* 56.3–5; 58.4–5.

Figure 1.10. Detail of Jesus washing Peter's feet.
Sarcophagus, Museo de l'Arles Antique, Arles.
Mid-fourth century. (Photo by author.)

Pilate washing his hands, which also could be a figure of baptism, perhaps of
Pilate in particular (a sign of his conversion).[166]

A baptism is a bath. Baptism is a ritual of cleansing as well as of physical and
spiritual healing. It washes away both external impurities and internal ones,
thus purifying recipients from both dirt and sin. The water in an ancient Christian baptismal font was blessed and prepared for this purpose, and candidates
were exorcised from demons, stripped, and apotropaically anointed at the
beginning of the ritual. Any evil spirits that remained somehow attached to
the person were rendered harmless, their wiles and weapons useless against the
wonder-working water. For example, Cyprian of Carthage claimed that like
scorpions and serpents, which can exercise their powers only on dry land, the
devil's malice persists only as far as the saving waters. In baptism his venom
loses all its poison.[167]

166. Pilate's conversion and subsequent martyrdom are described in the *Acts of Pilate* and
mentioned by Tertullian, *Apol.* 21.24.
167. Cyprian, *Ep.* 69.15.1–2.

Other elements of the baptismal ritual also contributed to this aspect of baptism, including the giving of salt to candidates, signing them with the cross, exsufflation of their facial orifices, and the washing of their feet. Candidates were also expected to prepare themselves for the ritual in ways that fortified them for the battle with demonic forces. They fasted, refrained from bathing and sexual intercourse, and went without sleep prior to their initiation. Most important, they renounced Satan before they professed their allegiance to Christ.

Baptism's cleansing property had parallels in both Jewish and Greco-Roman ritual practices, along with ordinary ancient bathing practices. Jesus was himself subjected to it, partly (according to early Christian writers) to purify the water itself for such a purpose, but ablutions of all kinds were well established in religious practice. Descending into water had a dual meaning even before John the Baptist came preaching an imminent baptism in the Spirit. Descent into water that was consecrated for the purpose conveyed both corporeal cleansing and spiritual purification.

According to early Christian writers, baptism had been prefigured in certain biblical stories, including narratives of destructive waters (e.g., the great flood, the drowning of Pharaoh's armies in the Red Sea) and healing waters (Naaman the Syrian, the paralytic, and the blind man). These types appear in both early Christian literature and visual art as allusions to the purificatory and healing properties of baptism. By undergoing actual ritual practices that embodied these properties, the newly baptized would have understood themselves to have been spiritually cleansed, their impurities left behind in the water, and both sin and Satan overcome.

This aspect of baptism remained primarily associated with the water bath and the prebaptismal anointing, which was completely understandable, as oil and water were ancient cleansing agents just as soap and water are today. For some early thinkers, the Holy Spirit was also transmitted through the water, invited at the consecration of the font. Nevertheless, the bath alone would come to be seen by some as only part of the ritual, and not complete in itself. Once cleansed, the person was made ready for the next set of actions associated with the initiatory rite.

2

Incorporation into the Community

In late Antiquity, the baptistery of the Lateran Basilica (San Giovanni in Fonte) was the preeminent place for baptism in Rome. Built sometime in the first quarter of the fourth century and remodeled in the fifth century, the basilica to which it belonged was the bishop's parish church and the earliest of Constantine's endowments to the ancient capital of the empire. Its original eight imposing porphyry columns were later joined by an octagonal architrave that supported another set of eight columns leading to a cupola above the font. Eight couplets, attributed to Leo the Great, are inscribed on this architrave:

> A people consecrated to the heavens is here born from a fruitful seed
> established by waters made fertile by the Spirit.
> Plunge in, O sinner, and be cleansed by the sacred flow.
> Whom it receives old, the wave returns new.
> No differences remain among the reborn,
> whom one font, one spirit, and one faith make one.
> By a virginal birth, Mother Church bears these children.
> Those whom she conceives by God's breathing she births by this
>   stream.
> You who wish to be innocent, wash in the bath,
> whether you are burdened by ancestral sin or your own.
> This is the fountain of life that cleanses the whole world;
> its origin is Christ's wound.
> Hope for the heavenly kingdom, once you are reborn in this spring.
> That happy life does not admit those who are only once-born.
> Let neither the number nor the kind of your sins frighten.
> Anyone reborn in the river will be holy.[1]

1. Trans. author. Scholars argue that Leo wrote this while he was archdeacon under Six-tus III. Some versions and translations use a different line order. A convincing argument for

This inscription poetically describes the many benefits of baptism: cleansing from sin, personal rebirth, and the constitution of a people or clan (*gens*). The people, "consecrated to the heavens," who are conceived in and born to the virgin Mother Church, comprise a new family, a new race, and a new class. Such an assertion lies at the heart of baptism as the establishment of both personal and corporate identity. Through baptism, neophytes were changed both in self-definition and social location. They attained a new identity, largely by setting aside certain other defining qualities (e.g., race, social class, gender) in at least a spiritual or eschatological, if not a practical or worldly, sense.

Several elements of the baptismal rite convey this transition. These include enrolling catechumens, assigning sponsors, sealing candidates, and embracing the new members with a holy kiss. In addition, certain symbols express the formation of the new community, including likening the neophytes to siblings, cohorts of soldiers, and members of athletic teams. The newly baptized are also referred to as flocks of sheep and schools or catches of fish. These analogies and metaphors allude not only to their incorporation into a new religious association but also to the marks, responsibilities, and benefits of that membership.

Christians as a New Race

When Christianity was an illicit sect and joining required renouncing the traditional Roman gods, taking on this new identity was risky. In some circumstances, Christian refusal to honor the gods was seen as sedition or treason. This perception remained despite the apologists' efforts to reassure traditionalists that Christians were still patriotic and morally responsible citizens. Receiving baptism undeniably required a new understanding of family relationships and civic loyalties, even though many aspects of daily life would not change. Now, having a dual identity (as both Roman and Christian), members of the baptized community found that when loyalties conflicted, they had to set one over the other. The second-century *Epistle to Diognetus* explains this revision of values: "For Christians are not distinguished from the rest of humanity by country, language, or custom. For nowhere do they live in cities of their own, nor do they speak some unusual dialect, nor do they practice an eccentric way of life. . . . [Yet] they live in their own countries, but only as nonresidents; they participate in everything as citizens, and endure everything as foreigners. . . . They live on earth but have their citizenship in heaven."[2] These lines assert the Christian experience of both dislocation and belonging. They portray Christians as continuing to be attached to the particular city or nation or family

---

Leo's authorship was made by Dölger, "Die Inschrift im Baptisterium S. Giovanni." See also Underwood, "Fountain of Life," 56–61.

2. *Diogn.* 5, trans. Holmes, *Apostolic Fathers*, 701–3, slightly adapted by author.

of their first birth, yet simultaneously holding a parallel familial identity of cobelievers and civic affiliation to a heavenly realm. Christians obey the laws of their earthly society while their faith supersedes the religious aspects of those laws.

This transition is an important baptismal motif. Certain aspects of the rite negotiated the way new Christians were incorporated into the group while relativizing their former obligations and loyalties. Moreover, this transition was necessarily public rather than purely secret, or it would not have been judged genuine. In the early centuries taking in this new identity could be perilous, sometimes resulting in hostile—even punitive—reactions from members of a candidate's family and the wider society. Christians were neither traditional Roman polytheists nor Jews; rather, they were a different subcultural group, which often made other citizens regard them with suspicion and even hatred.[3] Their gatherings were held in secret and closed to outsiders, which caused speculation about the degree of intimacy forged among the members. They were a heterogeneous group, mixing social classes, nationalities, and races. They were accused of spurning their birth families and cities, neglecting traditional religious duties, and joining a sect whose purpose was regarded with distaste or fear.[4]

The idea that Christians constituted another race, or *gens*, can be traced to Paul. This was one way early exegetes interpreted Paul's assertion that, through baptism, "there is no longer Jew or Greek, there is no longer slave or free, there is no longer male and female; for all of you are one in Christ Jesus" (Gal. 3:28).[5] The claim, put more constructively, that Christians are a distinct people is explicitly expressed by the author of 1 Peter, who describes Christians as "a chosen race, a royal priesthood, a holy nation, God's own people" (2:9a). The language and metaphors of baptism follow this pattern by referring to the community of Christians as a new family, a new nation, and a new (or distinct) ethnic group.

John Chrysostom's baptismal homilies urge neophytes to consider themselves strangers to the world around them without leaving it entirely. By their behavior, they should demonstrate their loyalty to and citizenship of a different

3. For example, Tertullian claims "death to the third race [Christians]" was a common cry in the circus (*Scorp.* 10). Here Tertullian distinguishes Christians from Jews or polytheists, possibly referring to the distinction between Jew and Greek of Gal. 3:28. The idea of creating a distinct (or "third") race or people is a complex matter in early Christianity, incurring as much negative reaction (and rejection) as acceptance. That Christians (including gnostics) employed the language and social strategies of breaking down boundaries, particularly of race and gender, is discussed more fully by Valantasis, "Question of Christian Identity"; Buell, *Why This New Race*; and Buell, "Race and Universalism in Early Christianity." See also Williams, *Immovable Race*.

4. For examples, see Minucius Felix, *Oct.* 8; Origen, *Cels.* 8.2; and Tacitus, *Ann.* 15.44. See also Markus, *Christianity in the Roman World*, 24–47.

5. Justin Martyr, *Dial.* 138, calls Christ the founder of a new race, generated by himself through water, faith, and the cross.

nation.[6] Although they live in the present, they should not judge this place or time to be their true home. They are to live one life outwardly, while keeping their true identity hidden from unbelievers. This identity was more boldly marked by their claim of a heavenly parentage and birth from the womb of a spiritual mother.

Church as Mother and God as Father

The Lateran baptistery inscription (cited above) employs the metaphor of creating a new birth family. The passage describes new Christians as being conceived in the womb (font) of the virginal Mother Church, fertilized by the breath or spirit of God (*spirante Deo*). Consecrating the water in the baptismal ritual assures the font's fecundity.[7] Moreover, presenting the font as a virginal mother, impregnated by God's breathing, recalls the conception of Jesus. Leo the Great's sermon on the nativity of Christ makes this connection explicit: "Each one acquires a spiritual birth in regeneration. To everyone who is reborn, the water of baptism is like the Virgin's womb. The same Holy Spirit fills the font as filled the Virgin, so that the sin that was nullified there by that sacred conception may be removed here by the mystic washing."[8]

Although the image of the font-as-womb was common among early Christian writers, who frequently referred to the church as the pure and virginal spouse of God and the mother of Christians, some offered an even more explicit description of the means of conception, gestation, and birth of the new believers.[9] Paulinus of Nola actually speaks of the Holy Spirit as mating with (*maritat*) the waters of the font.[10] The Syrian poet Ephrem describes the font as the second womb, a womb that "gives birth without pangs to the children of the kingdom," and the priest as the midwife "who ministers to this womb as it gives birth."[11]

6. John Chrysostom, *Catech*. 7.23 (Stav. 7).

7. See discussion of the font's fertility below, chap. 4, under the heading "Baptism as Rebirth in Early Christian Thought."

8. Leo I, *Serm*. 24.3 (SC 22:114), trans. author. See also Leo I, *Serm*. 25; 63.4 (*De Passione* 12). The impregnation of the font is still symbolized in some baptismal liturgies by the dipping of the paschal candle into the font as part of the blessing of the water in the Easter vigil. The similarities between this text and the inscription serves as evidence of Leo's authorship of the poem in the Lateran baptistry.

9. See Jensen, "*Mater Ecclesia* and *Fons Aeterna*"; and Plumpe, *Mater Ecclesia*.

10. Paulinus of Nola, *Ep*. 32 (to Severus). See partial text below, chap.4, under the heading "Birthing Metaphors in Fourth-Century Sermons on Baptism." Compare Didymus, who describes the baptismal pool as the organ of the Trinity and the mother of all through the Holy Spirit, while remaining a virgin, *Trin*. 2.263 (PG 39.692B), trans. Daniélou, *Bible and the Liturgy*, 48.

11. Ephrem, *Virg*. 7.7–8 (Hymn 7), trans. Brock, *Harp of the Spirit*, 49. In Ephrem's *Eccl*. (Hymn 36), Jesus's baptism in the river is described as a symbolic second conception: the "moist

Unlike the first birth, this second birth is a matter of conscious choice. Moreover, the offspring who emerge from a baptismal font share a single father and mother. They receive a new name and are siblings within a single "new birth" family. In his letters, Paul often addresses his readers as brothers and sisters (*adelphoi*) or as beloved children (*tekna mou agapēta*). Paul also refers to himself as their father in Jesus Christ (1 Cor. 4:14–15; cf. 1 Thess. 2:11).[12] Clement of Alexandria employs similar familial phrases in his exhortation to the Greeks, describing God as an affectionate father who admonishes his children and the church as composed of "first born offspring" (*prōtotokoi paides*) and "God's nurslings" (*trophimoi tou theou*).[13]

A Roman family was not limited to a married couple and their children, but included unmarried female relatives, clients, and slaves. All members were bound by filial obligation to revere the ancestors and domestic gods, as well as give absolute obedience to the paterfamilias. This basic societal unit had a kind of autonomy since the power of the father was recognized and respected in Roman law. Thus when early Christian writers compared the church to a family, they evoked an extended household, bound together by common piety and filial duties nurtured by a loving mother and governed by a divine father. However, unlike a birth family, this was a family one chose. Justin Martyr's *First Apology* elaborates on the Christian family as a "family of choice":

> Since at our birth we are born without our own knowledge or choice, by our parents coming together, and were brought up in bad habits and wicked training; in order that we may not remain the children of necessity and of ignorance, but may become the children of choice and knowledge, . . . there is pronounced over him who chooses to be born again and has repented of his sins, the name of God the Father and Lord of the universe; he who leads to the laver the person that is to be washed calls him by this name alone.[14]

The North African fathers characteristically typified the church as the mother of this family and thus the divine Father's spouse. The pattern is notable in the treatises of both Tertullian and Cyprian. Tertullian, for example, describes the family gathering after a baptism: "Therefore, blessed ones, for whom the grace of God waits, when you come up from that most sacred washing of the new birth, and for the first time you raise your hands with your brethren in your mother's house (*apud matrem*), ask of your Father, ask

---

womb of the water that conceived him [Jesus] in chastity, bore him in chastity, and made him ascend in glory."

12. Some of the same language appears in Heb. 2:10–17.

13. Clement of Alexandria, *Protr.* 9.

14. Justin Martyr, *1 Apol.* 61, ANF, 1:183, slightly adapted by author.

of your Lord, for special grants of grace and attributions of spiritual gifts."[15] Cyprian's language is more concrete: "The church is alone mother, plentiful in the results of fruitfulness: from her womb we are born, by her milk we are nourished, by her spirit we are animated. . . . He can no longer have God for his father who has not the church for his mother."[16] In a sermon on the Lord's Prayer, delivered to catechumens, Augustine explains why they should address God as "father." They are to think of themselves as babies still in the womb of their mother, the church. This mother, furthermore, remains a virgin (like Mary) even though she conceives and gives birth to children.[17] The children's birth was their emergence from the font, and for the first week following their baptism they would be referred to as infants.[18]

Baptism thereby gives Christians a new mother and father, as well as new sisters and brothers who are equal, none favored or advantaged over the others. Cyril of Jerusalem assures his catechumens that their enrollment for baptism makes them all sons and daughters of the same mother.[19] Zeno of Verona tells the candidates that, though they are different in age, sex, and stage of life, they soon will be joined in unity. One of Zeno's *Invitations to the Baptismal Font* particularly expresses this equalizing aspect of baptism: "From this [washing in the font], you who were diverse in age and different in race suddenly emerge siblings. Suddenly you emerge, infants from the same womb."[20] Naturally, this means that the newly baptized were like children, despite their age, when they entered the font. To illustrate this point, they are often identified as "infants" or "children" (*infantes* or *parvuli*).

This language of unity, or of transcending former differences, may be a conscious borrowing of Pauline theology, particularly that reflected in Galatians 3:26–28, which a very early baptismal formula might have been. Paul maintained this as an aspect of baptism, alongside that of the cleansing bath (1 Cor. 6:11), could have been Paul's expectation for the future time (at the new creation), when distinctions between persons would be dissolved.

15. Tertullian, *Bapt.* 20.5 (CCSL 1:295), trans. author.

16. Cyprian, *Unit. eccl.* 5–6 (CCSL 3:252–53), trans. author. Compare John Chrysostom, *Catech.* 4.1 (Stav. 4), where he mixes metaphors somewhat, describing the church as a loving mother who sees herself as a fertile field with a new, green crop of baptized children.

17. Augustine, *Serm.* 56. See also *Serm.* 119.4; 213; 216.7; 223.1; 228.1–2; and *Catech.* 1.2 for a few more instances of this common motif in Augustine's writings. On the fertility and maternity of the font, see below, chap. 4, under the heading "Birthing Metaphors in Fourth-Century Sermons on Baptism."

18. See Augustine, *Serm.* 228 and 376. This week was called the Octave of the Infants. For other examples of this language and more discussion, see below, chap. 4, under the heading "Birthing Metaphors in Fourth-Century Sermons on Baptism."

19. Cyril of Jerusalem, *Procat.* 13.

20. Zeno of Verona, *Tract.* 1.24 (II.38) (CCSL 22:71), trans. author. See also Zeno of Verona, *Tract.* 1.55; and cf. Cyril of Jerusalem, *Procat.* 13, "all of you who are enrolled are the sons and daughters of one mother" (*mias mētros gegonate huioi kai thygateres*).

Christians as Adopted Heirs

Paul also stressed the promise of a coming inheritance (cf. Rom. 8:17; Gal. 3:29; 4:1–2). Obviously, with regard to the rights and privileges of birth into a family, the primary heir has the highest status. Christians who share God as father and church as mother also share in the inheritance as legal children; however, the crucial inheritance of the newborn Christian is neither property nor wealth. This inheritance is eternal life and a place in the kingdom. In the Epistle to the Ephesians, the seal of the Holy Spirit acts as a pledge that guarantees this inheritance (1:13–14). In a sense, then, the promise is held in trust. Baptism provides an endowment whose full measure is realized in the future.

Borrowing several of these themes simultaneously, John the Deacon speaks of the two births of the Christian: "Thus, one whose first parentage brought perdition is restored by the boon of a second parentage and becomes the possessor of an eternal inheritance."[21] Similarly, John Chrysostom informs candidates of baptism's many benefits, among them a place in the family, with Christ as brother: "You are not only free, but also holy; not only holy, but also just; not only just, but also sons; not only sons, but also heirs; not only heirs, but also brothers of Christ; not only brothers of Christ, but also joint heirs; not only joint heirs, but also members; not only members, but also the temple; not only the temple, but also instruments of the Spirit."[22]

In Galatians 4:1–7, Paul refers to the rights of children while still under the power of the father in order to compare the state of the children of the family to that of slaves. The liberation offered is neither the manumission of a slave nor the attaining of the age of majority, but the act of adoption: "So you are no longer a slave but a child, and if a child then also an heir, through God" (v. 7).

This language appears in the baptismal rite when the candidate renounces Satan. For example, John Chrysostom characterizes the candidate's repudiation of Satan as a liberation from captivity or servitude that also bestows the status of a legal heir: "Only yesterday and the day before, these were slaves of sin, with no freedom to speak, subject to the domination of the devil; like captives, they were led to this place and that. Today they have been received into the rank of sons."[23] Here John also refers to a passage in Paul's Epistle to the Romans: "For you did not receive a spirit of slavery to fall back into fear, but you have received the spirit of adoption [*huiothesias*]. When we cry, 'Abba! Father!' it is that very Spirit bearing witness with our spirit that we are children of God, and if children, then heirs, heirs of God and joint heirs with Christ—if, in fact, we suffer with him so that we may also be glorified with him" (8:15–17).

---

21. John the Deacon, *Ep. Sen.* 3, trans. author. Wilmart, *Analecta reginensia*, 172.

22. John Chrysostom, *Catech.* 3.5 (Stav. 3, Pk. 4), trans. Harkins, *St. John Chrysostom*, 57.

23. John Chrysostom, *Catech.* 4.3 (Stav. 4). See also John Chrysostom, *Catech.* 2.18 and 29 (Stav. 2); and cf. Rom. 8:23.

Cyril of Jerusalem also cites this Pauline text and, more than Chrysostom, emphasizes the Roman practice of recognizing adopted children as equal heirs with children by birth: "If any one here is a slave of sin, let faith fit them for the new birth of adoption that will set them free. As they exchange the ignoble bondage of sin for the blessed bondage of the Lord, let them be counted worthy to inherit the kingdom of heaven."[24] In a similar manner, Basil of Caesarea admonishes the unbaptized for remaining slaves to sin. Their reluctance deprives them of the opportunity to be liberated, to become citizens of heaven on par with the angels, and to claim their inheritance as adopted children of God.[25]

Adoption was a common Roman practice. Adopted children inherited property and family obligations, including the duty to honor ancestors and practice filial obedience to the adoptive father. Wealthy Romans could even adopt adults (usually males). Augustus Caesar, the adopted grandnephew of Julius, in turn adopted his two stepsons, Tiberius and Drusus. The adopted child possessed all the privileges of a natural-born child, just as Paul claimed for Christians as adopted heirs of Abraham (Rom. 9:4; Gal. 3:18). Furthermore, as Paul indicates, freed slaves could be adopted and made legal heirs. Consequently, as *liberti*, these former slaves would take the family name.

According to custom, when persons of any age were legally adopted, their previous familial status was nullified. They renounced their former family name and kinship relations. All their prior liabilities were voided and their previous (or birth) family lost any claim to support or loyalty. The adoptee not only started a new life but was rendered debt free (cf. Col. 2:13–14: "God . . . erasing the record that stood against us with its legal demands"). Adoptees also took the social rank of their new father, possessed all the rights of succession and inheritance due any child of the family, and (like them) came under the power, control, and discipline of the paterfamilias, who would expect absolute allegiance.[26] In a hymn written for Epiphany (a baptismal day), Ephrem announces, "Today your debts are wiped out and your names are written down; the priest wipes them out in the water, and Christ writes your names in heaven. By the two actions your joy is redoubled."[27]

Although Paul's own purpose in using the language of adoption has been the subject of debate, its use by early Christian writers should be considered in light of contemporary Roman law.[28] Romans practiced two types of adoption,

24. Cyril of Jerusalem, *Cat.* 1.2, trans. McCauley and Stephenson, *Works of Saint Cyril of Jerusalem*, 1:92, slightly adapted by author.
25. Basil of Caesarea, *Bapt.* 3.
26. See article in *OCD*, "Adoptio," 8.
27. Ephrem, *Epiph.* 6.13, trans. Sebastian Brock, in Finn, *Early Christian Baptism*, 168.
28. See the work of Scott, *Adoption as Sons of God*; Peppard, *The Son of God in the Roman World*, 50–85; and a helpful but now dated summary of the debate about Paul's use of the idea in Cook, "Concept of Adoption."

the distinction made according to the adoptee's status. The first, *adoptio*, was simple and private, and applied to an individual who was under the power (*potestas*) of another paterfamilias. Because it required the ceding of rights at the core of the Roman family system (the role of the paterfamilias), the procedure was complicated. It involved the birth father's selling the child into slavery (a power held by the father), the child's being bought and manumitted by the adoptive father, and then, finally, adopted. The second type of adoption, *adrogatio*, applied to an individual who was not under any other person's power (*sui iuris*), and who might even have been a paterfamilias in his own right. This form brought both the persons and property that were under the adoptee's own control into the power of the new father, essentially dissolving the prior family.[29] In either case, certain legal aspects of adoption—such as the cancellation of debt (for baptism, the debt of sin); renunciation of former ties; release from slavery; and assuming a new name, family, and inheritance—all echo in the theology of baptism.

In his Epistle to the Romans, Paul describes the whole creation as groaning in labor. Christians, he says, also groan; they groan as they wait, though not for their birth. They await the adoption of their souls and the redemption of their bodies (8:22–23). Here, rather than the font, the creation is the mother's womb. Because natural birth is futile, leading only to decay and death, adoption alone offers hope of salvation.

In his baptismal homilies, Theodore of Mopsuestia cites this passage, interpreting it to mean that in baptism Christians receive adoption "in anticipation." That is to say, they must wait for the fulfillment of the adopted status, which will occur when they are resurrected from the dead. Theodore also speaks of this anticipated adoption as confirmed by the gift of the Holy Spirit, given by the bishop after the newly baptized emerge from the water.[30] This leads Theodore to add that such "adoption is far superior to Jewish adoption, which was subject to change. . . . This adoption remains firm and unshakeable, because anyone who is adopted in this way will remain immortal."[31]

Gregory of Nyssa likewise invokes the theme of adoption. Toward the end of his sermon on baptism, he calls his congregation to fashion themselves after the likeness of God, so that they may "appear true children of the one who calls us to the adoption according to grace." Thus they become "sons and daughters, fashioned in loving-kindness towards their kindred."[32] Both Theodore and Gregory equate baptism as adoption with baptism as birth

29. On the Roman practice of adoption, see Dixon, *Roman Family*, 112–13; Saller, *Patriarchy, Property, and Death*, 75–76 (definition of *familia* and discussion of *adrogatio*); Cobier, "Divorce and Adoption."

30. Theodore of Mopsuestia, *Bapt. hom.* 3.7, 25.

31. Theodore of Mopsuestia, *Bapt. hom.* 3.24, trans. Yarnold, *Awe-Inspiring Rites of Initiation*, 205–6.

32. Gregory of Nyssa, *Diem lum.*, NPNF², 5:524.

from a spiritual mother's womb. Both produce legitimate heirs, but the motif of adoption is additionally freighted with the idea that the one adopted was once enslaved and is now free.

Summarizing all these themes of family, parenthood, and adoption in a sermon to the catechumens about to be baptized (*competentes*), Augustine urges them, "Love what you will be. What you will be, you see, are children of God, and sons by adoption. This will be given you free, conferred on you for nothing . . . [then] God is Father, the Church is mother. You will be born of these parents very, very differently from the way you were born of [your human parents]. The birth of offspring here will not be accompanied by labor, by woe, by weeping, by death; but by easiness, by happiness, by joy, and by life."[33]

Joining the Church Likened to Membership in Other Associations

In addition to participating in the extended family unit, individuals participated in a variety of other social associations. While membership in certain kinds of groups (e.g., priests, athletes, soldiers) offered useful analogies to joining the church or to Christian life in general, outsiders often judged these private clubs with suspicion. They were perceived as potentially being comprised of members who met in secret for dubious purposes.

Private clubs (*collegia*) usually had some quasi-religious function, but people may have joined for the social or economic benefits more than for religious reasons. Members dined together, contributed to funds that would pay for eventual funeral expenses of their members, and formed professional or trade networks. Thus, clubs served as a base for supporting political or rank advancement of individuals.[34] The proliferation of these groups in the early centuries of the Common Era was due, in part, to the needs of immigrants who sought a community with whom they shared language, values, and religious practices.

To external observers, an early Christian congregation could have appeared as one such association, comprising individuals who met together to offer worship to a god, to dine together, and to provide mutual social and economic support.[35] This is how Pliny the Younger, governor of Bithynia-Pontus, describes Christians in a letter to the emperor Trajan.[36] In his letter, Pliny expresses fear that such associations could be socially disruptive or even politically seditious. Members might seek official sanction for their group,

33. Augustine, *Serm.* 216.8, trans. Hill, *Works of Saint Augustine*, 172. The translator (Hill) keeps "sons" here because it is a matter of both sexes having a share in the divine sonship of the Son.

34. On clubs and associations, see McCready, "*Ekklēsia* and Voluntary Associations"; Wilken, *Christians as the Romans Saw Them*, 31–47; MacMullen, *Roman Social Relations*, 88–120.

35. See also LaPiana, "Foreign Groups in Rome."

36. Pliny the Younger, *Ep.* 10.96.8.

but if they failed to obtain state approval, the group could be banned and its members arrested.

The perception of churches as secret societies caused trouble for their faithful. Tertullian, aware of the parallels, tried to allay concerns that Christians were immoral or disloyal. In his *Apology*, he acknowledges that Christians forge close bonds, and that they are joined by their professed faith, but, he assures his audience, they are also law-abiding and loyal citizens who pray for the emperors and magistrates, for world peace, and for the common good.[37]

Nevertheless, the ritual of baptism was a closed, secret rite. Those who received it were initiated into an exclusive group that allowed them entry to the similarly private table fellowship. Baptized Christians were required to repudiate other sorts of memberships as well as many ordinary social activities that would have brought them into contact with pagan idols. In many respects, the church acted (and appeared) as an alternative kinship group, a religious sect, or a private, voluntary association.

Priests, Prophets, and Kings

Baptism was understood also to impart (at least figuratively) the sacred order of anointed priesthood. Through the postbaptismal anointing, the candidate was initiated into these cultic roles. Drawing largely on the text of 1 Peter 2:9, which calls Christians not only a "chosen race" and a "holy nation" but also a "royal priesthood," the ritual of baptism admits the newly baptized to a certain kind of sacerdotal rank.[38] This idea, presupposing Israel's priestly classes, makes particular reference to the anointing of Aaron (Exod. 29:1–9). However, most gentile converts would have been more familiar with the colleges of Roman priests, having little knowledge of lived Judaism apart from the Scriptures, which describe (or refer to) the anointing of those ancient priests, prophets, and kings.

In his treatise on baptism, Tertullian specifically compares the candidate's anointing after coming up from the water to Moses's anointing of Aaron, which is why, he says, Aaron is called a christ (from the word 'chrism,' which refers to the anointing).[39] Nearly two centuries later, both Cyril of Jerusalem and Ambrose similarly compared the anointing of the newly baptized to the anointing of Aaron, as well as to that of kings David and Solomon (1 Sam. 16:13; 1 Kings 1:39). Cyril adds that both Moses and Solomon might be called

37. Tertullian, *Apol.* 38–39, *ANF*, 3:45–46, slightly adapted by author.

38. Here certain texts might be cited: Irenaeus, *Haer.* 4.8.3 (all the righteous possess the sacerdotal rank); Tertullian, *Exh. cast.* 7 (laymen must be ready at all times to act as priests); Origen, *Hom. Lev.* 9.1.3; John Chrysostom, *Hom. 1 Cor.* 3.7 (in baptism one becomes king, priest, and prophet).

39. Tertullian, *Bapt.* 7.

"christs," just as the newly baptized are called "christs."[40] Ambrose explains, "Each one is anointed into the priesthood, anointed into the kingdom, but into a spiritual kingdom and into a spiritual priesthood."[41] Thus the chrismation of the newly baptized, patterned after the anointings described in the Old Testament, inaugurates their "royal priesthood."

Augustine also emphasizes the sacerdotal aspects of the postbaptismal anointing, confirming that all who are anointed in baptism may be called "christs" inasmuch as the whole body with its head is one Christ. Referring to the Song of Hannah, he further remarks that, through this anointing, the ancient priesthood, begun with Samuel, had been fulfilled and extended.[42] Elsewhere, Augustine cites 1 Peter 2 to assert that not only presbyters and bishops are priests in the church, but also all the baptized may be called priests because of their having received the mystical chrism, and that all believers shall share Christ's thousand-year reign.[43]

Athletes

Anointing also prompted a comparison of the neophytes with another kind of tightly bonded group: athletes striving for victory. Athletes are models for Christians in Paul's Second Epistle to the Corinthians, in which he points out that all runners compete but only one receives a prize. Comparing the training a contestant receives to the formation of a Christian, he adds, "Athletes exercise self-control in all things; they do it to receive a perishable wreath, but we an imperishable one" (9:25). The author of 2 Timothy similarly compares himself to a winning contender who has earned his victory wreath: "I have fought the good fight, I have finished the race, I have kept the faith. From now on there is reserved for me the crown of righteousness, which the Lord, the righteous judge, will give me on that day, and not only to me but to all who have longed for his appearing" (4:7–8).

Thus the newly baptized were likened to teammates contending together against their opponents. This imagery would have resonated particularly well with the Roman love of sport. Just as in modern times, games and contests were not merely entertainments; they were also a central aspect of social life in almost every city. Athletes also were considered models of discipline and virtue in certain philosophical systems.[44] Deploying sport analogies, Ambrose describes the prebaptismal anointing: "You are anointed as if an athlete of Christ; as if a wrestler about to fight a match, you have agreed to fight your

40. Cyril of Jerusalem, *Myst.* 3.1, 6; Ambrose, *Myst.* 6.30.

41. Ambrose, *Sacr.* 4.3 (SC 25:103), trans. author. See also Ambrose, *Sacr.* 1.4.

42. Augustine, *Civ.* 17.4.9.

43. Augustine, *Civ.* 20.10. See also Augustine, *Enarrat. Ps.* 44.9. See also Gregory of Nazianzus, *Or.* 40.10.

44. See, for example, Epictetus, *Diatr.* 1.24.1–2; 3.15.1–13; and 4.4.11–13.

opponent. The wrestler has something to hope for; where there is a contest, there is a crown. You contend in the world, but you are crowned by Christ."[45] Ambrose's distinction between the worldly contest with a mortal opponent and the Christian athlete's contest with Satan lies in the reward; the crown of the one is ephemeral, while the crown of the other is enduring.

In contrast to Ambrose, John Chrysostom speaks less of the end reward than of the process itself, likening catechetical discipline to the training of an athlete. The catechumen faces a truly Olympian combat with the devil and must be in the best possible shape to prevail. The angels are spectators, but Christ is present both as judge and teammate.[46] However, like Ambrose, John compares those about to be baptized with wrestlers entering the ring. The nude and oiled candidate enters the font and must avoid being grasped and then held by an unseen, immensely strong, and devious adversary.[47]

Augustine also employs this metaphor, attending particularly to the oiling of the Christian athlete prior to the bout. In a passage where he elucidates the significance of Jesus's ascent from the Mount of Olives, Augustine reminds his audience that chrism is made from pressing olives, thus making the olive itself a messianic symbol. He adds that the reason for anointing the body at baptism was to strengthen the candidates as they wrestled with Satan. A slippery body would have given a special advantage in this kind of combat with the evil one.[48]

Soldiers

While the simile of athletic contests draws on a combat motif, the comparison of the baptized to military recruits focuses on the socialization of a cohort. Soldiers are socialized to bond tightly with their comrades in arms. Joining the ranks (e.g., a troop or a legion) required unwavering loyalty and obedience, and military service often required extraordinary courage and single-mindedness. The use of military metaphors for living the Christian life appears first in Ephesians 6:10–17, where the faithful are urged to put on the "whole armor of God," including the "belt of truth," the "breastplate of righteousness," the "shield of faith," the "helmet of salvation," and the "sword of the Spirit." A second reference to this idea appears in 2 Timothy, which urges the followers of Jesus to share in suffering like good soldiers: "No one

45. Ambrose, *Sacr.* 1.4 (SC 25:62), trans. author. See also Ambrose, *Hel.* 21.79, where he speaks in detail of the training of athletes as a model for the preparation of catechumens, including training every day, eating special foods, keeping chaste, refraining from drink, and anointing the body with oil.

46. John Chrysostom, *Catech.* 3.8–9 (Stav. 3, Pk. 4); also 2.23 and 9.28.

47. *Passio Perp. et Fel.* 10 also presents such an image. See also Narsai, *Hom. Epiph.* 306.

48. Augustine, *Tract. Ev. Jo.* 33.3. Note that Ephrem compares the prebaptismal anointing to the oil applied by divers after stripping and before entering the water; see *Hymn* 82 (on faith) 10. See also Ps. Dionysius, *Ecc. hier.* 2.3.

serving in the army gets entangled in everyday affairs; the soldier's aim is to please the enlisting officer" (2:4).

The word "sacrament" comes partly from this context. One of the several meanings for the Latin word *sacramentum* is the Roman soldier's oath, whereby the recruit pledged allegiance to the emperor and bound himself to his legion. This term was also used for initiation rituals in the Latin-speaking church. The first Latin Bible translated the Greek term *mystērion* with this borrowed military term.[49]

A soldier's tattoo identified him with his cohort and became a metaphor for the sign of the cross, made on the newly baptized person's forehead—a permanent mark. Theodore of Mopsuestia specifically alluded to this baptismal sign as a mark identifying one of Christ's soldiers. This was also their pass to receive the rest of the sacrament and "so acquire the full armor of the Spirit."[50]

Sacramentum also denotes other solemn oaths, such as the pledge of a surety or bond, deposited as security against a future judgment. When employed in a baptismal context, the word had a complex meaning. It referred to the candidate's vow of loyalty to Christ and to the neophyte's assurance of forgiveness of sin. Eventually it came to refer to the rite of initiation as a whole. The term appears in Pliny's epistle to the emperor Trajan to refer to Christians taking an oath (*sacramentum*) not to engage in immoral or criminal acts.[51] Tertullian, who was one of the first to use (and perhaps the originator of) this term for baptism, calls it the "sacrament of our water" (*sacramento aquae nostrae*).[52]

Another African, the anonymous author of the *Treatise on Rebaptism*, compares Christians initially baptized in the "true church" but who subsequently receive baptism in a heretical communion, to soldiers who desert their units after having sworn an oath. Their apostasy—the new oath they take in the camp of the enemy—renders the first sacrament null and void.[53] By their own actions, they not only excommunicate themselves but also are guilty of a capital crime. The original oath of loyalty they took becomes a testimony to their treacherousness and ultimately makes things worse for them.

49. On the Latin word *sacramentum*, see Mohrmann, "Sacramentum"; Kolping, *Sacramentum Tertullianeum*, 21–43. See also Van Roo, *Christian Sacrament*, 36–44; and Dölger, "Sacramentum militae."

50. Theodore of Mopsuestia, *Bapt. hom.* 2.17–18, 20, trans. Yarnold, *Awe-Inspiring Rites of Initiation*, 187–88.

51. Pliny the Younger, *Ep.* 10.96.

52. Tertullian, *Bapt.* 1.1. In his treatise *De corona*, Tertullian wrote about the role of a Christian in the military, and the symbolism of repudiating a soldier's crown by one who has taken an oath to God, rather than to his commanding officer. On Tertullian's view of military service, see Helgeland, "Christians and the Roman Army"; and Rordorf, "Tertullians Beurteilung des Soldatenstandes."

53. Anon., *Rebapt.* 16.

Augustine, following his predecessors, continued to speak about the mark or brand of the soldier: the *nota militaris*. Because this mark was permanent, it could not be (and should not be) repeated through another ritual of baptism. Thus Augustine employs the metaphor especially in his polemical works against the Donatists.[54] The indelibility of the mark means not only that one cannot renew it, but also that it remains, even when a person defects to a heretical party. For example, in his treatise *On Baptism*, he refers to the analogy of the military mark (*notae militaris*) and observes that it is borne by both the loyal and the deserter. And even though it should not be received outside the cohort, it should not be redone or renewed if the deserter is reclaimed for the legion.[55]

Among the Greek writers, John Chrysostom especially favors soldier metaphors for baptismal candidates, telling those about to be baptized that they have enlisted in Christ's army.[56] He elaborates on the metaphor in one of his catechetical lectures, noting the qualities the king of heaven needs for this special force:

> In the case of recruits for an army of this world, those whose task it is to induct them into the army, look for bodily size and health. Not only must the future soldier have these qualities, but he must also be a free man. . . . But the King of heaven looks for no such thing. He even receives slaves into his army, and those who are old and weakened in limb; and he is not ashamed of them. . . . But earthly kings recruit soldiers because of the service they will give. They lead their troops into war against a visible foe. He leads his troops into a spiritual battle.[57]

John's idea of baptism's benefits, however, would turn the slaves into the free and restore youthful strength to the old and weak. The postbaptismal army is thus spiritually armed and prepared for a successful campaign.

Cyril of Jerusalem similarly characterizes the preparation for baptism and the subsequent living of the Christian life in martial terms. According to Cyril, the foes are human challengers to the faith, not demonic or invisible enemies. The lessons the catechumens receive are, to them, both strategies and marching orders; the prayers and the creed are simultaneously armor and armaments. They are to deploy those weapons faithfully and courageously: "You are taking up arms against the enemy. . . . Your enemies are many; take plenty of ammunition; you have targets in plenty. You must learn how to shoot down the Greek and do battle with the heretic, Jew, and

54. Augustine, *Parm.* 2.29.

55. Augustine, *Bapt.* 1.4.5. On Augustine in particular but also for a good summary of the question, see Peper, "Augustine's Baptismal Analogy."

56. John Chrysostom, *Catech.* 2.1 (Stav. 2).

57. John Chrysostom, *Catech.* 12.30–32 (Montf. 2), trans. Harkins, *St. John Chrysostom*, 182. See also John Chrysostom, *Catech.* 2.1 (Stav. 2).

Samaritan. . . . Let this be included in your battle orders: study what you are told and guard it forever."[58]

Saints

Neophytes were also, at least provisionally, incorporated into the company of the saints and martyrs. In that it is not, precisely, a metaphor, this category is different from the others. Like winning athletes or victorious soldiers, martyrs earn crowns and, analogously, so do the newly baptized; thus the comparison. For example, John Chrysostom addresses the neophytes in one of Antioch's many martyria, urging them to imitate the saints in their zeal and to call to mind their brave deeds. He then asks his listeners to consider the reward they themselves would earn if judged worthy. Alluding to the saints' relics in the shrine, John prompts his audience to compare the water of baptism with the "spiritual fountains" that poured forth from the bodies of the heroes. Not only are the martyrs models for emulation, but their physical remains, like the water in the baptismal font, also have the power to cure physical ailments as well as heal souls.[59]

Because martyrs were baptized in their own blood, baptisteries were occasionally converted into martyria, and vice versa.[60] The fourth-century poet Prudentius composed a cycle of poems dedicated to martyrs, titled the *Crowns of Martyrdom*. One of these poems, written for a shrine/baptistery in Calahorra, Spain, explicitly compares martyrs' crowns with the crowns earned by the baptized:

> This is the place that Christ chose, which carries proven hearts
>   to heaven by blood, and which cleanses by water.
> Here two men, killed for the name of the Lord,
> bore the purple witness by means of a noble death.
> Here as well grace flows from the pure font,
> and washes old sins by a new stream.
> Let the one who desires to go up to the eternal kingdom of Heaven
> come here thirsty—for behold the way is provided.
> Before now the crowned witnesses ascended to high gates;
> now by their washing, souls seek the heights.
> Just as the Spirit, accustomed to descend perpetually

58. Cyril of Jerusalem, *Procat.* 10–11, trans. McCauley and Stephenson, *Works of Saint Cyril of Jerusalem*, 1:78–79.

59. John Chrysostom, *Catech.* 7.1–11 (Stav. 7).

60. On martyrdom as baptism, see Hippolytus, *Trad. ap.* 19; Tertullian, *Bapt.* 16 and *Apol.* 50; Origen, *Mart.* 30; Cyprian, *Ep.* 73.22.2 and *Dom. orat.* 24; anon., *Rebapt.* 14; Gregory of Nazianzus, *Or.* 39.15, 17; Basil of Caesarea, *Spir. Sanct.* 15.36; and Cyril of Jerusalem, *Cat.* 3.10. Baptisteries converted into shrines are found at the sites of Sufetula in Tunisia and Albenga in Italy. Saints' shrines that were equipped (subsequently) with baptisteries have been identified in Nisibis (Turkey), Bir Ftouha (Tunisia), Tarragona (Spain), and Qal'at Siman (Syria). See Jensen, "Baptism *ad Sanctos*?"

to bestow the palm, so also gives pardon.
The earth drinks the sacred drops, either of blood or from the spring,
and so drenched, she pours out both to her God.
He is the Lord of this place, the one from whose side wound two
    fluids—
    blood and water—gushed.
Each will go from here through the wounds of Christ, in the way he is
    able—
one by the sword and the other by water.[61]

The two kinds of cleansing (by the blood of martyrdom or the water of baptism) both achieve crowns. The recipients of baptism thus join the martyrs, a union made even more vivid by their having been baptized in the presence of the saints' remains.

Representations of saints bearing crowns appear in the dome mosaics of both the arian and orthodox Ravenna baptisteries (fig. 2.1). These saints circle the image of John the Baptist baptizing Christ that is placed directly over the font, perhaps to present their crowns to Jesus, as well as to indicate the victory of the font itself. As candidates entered the water, they could have gazed up to these images.[62] The dome mosaic of the earlier, fourth-century Naples baptistery of San Giovanni in Fonte shows the hand of God grasping a crown, presumably being offered to the neophyte standing in the font below (fig. 2.2). The Christogram just below the crown indicates that the triumph is both in and of Christ—a baptismal triumph over sin, death, and evil.

Other Symbolic Metaphors for the Christian Community

In addition to human associations (e.g., priests, athletes, soldiers, and saints), the early Christian community was likened to fish caught in the church's net and to a flock led by a caretaking shepherd. These metaphors were popular in both literary and visual art. Individual Christians were little fish swimming in water (caught either in nets or on hooks), or they were sheep marked so that their shepherd would know them. This same shepherd (Christ) was also a fisher or even the "big fish" himself. Surviving images of sheep, shepherds, fishers, and fish are mostly found in funerary contexts, but they also occur in baptismal chambers, indicating the neophytes' admission into the flock or reminding them of Jesus's invitation to the disciples to be fishers of people (cf. Matt. 4:19). The fish and the flock also appear with other symbolic references to the faith or to the benefits of membership: anchors, boats, and doves.

61. Prudentius, *Perist.* 8 (CSEL 61:366–67), trans. author.
62. See Engemann, *Die Huldigung der Apostel.* Engemann argues that the processing apostles acclaim the baptism of Christ in the center medallion.

Figure 2.1. Dome mosaic, Arian baptistery. Santa Maria in Cosmodian, Ravenna. Late fifth century. (Photo by author).

Figure 2.2. Dome mosaic, baptistery of Sta. Restituta, San Giovanni in Fonte, Naples. Late fourth century. (Photo by author.)

Fish

The fish is one of the earliest and most distinctive of Christian figures. Its precise meaning is almost impossible to define as it may refer to Christ, to the Christian, to an aspect of the faith, or to a specific biblical narrative. Although historians have found little evidence that the fish was a "secret sign" that identified early Christian meeting places, it was nevertheless a common symbol of membership, especially when combined with images of an anchor, a dove, or with loaves and a chalice (see fig. 2.5).

The ancient inclusion of fish in images of sacred meals or funeral banquets is a sign of its significance. Christ ate fish with the disciples at postresurrection meals, and it is possible that later meals of fish, bread, and wine (perhaps at funeral banquets) carried an eschatological significance: the fish symbolized the risen Lord. A late second-century epitaph, thought to have been written by the Christian bishop of Hieropolis Abercius, speaks of eating fish along his pilgrimage toward conversion: "Everywhere faith led the way and set before me for food the fish from the spring, mighty and pure, whom a spotless virgin caught, and gave this to friends to eat, always having sweet wine, and giving the mixed cup with bread."[63]

The earliest literary reference to the fish as a symbol comes from Clement of Alexandria, whose treatise *On the Instructor* urges readers to choose from among a small number of figures for their signet rings: "Let our seals be the dove, or the fish, or a ship sailing before a fair wind, or the lyre for music, which seal Polycrates used, or a ship's anchor, which Seleucus carved on his device, and if there be a fisherman, he will recall an apostle and children drawn from the water."[64]

When Clement refers to children being drawn from the water, he probably means baptism. It follows that the images he approves probably identified the seal's owner as baptized or at least as a catechumen. Clement does not say that the fish symbol represented Christ any more than the boat or the lyre, nor does he associate the fish symbol with an individual Christian. However, a hymn to Christ found at the end of Clement's treatise hails Christ as the "fisher of people, of those saved from the sea of evil, luring with sweet life the chaste fish from the hostile tide."[65]

Clement's Carthaginian contemporary Tertullian expanded this analogy. In his treatise *On Baptism*, he urges his hearers not to be fish out of water: "But we, being little fishes, as Jesus Christ is our great fish, are born in the water, and we are safe only so long as we remain in the water."[66] Here Tertullian inserts the Greek noun *ichthys* rather than the Latin *piscis*, suggesting that he was familiar with a well-known fish acrostic that considers each letter of the Greek word (*ichthys*) to signify one word of the title Jesus Christ, Son of God, Savior (*Iēsous Christos Theou huios sōtēr*).

Another ancient reference to this acrostic is in the Christian *Sibylline Oracles*, which, arguably, dated to the third or fourth century, although Tertullian's reference suggests that the acrostic at least was circulating by the late second century.[67] Later African theologians, Augustine of Hippo and Optatus of Milevis, as well

---

63. *Abercius Inscription*, text and trans, see Quasten, *Patrology*, 1:171–73. Also see a recent essay by M. M. Mitchell, "Looking for Abercius" (with excellent notes); and Wischmeyer, "Die Aberkiosinschrift als Grabepigramm."

64. Clement of Alexandria, *Paed.* 3.11, *ANF*, 2:285.

65. Clement of Alexandria, *Paed.* 3, trans. Annewies van den Hoek, 300–301.

66. Tertullian, *Bapt.* 1.3 (CCSL 1:227), trans. author.

67. *Sib. Or.* 8.217–50. Greek text of the oracles may be found in GCS 8.1:153–57 (Leipzig: J. C. Hinrichs'sche, 1902), 153–57. See J. J. Collins, "Sibylline Oracles," in *OTP*, 1:423–24. For more bibliography, see Jensen, *Understanding Early Christian Art*, 191n64; or esp. Stroumsa, "Early Fish Symbol Reconsidered."

as Maximus of Turin and Eusebius of Caesarea also knew and cited the fish acrostic.[68] Of these, however, only Optatus unequivocally interprets the acrostic as an allusion to baptism. Speaking of the baptismal font as the "ancient fish pond," he writes:

> I don't know if it came with that fish, which is understood as Christ, which in the recitation of the patriarchal narratives is said to have been caught in the Tigris, whose gall-bladder and liver Tobias took to guard the woman Sara and to bring light to the blindness of Tobias; by the insides of the same fish the demon Asmodeus was driven away from the girl, Sara, who is understood as the Church. . . . This is the fish, which in baptism is introduced into the waves of the font, so that what was water may also be called a fish pool because of the fish. The name of this fish according to its Greek appellation *ichthys* contains a host of holy names in its individual letters, being in Latin, *Jesus Christus dei filius Salvator*.[69]

Optatus's writing connects the fish in the acrostic with the fish of Tobias (Tobit 6:9 and 6:19) and with the fish "placed into the baptismal font" at the invocation over the water. He remarks on the fact that baptismal fonts are often called *piscinae* (fishponds) and argues that the font is thus still a fishpond, filled with the Spirit of the sacred *ichthys*. This Spirit leads to the healing and exorcism of the baptized, just as Tobit's fish had miraculous properties to heal the blind and exorcise demons.

By far the most famous biblical "fish story" is the calling of the disciples away from being fishers of fish to become "fishers of people" (Matt. 4:18–19 and parallels). Origen's *Commentary on the Gospel of Matthew* draws a connection between this story and another Matthean story in which Peter finds a fish with a coin in its mouth (17:27). According to Origen, the fish is a type for the Christian convert, willingly caught on the hook of Peter, the commissioned fisher for new converts.[70] Cyril of Jerusalem apparently has this in mind when he tells his catechumens that they are fish, caught in the net of the church. He urges them, "Let yourself be taken alive; don't try to escape. It is Jesus who is playing you on his line, not to kill you, but by killing you, to make you alive."[71]

Ambrose likewise encourages baptismal candidates to be like fish, emulating those living things brought forth from the waters on the fifth day of creation, those enduring creatures that swim and survive even in terrifying situations: "Imitate that fish which, although it received less grace, should be a marvel to

68. Augustine, *Civ.* 18.23; Optatus of Milevis, *Parm.* 2.1; Maximus of Turin, *Contra pag. trac.* 4; Eusebius, *Coet. sanct.* 18–19, includes this text in his account of Constantine's oration to the assembly of the saints.

69. Optatus of Milevis, *Parm.* 2.1, trans. Edwards, *Optatus*, 58–59, slightly adapted by author.

70. Origen, *Comm. Matt.* 13.10.

71. Cyril of Jerusalem, *Procat.* 5, trans. McCauley and Stephenson, *Works of Saint Cyril of Jerusalem*, 1:74–75.

you. It is in the sea and over the waves; it is in the sea and swims above the tide. On the sea, the tempest rages, hurricanes roar, but the fish swims. Similarly, this world is a sea to you. It has varying currents, huge surges, and fierce gales. And you must be a fish, so that the waves of the world cannot drown you."[72]

Augustine merges the story of the miraculous catch of fish in Luke 5:1–11 with the postresurrection episode in John 21:1–14 in which Jesus directs the disciples from the beach. In the former story the disciples haul in teeming nets; in the latter story they make a similarly significant catch, but one with a specified number of fish, all caught from the right side of the boat. Augustine interprets Luke's two boats in 5:2 as symbolizing the two "churches" (of the Jews and of the gentiles), and the single boat in John's story as representing the unity of a single church. Thus the second catch, according to Augustine, symbolizes the holy church, existing in a limited number among the wicked multitude. Nevertheless, he says, all the fish in this net are "big fish" because they are destined for immortality. They do not strain or tear the nets, like fish in Luke's narrative, because they, like the true church, are not strained or fractured by schism or heresy, but live together in peace and love.[73]

A late fourth-century Greek inscription found in southern France, the Epitaph of Pectorius, addresses the Christian reader as a "divine child of the heavenly fish" and uses fish metaphors that refer to both baptism and the Eucharist. Its first five lines also form an acrostic for the word *ichthys*.

> Divine race of the heavenly fish (*Ichthys*), keep (*chrēse*) your heart holy,
>   having received the immortal spring of divine (*thespesiōn*) waters.
> Comfort your soul, friend, with the ever-flowing water (*hydasin*) of
>   wealth-giving wisdom.
> Take the honey-sweet food from the Savior of the holy ones.
> Eat with joy and desire, holding the fish in your hands.
> Give the fish as food, I pray, Lord and Savior.
> Fill me with the fish, this is my desire, O my Lord and Savior.
> Soft may my mother sleep; I beseech you, O Light of the dead.
> Aschandius, my father, beloved of my heart, together with the dear
>   mother and my brothers, in the peace of the fish, remember
>   Pectorius.[74]

72. Ambrose, *Sacr.* 3.3 (SC 25:92), trans. author.

73. Augustine, *Serm.* 229M.

74. *Pectorius Epitaph*, trans. author, based on Greek text and translation in Morey, "Origin of the Fish Symbol." Compare the eucharistic overtones here with a passage from Paulinus of Nola, *Ep.* 13.11 (CSEL 29:92–93): "I see the congregation, arranged in order on the couches and all filled with abundant food, that before their eyes appears the richness of the gospel's blessing and the image of the people whom Christ fed with five loaves and two fishes, himself being the true bread and fish of the living water" (trans. author). See also Augustine, *Conf.* 13.21.29 (CCSL 27:258.17–19): "These the earth does not need, although it eats the fish, raised from the deep, on that table, which you have prepared in the sight of the faithful" (trans. author).

Figure 2.3. Funerary inscription of Licinia Amias, Museo Nazionale, Rome. Early third century. (Photo by author.)

In visual art, fish often appear on funerary epitaphs, lamps, gems, glass, pottery dishes, frescoes, and relief sculptures. The fish are often shown with an anchor, a symbol suggesting the Christian hope of salvation. Together the two signs indicate that a certain deceased Christian was caught by the apostles' preaching, like the fish of Matthew 4:18–19, and adhered to the faith as life's anchor. One example, the Epitaph of Licinia, which is currently in Rome's Museo Nazionale, shows two fish on either side of an anchor (fig. 2.3). Above them are the first two letters of a typical Roman funerary legend: the two letters D and M on either side of a wreath. The next line of the inscription contains the two Greek words *ichthys zōntōn* ("fish of the living ones"). The lower part (beneath the fish and anchor) is incomplete but identifies the deceased: LICINIAE AMIATI BENE MERENTI VIXIT, "To Licinia Amias, of worthy merit, she lived . . ."

Related to these simple, symbolic funerary epitaphs are visual representations of fishers standing on the banks casting lines into the water or aboard boats and tossing nets. These are found among the wall paintings in the Christian catacombs and on sarcophagus reliefs. The so-called Jonah Sarcophagus has a prominent image of a fisherman, perhaps Tobit himself (fig. 4.4). The frieze of the sarcophagus of Sta. Maria Antiqua has several scenes unified by a flow of water: the river god pouring out his jug, Jonah being cast overboard, John baptizing Jesus, and two men lowering nets from a boat (fig. 1.1).

Fish also show up frequently in meal iconography, with bread and wine. In one instance the banquet is depicted next to a scene of baptism (fig. 2.4). Fish or fishermen were another common motif. Chamber 22 of the Catacomb of

Figure 2.4. Baptism with funerary banquet. Sarcophagus fragment, Museo Pio Cristiano, Vatican. Late third century. (Photo by author with permission from the Vatican Museum.)

Callixtus contains a three-part scene on its back wall depicting a man fishing from the bank, Jesus's baptism, and (on the right) a healed paralytic carrying off his bed. The next chamber (21) has a similar combination of scenes. The baptism is adjacent to images of Moses striking the rock, a fisherman, and seven persons eating a meal of fish, bread, and wine. The same catacomb's Crypt of Lucina has two fish, each bearing a basket of bread and chalice on its back (fig. 2.5). The prominent sacramental symbolism of these images has led to a traditional labeling of these cubiculi as "sacraments chambers."

Baptistery décor also often features images of fish. The iconographic program in the dome of the baptistery of San Giovanni in Fonte in Naples includes the miraculous catch of fish from John 21 (fig. 2.6). This image occurs just below depictions of Jesus walking on the water (filled with leaping fish) and his stilling the storm. Baptismal fonts also were decorated with fish motifs. One in particular stands out: the sixth-century baptistery from Kélibia in modern-day Tunisia. Here several varieties of fish appear along with fruit trees, flowers, and a set of Christian symbols (e.g., a chalice, the ark, and a cross under a ciborium; see fig. 5.4).

Flock

A flock of sheep, like a school of fish, symbolizes the community of faith. The prevalent biblical images of the shepherd and flock include the Twenty-Third Psalm and Jesus's identification of himself as the Good Shepherd who lays down his life for his sheep (John 10:11). The parable of the lost sheep (Matt.

Figure 2.5. Fish with loaves. Painting, Catacomb of Callixtus, Rome. Third century. (Photo © Estelle Brettman, The International Catacomb Society.)

Figure 2.6. Catch of fish and Jesus stilling the storm. Mosaic, baptistery of Sta. Restituta, San Giovanni in Fonte, Naples. Late fourth century. (Photo by author.)

18:12–13; Luke 15:3–7) symbolizes the faithful care of the shepherd, even for the member of the flock who goes astray. These metaphors were continually invoked in early Christian literature in homilies, theological treatises, poetry, and catechetical instruction. A late second-century hymn attributed to Clement of Alexandria addresses Jesus as the shepherd of the royal lambs, of the holy flock, and of the sheep of the Logos.[75] The second-century seer Hermas had a vision of a shepherd who explained that Hermas must answer to the Master of the flock for the safety of all the sheep.[76] Abercius's epitaph describes himself as a disciple of the chaste shepherd, one who feeds his flocks on mountains and plains.[77] Insisting on the singularity of the church, Cyprian asserts that the true community is a solitary flock with only one shepherd.[78]

In a rare early allusion to Christian material culture, Tertullian objects to Christians using drinking cups decorated with depictions of Jesus in the guise of the Good Shepherd.[79] Surviving examples of small domestic objects with depictions of the Shepherd carrying a sheep over his shoulders are also found on terra-cotta lamps and bowls as well as etched into gems and set into rings. The daily use (or wearing) of these items would have reminded their owners of their belonging to the flock or of their caretaking Savior.

75. Clement of Alexandria, *Paed. Hymn* 1.7. Here he also describes Christ as the fisher of people and the chaste fish. See the recent translation of this hymn by Hoek, "Hymn of the Holy Clement," 300–301. See also Clement of Alexandria, *Protr.* 11.

76. Herm. *Sim.* 9.31.5–6.

77. *Epitaph of Abercius*, 3–4.

78. Cyprian, *Ep.* 69.5 (an argument against Novatian).

79. Tertullian, *Pud.* 7.1–4.

The symbolic use of lambs entering a flock for the newly baptized is also commonplace in the literature of the fourth century. Ambrose, citing a line from the Song of Songs, compares the neophytes with flocks of shorn sheep coming up from the washing (Song 4:2; 6:6).[80] Cyril of Jerusalem, also referring to passages from the Song, proposes that the ewes big with twins (Song 4:2) represent the two grace-bearing gifts of baptism: the water bath and the Spirit's descent.[81] Augustine likewise associates this passage from the Song with baptism. He explains that their being newly shorn indicates that the sheep (the neophytes) have shed their earthly sins by being washed in the water of the font.[82]

The metaphor of a shepherd with his flock was widely associated with baptism and incorporated into early baptisteries. Prudentius composed a hymn for the Feast of Peter and Paul in which he described the fourth-century basilica of St. Peter in Rome and, in particular, its spring-fed baptistery, which seems to have had a colored mosaic image of the great Shepherd bathing his sheep in an icy pool.[83] Paulinus of Nola similarly wrote a poem, intended for the baptistery built by his friend Severus. The first verses recall the lines of the Lateran inscription (cited above) and its assertion of the font's maternity. They also echo the images found in the Twenty-Third Psalm:

> From the font, the bishop—as parent—leads
> babes, snowy white in body, heart, and garb.
> And circling the novice lambs around the festive altar,
> the priest initiates their tender mouths with health-giving food.
> Here the older members of the community rejoice together in a noisy
>   throng,
> and the flock bleats a new chorus, Alleluia![84]

Ephrem includes a similar image in a hymn written for Epiphany, where he describes the older sheep of the fold running to embrace the new lambs that have been added to the flock.[85]

This use of sheep/shepherd imagery has led some scholars to conclude that the newly baptized recited the Twenty-Third Psalm as they processed from the font back into the main church. In fact, much of the language of that psalm may be applied to the baptismal liturgy, including the anointing of the forehead and the first reception of the Eucharist (the overflowing—or

80. Ambrose, *Myst.* 7.38; see also *Sacr.* 5.3.13; Cyril of Jerusalem, *Cat.* 16.
81. Cyril of Jerusalem, *Cat.* 3.16. The twins also signify the twofold grace announced in the Old and the New Testaments.
82. Augustine, *Serm.* 313B.3; idem, *Enarrat. Ps.* 3.7; 94.11.
83. Prudentius, *Perist.* 12.43 (CSEL 61:420–23).
84. Paulinus of Nola, *Ep.* 32.3.4 (CSEL 29:280), trans. author.
85. Ephrem, *Epiph.* 6.15.

inebriating—cup).[86] The practice is almost certainly confirmed in one of Ambrose's catechetical lessons, in which he initially asks the catechumens how many times they have heard the psalm recited but, prior to their preparation for baptism, never understood its meaning.[87] After their baptism he refers again to the psalm as he describes the candidates' coming into the church to receive their first Eucharist.[88]

An almost exact parallel to this is found in Cyril of Jerusalem's catechetical and mystagogical lectures.[89] As further evidence, an inscription in the Orthodox Baptistery at Ravenna contained an inscription referring to the psalm.[90] Another recorded inscription, commonly assigned to the fourth-century baptistery at the Basilica of St. Peter (possibly written by Pope Damasus) appears in a collection of Roman inscriptions compiled by pilgrims. It speaks of Christ as the chief shepherd:

> Here in this place, innocent lambs, having been washed in the celestial
>   stream,
> are signed by the right hand of the chief shepherd.
> Come here, you who have been reborn in the waters,
> because the Holy Spirit calls you into unity, so that you may receive his
>   gifts.
> You, having been signed with the cross, shun the temptations of the
>   world,
> being profoundly admonished by consideration of this place.[91]

The text of an inscription written by Venantius Fortunatus in the early sixth century for the Cathedral of Mainz joins the themes of cleansing by similarly referring to the shepherd washing his flock:

> Shine, high hall of sacred baptism!
> —where Christ washes away the sins of Adam by a river.
> Here the flock is plunged into the pure waves by the shepherd God,
>   as long as the sheep's wool still shows stains.
> Birth by human seed brought death, but you, Father of the world,
> cleanse mortal sins by the medicinal waters.[92]

---

86. Quasten makes this argument, particularly in reference to the liturgy at Naples, "Das Bild des Guten Hirten." Quasten also notes that shepherds brand their sheep and associates this branding with the seal (*sphragis*) given to the baptized. Regarding the cup, the Vulgate describes the cup in v. 5 to be inebriating, not "running over," *calyx meus inebrians*, a translation supported by both Greek (LXX) and Hebrew texts.

87. Ambrose, *Sacr.* 5.13.

88. Ambrose, *Myst.* 8.43.

89. Cyril of Jerusalem, *Cat.* 1.6 and *Myst.* 4.7.

90. The text reads: "In locum pascuae ibi me conlocavit super aqua reflectionis edocavit me" ("He set me here, where there are pastures. He led me beside reflecting waters").

91. Text in de Rossi, *ICUR* 2.139, no. 36, trans. author. Gregory of Nyssa also refers to himself in this way, *Diem lum.* On the baptistery at St. Peter's, see C. Smith, "Pope Damasus' Baptistery."

92. Fortunatus, *Carm.* 2.11 (MGH.AA 4.1.40–1), trans. author.

In the same Epiphany hymn (noted above), Ephrem likens the sealing or marking with the cross (*sphragis*) to the branding of the sheep: "The sheep leapt with joy to see the hand in readiness to baptize. O lambs, receive your marking, enter in and mingle with the flock; today the angels rejoice in you more than in all the rest of the sheep." A little further on, the congregation is described as the flock awaiting the new arrivals: "The older sheep within the fold ran to embrace the new lambs that have been added."[93]

The Shepherd was a popular motif in early Christian art as well as in literature. The Shepherd's standard appearance—youthful and beardless, wearing a short tunic and boots, and carrying a sheep (lamb, ewe, or ram) over his shoulders—exists in almost every kind of medium from the most precious to the commonplace: frescoes, sculpture, glass, mosaic, gems, and pottery lamps and bowls. The figure appears more than 120 times in catacomb paintings alone, often in the center of the dome of a small private family burial chamber (fig. 2.7).[94] It also was a popular motif for sarcophagus reliefs (fig. 1.1). Art historians have long pointed out that the Shepherd image was not new or unique to Christianity, but was borrowed from the corpus of classical imagery, particularly that of Hermes the sheep-bearer (*kriophoros*), who was thought to have guided and tended the soul as it entered the underworld. In general, shepherds and pastoral imagery were widely popular for pagan funerary art, perhaps because they suggested a kind of bucolic peace, or possibly to represent the divine guide for souls making their postdeath journey.[95]

The association of shepherd/flock with baptism is particularly signified in a painting in the Roman catacomb of Callixtus. Partially destroyed to make room for another tomb, the image portrays a shepherd between two sheep that stand under showers of water. The waterfalls refer also to the miracle of the rock (Exod. 17:6). The sarcophagus of Sta. Maria Antiqua presents the shepherd carrying a ram and with two sheep at his feet, directly next to the image of Jesus's baptism by John (fig. 1.1). Across the front of the sarcophagus flows the water, poured from the jug of the river god. This water that floats the boats of Noah (on the left) and the fishermen (on the right end) also represents the Jordan, in which the childlike Jesus stands.

Shepherds and flocks also appear on the walls and domed ceilings of baptisteries. For instance, a shepherd appears over the font at Dura Europos (fig. 2.8) and another among the mosaic themes in the baptistery of San Giovanni in Fonte in Naples (fig. 2.9). The sixth-century baptistery in Albenga, Italy,

---

93. Ephrem, *Epiph.* 6.6.15, trans. Brock, in Finn, *Early Christian Baptism*, 167–68. See discussion of the *sphragis* below, under the heading "Marking with the Sign of the Cross."

94. Leclercq identified more than three hundred examples in Christian art between the third and fifth centuries in his 1924 article "Pasteur (Bon)," in *DACL* 13.2, 2272–390.

95. See Himmelmann, *Über Hirten-genre in der antiken Kunst*; Schumacher, *Hirt und "Guter Hirt"*; and Klauser, "Studien zur Entstehungsgeschichte." One should note that shepherds and other bucolic or pastoral imagery were widely popular in pagan funerary art.

has an extant mosaic in one of its
four rectangular niches that show
two sheep on either side of a jeweled
cross (fig. 3.3). At least two African
baptisteries, Henchir Sokrine and
Sidi Jedidi, display images of lambs
in their mosaic pavements. Finally,
one of the niches in Ravenna's fifth-
century Neonian baptistery (the
baptistery of the Orthodox) quotes
the Twenty-Third Psalm above a
now-missing mosaic that may have
once held an image of a shepherd
and sheep.

Figure 2.7. Shepherd with milk. Painting, Catacomb
of Callixtus, Rome. Third century. (Photo © Estelle Brettman,
The International Catacomb Society.)

Figure 2.8. Good shepherd with flock; Adam and
Eve. Painting, Dura Europos baptistery. Mid-third
century. (Photo from Marsyas/Wikimedia Commons.)

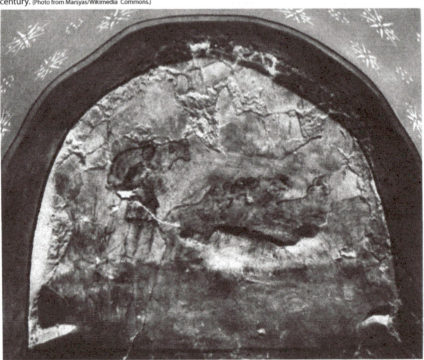

Figure 2.9. Shepherd with sheep. Mosaic, Baptistery of Sta. Restituta, San Giovanni in Fonte, Naples. Late fourth century. (Photo by author.)

A Christ-lamb (*Agnus Dei*) standing alone (without the flock) began to appear in Christian visual art in the mid-fourth century, while the enthroned lamb described in Revelation 5:6–14 emerged even later. According to the *Liber Pontificalis*, Constantine endowed the Lateran Basilica with a solid-gold lamb designed as a waterspout.[96] Rome's Catacomb of Commodilla has a painting of a lamb performing the multiplication of the loaves and fishes, a motif that also appears on the sarcophagus of Junius Bassus (ca. 359) along with images of the one lamb baptizing and raising Lazarus. In his above-mentioned letter to Severus, Paulinus describes the (now-lost) apse fresco of his own basilica at Fundi in a poem dedicated to the decoration of the vault. His description juxtaposes the shepherd and flock imagery with the metaphor of the sacrificial victim. Christ, as a snowy white lamb, stands directly under the cross, presiding as a judge, separating the goats from the sheep (whom he welcomes with his right hand).[97] Beginning in the sixth century, visual depictions of the Christ-lamb came to include a group of lambs (usually twelve, representing the apostles). This composition was especially popular for later Roman apses (e.g., Ss. Cosmas e Damiano, S. John Lateran, S. Praessede, S. Clemente—fig. 2.10).

The representation of Christ as a lamb raised concerns that led to its banning by the late seventh-century Council of Trullo (the Quinisext Council), which argued that the figure of the lamb (instead of a human) undermined the reality of Christ's human incarnation and human suffering.[98] Nevertheless, the lamb continued to be a popular visual metaphor for the Christian savior and a reference to his pastoral care for his flock—the baptized faithful.

---

96. *Lib. Pont.* 34.14. On the gift, see Brandt, "Deer, Lambs, and Water."
97. Paulinus of Nola, *Ep.* 32.17.
98. Council of Trullo, *Can.* 82, NPNF², 14:401.

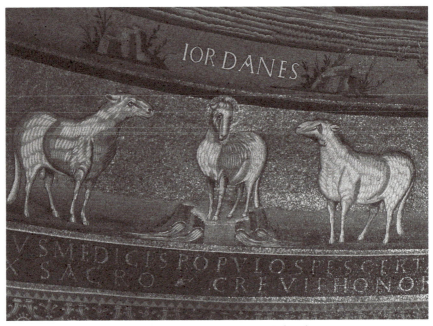

Figure 2.10. Mosaic, apse of Ss. Cosmas e Damiano, Rome (Agnus Dei). Early sixth century. (Photo by author.)

Rituals of Incorporation

Certain critical moments in the baptismal rite enacted the transition from catechumen to full membership in the Christian community. At the beginning of their final preparation, candidates were enrolled by having their names inscribed on a list of those who sought baptism. They were expected to obtain sponsors who would guide them through the process and vouch for their sincerity and character. They attended lessons and received spiritual, disciplinary, and intellectual formation through scrutinies, exorcism, ascetical exercises, and catechesis. Anointing with oil on the forehead signified the moment the newly baptized individual entered holy (and "royal") sacerdotal orders. When they emerged from the font the candidates were dressed in identical (and identifying) garments; they were urged to think of their fellow initiates as brothers and sisters and of the church as their new home. The ritual actions that particularly marked the steps toward their incorporation into the Christian family were the enrollment and role of their sponsors, the marking with the sign of the cross, and the welcoming kiss of peace.

Enrollment

Prior to being given final instruction, candidates for baptism were officially enrolled for the rite. This enrollment initiated the individual's separation from his or her old life. It began with an examination of the candidates' seriousness of purpose and suitability for membership in the church. This included obtaining good character references, approving their profession, and, if they were slaves, verifying that they had obtained their master's permission to proceed.[99]

According to Egeria's account of the enrollment process in fourth-century Jerusalem, candidates gave their names to a priest on the day before Lent began. The next day, those on the roster arrived at the cathedral and had their first official meeting with the bishop. One by one they approached the bishop on his throne with their sponsors ("fathers" for the men and "mothers" for the women), who vouched for their good character. The bishop asked the initiate several specific questions; if his inquiries turned up nothing of bad repute, he formally enrolled the aspirant.[100] By the fourth century, Lent was the most appropriate season for the catechetical process to begin. Augustine echoes the timing of this ritual in a sermon that addresses the catechumens in his congregation, urging them to proceed with their initiation: "See, it is Easter time; give your name for baptism."[101]

Fourth-century catechetical sermons elucidate the symbolism of this rite. John Chrysostom equates the enrollment to being inscribed on the citizen lists of heaven, an expression that echoes the idea of becoming members of a heavenly *gens* that was expressed in the Lateran Baptistery.[102] Cyril of Jerusalem and Theodore of Mopsuestia also use the language of citizenship in reference to the candidates. Cyril provides more information on a ceremony that followed the registration, including a procession of candidates carrying lit tapers, probably into the church or oratory where they would hear the bishop's catechetical lectures. He says, "Now you have enlisted, now you have been called to the colors. You have walked in procession with the tapers of brides in your hands and the desire of heavenly citizenship in your hearts; with a holy resolve also, and the confident hope which that brings in its train."[103] A little further on he exclaims, "What honor Jesus bestows! You used to be called a catechumen, when the truth was being dinned into you from without. . . . [Now] you, a pitiable creature, are receiving the family name of God."[104]

99. See Hippolytus, *Trad. ap.* 16. Rejected professions included actors, charioteers, gladiators, military commanders, and civic magistrates. Candidates holding such professions had to desist or be rejected. Magicians were rejected outright.

100. Egeria, *Itin.* 45. For other places where the term "enrollment" appears in a baptismal context, see John Chrysostom, *Catech.* 2.9 (Stav. 2); Ephrem, *Epiph.* 6; and Narsai, *Hom. Epiph.* 141–45.

101. Augustine, *Serm.* 132.1 (PL 38:735), trans. author; see also *Cur.* 1.15 (CSEL 41:646.11).

102. John Chrysostom, *Catech.* 4.6 (Stav. 4). Compare with Clement of Alexandria, *Protr.* 9.

103. Cyril of Jerusalem, *Procat.* 1, trans. McCauley and Stephenson, *Works of Saint Cyril of Jerusalem*, 1:70.

104. Cyril of Jerusalem, *Procat.* 6, trans. McCauley and Stephenson, *Works of Saint Cyril of Jerusalem*, 1:75.

Ambrose describes a special ceremony for enrollment in Milan. There, as the bishop entered the candidates' names, he took mud and smeared it over their eyes, recalling the healing of the man born blind in John 9. According to Ambrose, this gesture signified that the person had confessed his or her sins and thus had come to recognize the fallen human condition. The act also indicated the metaphorical giving of sight (opening of the mind) and therefore seems to typify the rite of opening (*ephphetha*) that was performed on the day of baptism itself.[105]

Basil of Caesarea describes the rite of enrollment in terms of all those social groups discussed above (soldiers, athletes, citizens): "Give your name, be enrolled in the Church. A soldier is enlisted in the army rolls; an athlete enters his name before he competes in the games; a citizen when he takes out citizenship is registered in one of the tribes. You are liable on all these counts—as a soldier of Christ, as a religious athlete, as one whose citizenship is in heaven. Be inscribed in this book so that you may be transcribed into the book of heaven."[106] Basil completes this exhortation by reminding his listeners that these roles also require discipline and training. No one ever won a crown by being self-indulgent or a trophy in his or her sleep: "One does not bring off the prize without running. Effort produces glory, victory garlands come with perspiration."

The fifth-century *Gelasian Sacramentary* includes a prayer for the making of a catechumen, an excerpt of which reads, "God, who established the human race that you might restore it, look with favor on your adopted people, and enroll the offspring of your new race in your new covenant, so that what these children of promise could not achieve by nature, they may joyfully receive by grace."[107]

Sponsors

The role of the sponsor was neither temporary nor merely ceremonial. The Latin word "sponsor" had a fiduciary connotation, akin to guaranteeing a note or posting bail. Christians who desired baptism had to find someone to vouch for them and serve as their guarantor. Tertullian is especially concerned that sponsors realize that they may themselves be put in peril should their candidates subsequently develop an evil character and fail in their promises. For this reason, Tertullian urges those who wish to be baptized to delay until they are firmly established in their convictions and able to live the life expected of them after baptism, including the observance of sexual continence.

---

105. Ambrose, *Sacr.* 3.12. On the ceremony of the *ephphetha*, see above, chap. 1, under the heading "The Paralytic and the Man Born Blind."

106. Basil of Caesarea, *Bapt.* 7, trans. Thomas P. Halton, in Hamman, *Baptism*, 84–85.

107. *Gel. Sac.* 1.30, trans. Finn, *Early Christian Baptism*, 92.

He emphasizes that "those who understand the burden of baptism will fear obtaining it more than postponing it."[108]

John Chrysostom lays out the duties and responsibilities of sponsors, comparing their situation to cosignatories to loans. Like Tertullian, he warns that those who act as surety for others' debts put themselves at even greater risk than the debtors do, as they are responsible for the whole sum if the borrower defaults. Yet if the borrower proves worthy, his good credit reflects on his guarantor. Thus John urges sponsors to encourage, instruct, counsel, and correct their candidates. This paternal approach earns them the title "spiritual fathers" (*pateres pneumatikoi*), and those whom they sponsor are called "spiritual sons" (*tekna pneumatika*).[109]

Similar to Cyril of Jerusalem and John Chrysostom, Theodore of Mopsuestia entreats candidates to strive to be citizens of a new and great city, and to give careful thought to all that is required before being received by the duly appointed person who registers their names. And, as elsewhere, the registrar will probe, asking about their habits and character to see if they meet the requirements for heavenly citizenship. Theodore recognizes that a candidate for baptism, like any stranger desiring to be admitted to citizenship of an earthly city, would need a specially appointed person: someone who is from the city and knows its mores, and who can testify that the stranger is worthy of being received.[110]

Theodore, however, changes the role of sponsor slightly, saying that it does not include their taking responsibility for any future misbehavior of the baptized. He also notes a few additional ritual details in regard to their role. According to Theodore, sponsors' names were inscribed in the church's registry along with their candidates', and after the first sealing (on the forehead—following the initial renunciation of Satan), sponsors were privileged to spread linen stoles (*oraria*) over their kneeling candidates' heads and raise them to their feet.[111]

Augustine asks sponsors to be responsible for helping candidates memorize the creed.[112] Because the creed was kept a secret, it could not be written down. It was delivered orally by the bishop and explained in a series of lectures, referred to as the handing over of the symbol (*traditio symboli*). Just before Easter, the candidates stood before the bishop and repeated the creed from memory (*redditio symboli*), a ceremony that often took place on the Saturday before Holy Week. Egeria likewise observed candidates reciting the creed be-

---

108. Tertullian, *Bapt.* 18.6 (CCSL 1:293.39), trans. author.
109. John Chrysostom, *Catech.* 2.15–16 (Stav. 2).
110. Theodore of Mopsuestia, *Bapt. hom.* 2.
111. Theodore of Mopsuestia, *Bapt. hom.* 2. See Mingana, *Commentary of Theodore of Mopsuestia*, 24–31, 47.
112. Augustine, *Serm.* 213.11. Here Augustine uses the term *parentes* rather than *sponsores*. Other instances turn up in *Serm.* 294.17 and *Ep.* 98.

fore the bishop of Jerusalem, and she notes that their sponsors accompanied them as they did so.[113]

Marking with the Sign of the Cross

Like the circumcision of Jewish men, the sign of the cross or sealing identified members of the Christian community with an invisible but nonetheless ineradicable mark. Although these acts, when given to candidates just before the baptism, had an exorcistic function, they also signified ownership, just as lambs were branded, or slaves and soldiers were tattooed. The text of Galatians 6:17 reflects this idea: "From now on, let no one make trouble for me; for I carry the marks of Jesus branded on my body." Similarly, in Revelation 7:3–4, the saints bore the seal of the lamb on their foreheads, while the servants of the demon bore the mark of the beast (Rev. 13:17). Another possible scriptural source for such identification marks comes from Ezekiel 9:4. Here the members of the future Israel receive a special mark on their foreheads that protects them from being slain (cf. also the mark of Cain, Gen. 4:15).

Early Christian documents noted the parallels between baptism and circumcision. The Epistle to the Colossians draws the two rituals together: "In him also you were circumcised with a spiritual circumcision, by putting off the body of the flesh in the circumcision of Christ; when you were buried with him in baptism, you were also raised with him through faith in the power of God, who raised him from the dead" (2:11–12). In his Epistle to the Romans, Paul disputes the value of circumcision, saying that real circumcision is an inward and spiritual matter of the heart (2:25–29). Further on, he proclaims that Abraham's righteousness was due to his faith, not his circumcision (4:9–12).

The early church incorporated these ideas into the ritual of baptism in respect to its imparting a mark of belonging. In his dispute with the Jew Trypho, Justin Martyr declares that only Christian circumcision (i.e., baptism) was of any value.[114] Two centuries later, Cyril of Jerusalem cites Paul's text to contrast Abraham's circumcision with the mark given to the newly baptized. Cyril argues that this sign also designates Christians as adopted sons of Abraham and members of the New Israel for, like them, "we receive the spiritual seal, being circumcised by the Holy Spirit through the laver of baptism, not in the foreskin of the body, but in the heart."[115] Cyril then cited the text of Jeremiah 4:4: "Circumcise yourselves to the LORD, remove the foreskin of your hearts."

This same reasoning appears frequently in Augustine's sermons. For example, in a sermon preached to the newly baptized on the octave of Easter, Augustine tells his neophytes that they must understand that the circumcision

---

113. Egeria, *Itin.* 46.
114. Justin Martyr, *Dial.* 19.
115. Cyril of Jerusalem, *Cat.* 5.6, trans. McCauley and Stephenson, *Works of Saint Cyril of Jerusalem*, 1:142–43.

of the flesh, which once took place on the eighth day after birth, is now on the eighth day after their baptism and is transformed into a circumcision of the heart. Whereas the old instruction was to circumcise with a knife of rock (flint), now the rock is Christ himself (cf. 1 Cor. 10:4). This sign of membership, though invisible to the external eye, is no less a physical mark on the body.[116]

Certain Christian sects may have practiced actual bodily marking as a part of religious initiation. In his refutation of gnostic sects, Irenaeus claims that Carpocratians branded their followers on the right earlobe.[117] Augustine similarly mentions Montanists pricking their infants with needles, which may have been related to baptismal tattooing.[118] Epiphanius claims that Pepuzians and certain other groups (perhaps imagined by him) also marked—possibly by tattooing—their followers.[119]

Christian writers frequently pointed out the parallels between baptism's ritual sealing with the sign of the cross and the branding of livestock or military recruits. Such a sign not only serves as a mark of ownership and of belonging but also serves as protection for the one who bears it. Cyril of Jerusalem urges catechumens to receive the sacramental seal so that the Lord might recognize them. He also compares the seal to an engraving on a signet ring.[120] Gregory of Nazianzus promises, "This [seal], even while you live, will greatly contribute to your sense of safety (for a sheep that is sealed is not easily snared, but that which is unmarked is an easy prey to thieves)."[121]

Basil of Caesarea warns the unbaptized that without the baptismal mark, no one will recognize to which side they belong on the field of battle; the rescuing angel will not be able to distinguish the soldiers of Christ from the enemy troops. He also recalls the Exodus story of the destroying angel who passed over the houses with the sacred sign (Exod. 12:23). Finally, he reminds them that as unmarked treasure can easily be stolen, unbranded sheep can easily be raided.[122] Like Basil, John Chrysostom warns catechumens that they are like vulnerable sheep without the brand; however, when they are anointed and signed, they become like athletes chosen for the spiritual arena. When they receive the sign, they become fully equipped soldiers.[123]

Theodore of Mopsuestia takes a similar tack. He identifies the episcopal sealing and anointing performed prior to the descent into the font as a virtual identification with the holy flock and a member of the Christian militia:

116. Augustine, *Serm.* 260.1; 260A.4.

117. Irenaeus, *Haer.* 1.25.6; repeated by Epiphanius, *Pan.* 27.5.9.

118. Augustine, *Haer.* 26. On Montanist tattooing, see Tabbernee, "Revelation 21."

119. Epiphanius, *Pan.* 48.14–15.

120. Cyril of Jerusalem, *Myst.* 4.7. See also Cyril's discussion of the sign of the cross, made throughout the day, as an apotropaic action that warded off demons: *Cat.* 13.36.

121. Gregory of Nyssa, *Diem lum.* 15, NPNF², 7:364.

122. Basil of Caesarea, *Bapt.* 4.

123. John Chrysostom, *Catech.* 10.16 (sheep without brands; Pk. 2); 2.22 (athletes; Stav. 2); 12.60–61 (soldiers; Montf. 2).

The seal that you receive at this point marks you out forever as the sheep of Christ, the soldier of the King of Heaven. As soon as a sheep is bought, it is given a mark to identify its owner; it feeds in the same pasture and lives in the same fold as the other sheep that bear the same owner's mark. And when a soldier is chosen for his height and build to serve the empire, he is at once given a tattoo on his hand to show the name of the emperor in whose service he has enlisted. You have been chosen for the kingdom of heaven; you too can be identified as a soldier of the King of Heaven . . . [a member of] his household and soldiers of Christ the Lord.[124]

The Holy Kiss

At the end of his First Epistle to the Corinthians, Paul commanded them to "greet one another with a holy kiss" (16:20). Similar salutations occur at the end of other Epistles (e.g., Rom. 16:16; 2 Cor. 13:12; 1 Thess. 5:26; 1 Pet. 5:14). Justin Martyr's *First Apology* also offers evidence of this custom of Christians greeting one another with a kiss. According to Justin, it is given just prior to the offering of the eucharistic gifts.

The gesture must have led to some problems. Clement of Alexandria worried about abuses that would turn the holy gesture into a shameless act. Similarly expressing concern about the appearance of sexual indecorum, the *Apostolic Tradition* limits the exchange to members of the same sex.[125]

A kiss is also recorded as one of the last postbaptismal actions that signaled the reception of neophytes into the community and was offered to each as a sign of welcome. According to the *Apostolic Tradition*, this kiss was exchanged with the whole gathered congregation, after the candidates entered the nave of the church and just before they received the Eucharist for the first time. Earlier, however, they were warned not to give this kiss prior to baptism, for their "kiss [was] not yet pure."[126] One of Cyprian's letters testifies to an otherwise unknown custom of kissing the feet of newly baptized babies. He notes that people might find the act repellant, especially when the infant is "fresh from birth," but assures that no one need worry. Since the baby was so recently formed from the very hands of God, kissing its feet is like kissing God's hands and embracing God's creation.[127]

John Chrysostom is less definite about whether this kiss is given inside the baptismal room or shared with the newly baptized after they were brought into the church proper. He does provide some detail, saying, "As soon as they come forth from those sacred waters, all who are present embrace them, greet them, kiss them, rejoice with them, and congratulate them, because those

---

124. Theodore of Mopsuestia, *Bapt. hom.* 2.17, trans. Yarnold, *Awe-Inspiring Rites of Initiation*, 186–87.

125. Justin Martyr, *1 Apol.* 65; Clement of Alexandria, *Paed.* 3.11.81; Hippolytus, *Trad. ap.* 19. On the holy kiss, see Penn, *Kissing Christians*; idem, "Performing Family"; Phillips, *Ritual Kiss*.

126. Hippolytus, *Trad. ap.* 18; 22.3–4.

127. Cyprian, *Ep.* 64.4.1.

who were heretofore slaves and captives have suddenly become free, and have been invited to the royal table." Later, he offers a deeper explanation of the significance of the kiss: "Since I mentioned a kiss, I wish now also to speak to you of this. When we are about to participate in the sacred table, we are also instructed to offer a holy greeting. Why? Since we have been divorced from our bodies, we join souls with one another on that occasion by means of the kiss, so that our gathering becomes like the gathering of the apostles when, because all believed, there was one heart and one soul."[128]

The kiss given to the newly baptized cannot be distinguished easily from the kiss exchanged by members of the congregation just before the offering of the eucharistic gifts. Cyril of Jerusalem's description of the ritual places the kiss between the washing of the celebrant's hands and the offering of the gifts. It is not, he insists, an "ordinary kiss" like those exchanged on the streets by friends; rather, it is a sign of the "true union of hearts, banishing every grudge," a symbol of reconciliation and charity.[129]

Theodore of Mopsuestia, however, makes an explicit connection between the kiss exchanged just before the Eucharist (which was actually after the offering of the gifts and before the hand washing in his liturgy) and the transformation that takes place through baptism. He describes the act as a sequence in which each person kisses only the person next to him or her. This chain allows one kiss to be shared essentially with the whole assembly as a sign that they are the single body of Christ. Thus, for Theodore, the kiss symbolizes the unity and charity that connects the whole community, leading each to care for the others' needs, share in their sorrows, and celebrate their joys as common to all. Because this has also taken place in baptism, the sign confirms their unity; everyone comes to the same family table to share a common meal. To this last point, Theodore quotes Paul: "Because there is one bread, we who are many are one body, for we all partake of the one bread" (1 Cor. 10:17).[130]

Augustine likewise associates the unity expressed in the Eucharist with the holy kiss. As he explains to the newly baptized, the kiss is a sign of peace, and what is performed by the lips should indicate what is in the heart: a desire for unity, which is also symbolized in the one loaf and one body of Christ.[131] Becoming a part of the one body is also both an inclusionary and an exclusionary act, of course. Kissing is not something shared by all but is extended only to members of one's immediate family, in this case a family constituted through baptism rather than by earthly birth.

128. John Chrysostom, *Catech.* 2.27 (Stav. 2); 11.32 (Pk. 3), trans. Harkins, *St. John Chrysostom*, 53, 171. Compare Ambrose, *Myst.* 5.5–6, which cites the Song of Songs 1:2: "Let him kiss me with the kisses of his mouth!"

129. Cyril of Jerusalem, *Myst.* 5.3, trans. McCauley and Stephenson, *Works of Saint Cyril of Jerusalem*, 2:192–93.

130. Theodore of Mopsuestia, *Bapt. hom.* 4.39–40.

131. Augustine, *Serm.* 227. See also *Serm.* 229 and 229A.

Through baptism, Christians became members of a community that understood itself as both separate and secure. They had crossed a social boundary, joining an exclusive group that functioned like a family and provided them spiritual nurture and support. Like orphaned children adopted into a privileged and happy extended family, they left their old lives and identities behind. This adoption afforded them the name, the parental and filial love, and the due inheritance promised to any child by birth. In the church, at least, social class, ethnicity, or race no longer divided them, since all were brothers and sisters of a single set of parents.

They had also crossed a spiritual boundary, being enrolled in a group that not only offered companionship and encouragement in this life but also certain assurance of a blessed afterlife. These rewards were equated to those earned by the martyrs, but they were also likened to the victories of courageous soldiers who battled earthly enemies or athletic champions who trained for the games. Those victories earned them worldly crowns, while the newly baptized were awarded heavenly ones. By becoming Christians they had, in effect, become members of a new race, citizens of a new state, and affiliated with an exclusive class (both royal and priestly).

The rituals that embodied this transformation included the enrolling of new candidates, their being assigned sponsors, their sealing with a mark of their owner (and their new identity), and the extension of the kiss of peace that expressed the mutual love of the community. They were to consider their coreligionists as sisters or brothers, the church as their sacred mother, and God as their heavenly father. Like little fish, they needed to remain in the water of their baptism to survive. Like sheep in a flock governed by a loving shepherd, they were protected and cherished, rescued when in danger, and persistently herded toward their place of safety.

3

Baptism as Sanctifying and Illuminative

John the Baptist preached a baptism for repentance. He also announced that someone would come after him who would baptize with the Holy Spirit (and fire). This promised that something more—or different—was about to be offered. John's baptism prompted sinners to live righteous lives in the face of a coming messianic judgment, and receiving it appears to have been the basis for becoming one of his disciples (cf. John 4:1; Acts 19:3–4). Yet John's prophecy of a coming baptism of the Holy Spirit described a ritual that was more than purification from sin or initiation into a religious community. Such a baptism is described in the Acts of the Apostles, where the Spirit's gift is presented as a distinct benefit, delivered through the imposition of hands by authorized disciples of Jesus. In subsequent early Christian writings, the Spirit's gift was an essential part of the baptism ritual; it sanctified and enlightened its recipients. Thus from the earliest days of the Christian movement, the gift of the Holy Spirit was essential for baptism and was transmitted through a specific rite, separate from the water bath but performed alongside it. In certain heterodox communities, this gift was judged to be the essence of the entire ritual and so crucial that the cleansing bath in water might even become a preliminary or dispensable act.

This chapter considers the baptismal gift of the Holy Spirit as it occurs in early Christian documents, religious practice, and in Christian iconography and architecture. It also attends to variants in the ways that the Spirit's gifts were transmitted, differences of opinion about the validity of material substances to convey those gifts, and contradictory views about the water's indispensability in the ritual. The diversity of practices sometimes resulted in alternative and competing rituals as well as "orthodox" repudiation of some rituals as heretical or invalid.

The Holy Spirit at Jesus's Baptism

According to the Synoptic Gospels, the Holy Spirit descended on Jesus immediately after his baptism. Retrospectively, this elementally changed the Baptist's exclusively water-based rite into a more complex ritual (at least as most early Christian communities practiced it). The Holy Spirit's descent added an element to John's purificatory ritual and fulfilled his prediction that the one who came after him would baptize with "the Holy Spirit and fire" (Matt. 3:11//Luke 3:16). Nevertheless, in the Gospel accounts, the meaning of John's prophecy is ambiguous; he does not explain how this would be accomplished. Only the Acts of the Apostles, which describes different means for the imparting of the Spirit, shows the ritual to have evolved and adapted to the circumstance of Jesus's having appeared and formed his own group of followers.

The role of the Holy Spirit is more theologically nuanced in the New Testament Epistles, which emphasize the role and place of the Spirit at baptism, characterize its transmission as offering enlightenment, and compare it to the anointing of kings and priests. The Epistles allude to the use of oil for this latter purpose only analogically, as an ancient religious symbol. Thus anointing may have been practiced, but the evidence for it is not definitive.

The Holy Spirit at Baptism in the Acts of the Apostles

Jesus himself did not baptize, although both John's Gospel and Acts maintain that Jesus's disciples did (cf. John 4:2). Yet how these baptisms were administered and what they signified change from case to case. The apostles received the promised baptism of the Holy Spirit at Pentecost (Acts 1:5), a baptism that Peter extended to three thousand others, presumably in some unspecified body of water (Acts 2:38–41). According to Acts, other baptisms performed by Jesus's followers also involved water (cf. Acts 8:36; 10:47) but with the Holy Spirit sometimes given before, sometimes given after the recipient's immersion. For example, Paul was filled with the Holy Spirit prior to being baptized by Ananias (Acts 9:17; 22:16). This order (pouring out of the Spirit first, water immersion second) also characterizes Peter's baptism of the gentiles (Acts 10:44–48).

Other examples show the same variation in relative order of water and Spirit. When Philip baptized the Ethiopian, the Holy Spirit appeared after the immersion and, seemingly, only in order to snatch Philip away (Acts 8:39). The Spirit is not specifically mentioned in the baptisms of Lydia and her household (Acts 16:15), of Paul and Silas's jailer (Acts 16:33), or of Crispus and the other Corinthians (Acts 18:8). By contrast, Philip's baptism of the Samaritans needed to be completed by Peter and John, who subsequently performed an imposition of hands so that they could receive the Holy Spirit (Acts 8:12–17). Although this special gesture (the imposition of hands) is merely mentioned here, its necessity is confirmed in Acts 19 when Paul baptizes and lays hands on some disciples of John the Baptist (vv. 1–6).

Based on these texts, the primitive, first-century ritual appears to have been evolving and eventually encompassed two distinct signs: application of water (whether by immersion or by some other means) and an imposition of hands. These two actions initially corresponded to two distinct gifts: forgiveness of sin and the receipt of the Holy Spirit. "Baptism" originally conveyed the sense of water's application (if not also immersion) in its very definition, but this definition was expanded to include a waterless element that instantiated John's promise that one coming after him would baptize with the Holy Spirit (and fire).[1] In fact, in every instance following the Pentecost baptism of the three thousand, the sign of repentance is only one of baptism's benefits. From this point, baptism also indicated conversion to the good news of Jesus and the kerygma of the gospel as much as (or possibly more than) personal contrition and renewed resolve to live in a righteous manner (cf. Acts 8:12–13; 10:34–43). Baptism's moral implications were balanced or even displaced by its function as demonstrating adherence to Christ. Therefore, baptism was for believers as well as for penitent sinners.

This twofold purpose potentially divided the rite into two distinct parts: one, an act of cleansing, and the other, the giving of the Spirit. The order of these parts is variable along with their relative significance. The latter action also differs in time and place in regard to how and where it was conveyed and what it was interpreted to mean.

Anointing and the Seal of the Holy Spirit in the Epistles

The New Testament Epistles refer numerous times to a spiritual anointing or signing that Christians receive. One such reference occurs in Paul's Second Epistle to the Corinthians, assuring readers of God's faithful care: "But it is God who establishes us with you in Christ and has anointed [*chrisas*] us, by putting his seal on us and giving us his Spirit in our hearts as a first installment" (1:21–22). Two others come from the Epistle to the Ephesians. In the first of these (1:13–14), the seal of the Holy Spirit follows (rather than precedes) the hearing and believing of the gospel. The second (4:30) admonishes readers to resist evil talk lest they grieve the Holy Spirit with which they were "marked with a seal for the day of redemption." In each of these Ephesians passages, the verb "to seal" is formed from the Greek noun *sphragis*, which denotes a

---

1. See McDonnell and Montague, *Christian Initiation*, 23–41. Arguments about the validity of John's baptism are evident in the early literature. See Tertullian, *Bapt.* 10–11, and Cyprian, *Ep.* 69.11.2 and 73.9.1–2.

seal like that made by a signet ring and which indicates ownership. However, these texts do not connect this sealing with water with either baptism or washing (cf. Eph. 5:26), or with any other ceremony associated with the gift of the Holy Spirit (e.g., anointing with oil or the imposition of hands).[2]

Although the phrasing in the Epistle to Titus is similar, the word *sphragis* does not appear and the context is more explicitly baptismal. The passage reads, "But when the goodness and loving-kindness of God our Savior appeared, he saved us, not because of any works of righteousness that we had done, but according to his mercy through the water [*dia loutrou*] of rebirth and renewal by the Holy Spirit. This Spirit he poured out on us richly through Jesus Christ our Savior, so that, having been justified by his grace, we might become heirs according to the hope of eternal life" (3:4–8).

The gifts of the Spirit come up in Paul's First Epistle to the Corinthians (12:3–7, 12–13), which claims that all are equally members of the one body, whether Jew or Greek, slave or free, since all are baptized in one Spirit and given to drink of that one Spirit. In 1 John 2:20, 27, the gift of the Spirit seems to be the comprehension of truth. The association with baptism is not clear: "But you have been anointed by the Holy One, and all of you have knowledge." In this and the previous Epistle texts, no particular action or element is described in association with the sealing, anointing, or "pouring out." Neither the imposition of hands (as in Acts) nor an actual ritual of anointing is specified. Although opinions differ, most New Testament scholars see no evidence for the application of oil in earliest Christian baptismal practice.[3]

Furthermore, whether these Epistles' authors intended water baptism, imposition of hands, or application of oil when they referred to an anointing, sealing, or pouring out of the Holy Spirit is also ambiguous. References to sealing never occur in direct connection with baptism or allusions to baptism. Also, any evidence for baptismal application of actual oil depends on the way in which the words "anointed" and "sealed" (variations of the verbs *chriō* and *sphragizō*) are related to specific Gospel narratives or perceived apostolic practice.[4] The words might be understood literally or figuratively. Nevertheless, anointing was not without apostolic and biblical justification, if only a linguistic one.

Anointing in Ancient Religious Practice

Oil was an indispensable substance for life in the ancient world. It was used as a cleansing agent, a healing balm, a lubricant, a preservative, a fuel (especially for lamps), an embalming substance, and a basic food. It also played an

---

2. For a detailed, if rather old, discussion of the issues, see Lampe, *Seal of the Spirit*, 3–18.
3. L. L. Mitchell, *Baptismal Anointing*, 16–17.
4. See the arguments of Kavanagh, *Shape of Baptism*, 25–29.

important role in religious rites in pre-Christian religions of the ancient Near East and the Greco-Roman world. Oil was a sacrificial offering to the gods, as were milk, wine, grain, incense, and blood. Oil also was poured over objects or persons as a means or symbol of solemnly consecrating them. Brides were anointed before marriage, and bodies were anointed before burial; altars and crossroads were anointed in order to mark a sacred event that happened there or merely to make them safe.[5]

The Hebrew Scriptures indicate that oil was a sacrificial gift (cf. Lev. 2; Mic. 6:7) as well as an anointing substance. The application of oil consecrated certain places, setting them apart for sacred functions or roles (e.g., Jacob's pillar of Bethel, Gen. 28:18), objects (e.g., the tent of meeting and the ark of testimony, Exod. 30:25–46), and persons (e.g., Aaron, Exod. 29:7; Saul, 1 Sam. 9:15–10:1).

The ancient Israelite ritual of anointing was reserved in particular for priests (especially the high priest) and kings. Although both might be called "the Lord's anointed," the title "Anointed One" generally referred only to the king.[6] These rites required special, scented oil that was perfumed with a combination of olive oil, spices (cinnamon, cane, cassia), and myrrh. Using this for ordinary persons was prohibited, and only an authorized individual was allowed to prepare it (Exod. 30:22–33). Such a compound of perfume, spices, and oil probably was the basis for the special oils (chrism) used for spiritual sealing in the baptismal liturgy. It was substantially distinguished from ordinary olive oil, which was used for exorcism and strengthening. Jews also anointed their dead for burial (as they still do). According to the Mishnah and the Tosefta, corpses must be anointed prior to being wrapped with a linen shroud. This use of oil is evident in the accounts of the treatment of Jesus's body (cf. Mark 16:1; John 19:39–40).[7]

Oil's primary use in the New Testament was for anointing the sick (cf. Mark 6:13; Jas. 5:14) or anointing the body before or after death (cf. Mark 14:8; 16:1; John 19:39). Mark 6:7 records that Jesus gave the apostles authority over unclean spirits, whereas Mark 6:13 says that they not only cast out demons but also anointed with oil to cure the sick. The New Testament never mentions Jesus using oil for healing, although in one instance he uses spittle (John 9:6). The Gospel accounts of the woman who anointed Jesus describe her using a costly ointment (pure, fragrant nard, according to both Mark and John) with which she anointed either Jesus's head (Matt. 26:6; Mark 14:3) or his feet (John 12:3).

Use of fragrant oil for consecration and burial may underlie Paul's assertion that "we are the aroma of Christ to God among those who are being saved

5. See Bowie, "Oil in Ancient Greece and Rome."
6. See Porter, "Oil in the Old Testament."
7. For an excellent discussion of Jewish burial practices and good references, see Green, "Sweet Spices in the Tomb."

and among those who are perishing" (2 Cor. 2:15), and this is what many early Christian writers took it to mean.[8] Cyril of Jerusalem, for example, cites this text to comment on the significance of scented or perfumed oil for chrism (he called it the "mystical oil of gladness"), which was placed first on the forehead, then on the ears, the nostrils, and, finally, on the breast. The scent reminded the newly baptized that they were like incense, being offered by Christ to God.[9] The *Apostolic Constitutions* records a prayer offered after the chrismation of the newly baptized that similarly emphasized the importance of the perfume mixed into the unction used for this rite. It reads: "O Lord God, who is without generation, and without superior, the Lord of the whole world, who has scattered the sweet odor of the knowledge of the gospel among all nations, grant that this chrism may be efficacious upon the baptized, so that the sweet odor of your Christ may remain firm and fixed; and that now having died with him, she or he may arise and live with him."[10]

Baptism and the Holy Spirit in Post–New Testament Christian Documents

Despite the importance of oil in the later tradition, a survey of the earliest literature offers little evidence for baptismal anointing. For example, the *Didache*, which offers instruction on how to baptize, specifies the kind and quality of the water for the ritual, and commands baptism in the triune name, but it makes no mention of an imposition of hands or of any other ceremony especially associated with the gift of the Spirit.[11] If any transmission of the Spirit took place, the water alone seems to have been sufficient for the purpose.

Such sufficiency of water for the imparting of the full benefits of baptism is indicated in the second-century *Acts of Paul and Thecla*. After her first rescue from the fires of martyrdom, Thecla finds Paul in his desert tomb, expresses a desire to follow him, and then begs that he give her "the seal in Christ" so that she might resist temptation. Paul refuses, saying, "Have patience, Thecla, and you will receive the water." Eventually, Thecla does receive the water when she baptizes herself in a pit filled with water and flesh-eating seals. When she next sees Paul, Thecla announces that she has "taken the bath."[12] Evidently,

8. See discussion by J. John, "Anointing in the New Testament."

9. Cyril of Jerusalem, *Myst.* 3.4.

10. *Const. ap.* 7.44.2, ANF, 7:477, slightly modified by author. See the importance of the sense of scent in gnostic anointing (below).

11. *Did.* 7.

12. *Acts of Paul*, 25, 34, 40. Lampe cited the story of Paul and Artemylla in this document to point out that here baptism in water is similarly identified with the term "seal." In both stories (of Thecla and of Artemylla) no additional act confers the gift of the Spirit. Lampe further cites several other early documents in which the seal is conferred through the washing in water alone, *Seal of the Spirit*, 108–9.

Paul sees no need to add an additional sign to Thecla's baptism and instructs her to go and teach the word of God.

The seer in the *Shepherd of Hermas* draws a highly metaphorical picture of baptism, which includes receiving a seal. In his vision, the seal seems to be equated with immersion in water, however. The church is likened to a tower built on saving water, and the Shepherd explains that the various stones used in its building are those the builders kept because of their purity and faithfulness (cf. Matt. 21:42; Acts 4:11; 1 Pet. 2:4–8); those stones first needed to emerge from water, which is referred to as a "seal."[13]

Justin Martyr describes an actual baptismal rite that takes place in water but makes no mention of any separate sign or ritual to convey the gift of the Spirit. Admittedly, Justin's brief description of baptism in his *First Apology* lacks details, perhaps to protect its secrecy. Nevertheless, Justin summarizes the rite's benefits, saying that a neophyte received forgiveness of sin and became an "illuminated one" (*ho phōtizomenos*).[14] Elsewhere, in his *Dialogue with Trypho*, Justin refers to baptism as the washing of repentance and knowledge of God, and argues that Christian baptism is better than Jewish ablutions or circumcision because baptism alone cleanses both soul and body.[15]

Likewise, Irenaeus is silent about any discrete baptismal act added to the water bath for the purpose of conveying the Holy Spirit. In his *Treatise on Apostolic Preaching*, he claims that Christians are given simply a baptism of water in which they receive the Holy Spirit. Christ's anointing, he says, was accomplished by the Spirit's descent at his baptism. By extension, it appears that Irenaeus understands the Spirit as descending upon the newly baptized as they rise from the water. In a further association of the Spirit with water, Irenaeus adds that nonbelievers had not yet been given the Holy Spirit to drink, even though God created rivers in abundance to disseminate the Holy Spirit on earth.[16] Irenaeus's treatise *Against Heresies* simply identifies the saved as those who "have been washed, believing in the name of the Lord and receiving his Spirit."[17]

Thus, according to the earliest noncanonical records, baptism conferred two distinct benefits: a cleansing from sin and a sealing of the Spirit. Yet these benefits apparently were not conveyed by two separate ritual actions, since the Spirit was integrally connected with the water. Although an associated action (e.g., the imposition of hands) may have served the purpose, such an action was neither the sole means for imparting the Holy Spirit nor necessarily one that followed a bath whose primary function was cleansing.

13. *Herm. Vis.* 3.3.5, 3.7.3; *Herm. Sim.* 9.16.
14. Justin Martyr, *1 Apol.* 61.
15. Justin Martyr, *Dial.* 14 ("dia tou loutrou oun tēs metanoias kai tēs gnōseōs tou theou"), and cf. 19.
16. Irenaeus, *Epid.* 41, 42, 47, 89.
17. Irenaeus, *Haer.* 5.11.2, ANF, 1:537.

The earliest surviving references to anointing with oil at baptism occur in two late second- or early third-century sources: Tertullian's treatise *On Baptism* and the *Apostolic Constitutions*. A third source, the *Apostolic Tradition*, may reflect early practices, although the dating of this document is highly controversial.[18] These documents vary regarding the oil's purpose, however.

Tertullian's baptismal rite mentions no anointing prior to the bath and, citing the Holy Spirit's descent at Jesus's baptism, describes a spiritual anointing of the body after it emerges from the water, followed by an imposition of the hand to invite and welcome the Holy Spirit.[19] Thus Tertullian's treatise *On Baptism* is somewhat contradictory about the relationship of water cleansing and the gift of the Spirit. Its opening paragraphs stress the "sacred significance" of water and insist that Christian baptism cannot take place without water (or at least without the effort to obtain water).[20] Tertullian argues that the Holy Spirit's moving over the face of the waters in the creation account (Gen. 1:2) shows that water was created to be a resting place for the Spirit and thereby derives its sanctity. Since matter is qualitatively transformed by a substance set over it, he says, the hovering Spirit makes the water into a sacred thing (*sanctum*). This original act, according to Tertullian, grants water the unique ability to convey the Spirit; individuals washed in consecrated baptismal water (of any kind) will find that their spirits are "corporally washed" and their bodies are "spiritually cleansed."[21]

Nevertheless, Tertullian distinguishes between the water bath and a following rite for the gift of the Spirit. He asserts that although the Holy Spirit was not precisely given in the water, it was present through the act of invocation or consecration. In this consecratory act (paralleled by the action of the angel in John 5:1–9), the water of the font is cleansed and the baptized person is made ready to receive the Holy Spirit. Here Tertullian points to the model of Jesus's baptism to support his argument. John baptized with water in order to prepare the way for the Holy Spirit, who was to come next. Therefore, John's baptism was not so much invalid as it was simply incomplete and not "heavenly." Once Jesus had come, John's preparatory baptism was no longer needed.[22] This is why, according to Tertullian, neophytes are anointed with unction to signify

18. Although for a long time the *Apostolic Tradition* was considered to be evidence for third-century Roman practice, recent scholarship has convincingly demonstrated that the material in the document is the work of a later compiler and thus a synthesis of practices from different places and eras, some of them likely to have been fourth-century developments to the rite. See Bradshaw, Johnson, and Phillips, *Apostolic Tradition*.

19. Tertullian, *Bapt.* 7.

20. See discussion of the controversy over waterless baptism below, under the heading "Early Controversies about Water and Spirit Baptism."

21. Tertullian, *Bapt.* 4.4 (CCSL 1:280), trans. author.

22. Tertullian, *Bapt.* 10–11. On the question of John's baptism, see also Gregory of Nazianzus, *Or.* 39.17, where he makes a similar argument about John's baptism: while better than the Jews', since it was for repentance, it was not entirely spiritual.

the gift of the Spirit and then receive the imposition of hands in benediction. The administrator makes the sign of the cross upon them, a sign that invites and welcomes the Holy Spirit to come again and rest, as though revisiting its primal dwelling place.[23]

Dated a decade or so later, the Syrian *Didascalia Apostolorum* records two ritual anointings: one of the head by the bishop and the other of the whole body prior to—or perhaps during—immersion in the font. The episcopal anointing of the head only seems to precede the candidate's entering the font and is compared to the anointing of kings and priests in ancient Israel. No postimmersion ceremonies of anointing or imposition of hands are specified.[24]

A quite different late second-century or early third-century document with a Syrian provenance, the apocryphal *Acts of Thomas*, includes a mention of baptismal anointing. Most likely originating from Edessa, the text narrates the adventures of the apostle Judas Thomas, whose evangelizing work in India included a number of baptisms. The first of these, the baptism of Gundaphorus, incorporates a postbaptismal anointing that invokes the divine by many names, including the "Power of the Most High" and the "Compassionate Mother." It concludes with the invocation of the Holy Spirit to cleanse and seal the candidates through the triune name.[25] A second baptism described in these *Acts* may have been waterless, consisting only of the apostle's imposing hands and sealing the candidate in the triune name.[26]

Unlike Tertullian or the *Didascalia*, the *Apostolic Tradition* often attributed to Hippolytus gives detailed instructions, first, for a prebaptismal anointing with the oil of exorcism and, second, for a postbaptismal anointing with the oil of thanksgiving. After the candidates are dried and dressed, they receive both the imposition of hands from the bishop, which invites the presence of the Holy Spirit, and a final anointing or sealing on the forehead (probably the sign of the cross, made with oil).[27] The *Apostolic Tradition* describes the bishop laying hands on the neophytes and giving thanks for the remission of sins delivered through the "washing of the regeneration of the Holy Spirit" (cf. Titus 3:5). Notably, neither in this prayer nor in the anointing that follows does the bishop specifically invoke the Holy Spirit's presence or imply that he is transmitting the Spirit's sanctity to the newly baptized through this gesture.

---

23. Tertullian, *Bapt.* 8. Tertullian likens this signing with the cross to Jacob's cross-handed blessing of Ephraim and Manasseh, a prefiguration of Christ's blessing in baptism.

24. *Did. Apos.* 16 (contained within an argument about what to do with women candidates when no woman deacon is present).

25. *Acts Thom.* 25–26. The baptisms in this text are discussed in more detail below, under the heading "Baptism in the Acts of Thomas."

26. *Acts Thom.* 49. Three other baptisms described in these acts were rituals of anointing first and water bath second. Cf. the baptism of Mygdonia.

27. Hippolytus, *Trad. ap.* 21–22.

Presumably, the neophytes receive the Spirit in the font and the subsequent actions were signs confirming the completion of the rite.

Thus a ritual of anointing with oil seems to have appeared almost suddenly, toward the end of the second century, and to have varied in form, purpose, ritual placement, and relative importance to the water bath.

Early Controversies about Water and Spirit Baptism

To the extent that certain early Christians perceived baptism to be a two-stage ritual with parts that could be separated by time and space, they may have wondered about those parts' relative efficacy.

Tertullian's treatise *On Baptism* may have been written in direct refutation of a group whose members practiced waterless baptism.[28] He condemns a certain woman for the heresy of the Cainites, who apparently not only baptized without water but also presumed that she, as a woman, had authority to perform the rite. Tertullian, referring to Matthew 12:43, accuses the Cainites of "demolishing baptism" like asps or vipers who inhabit "dry and waterless places." Tertullian's treatise further likens faithful Christians to fish who must remain in water to live. He adds that the Cainite heretics know how to kill fishes: by taking them out of the water.[29] Yet Tertullian admits that the efficacy of the water is invisible and thus subject to mockery by those who would undermine the faith. This leads Tertullian to defend the liquid element of baptism quite vehemently and to prove its divinely ordained purpose by reference to Scripture.

The author of the third-century *Treatise on Rebaptism* argues against the need for repeating the water baptism of converted schismatics or heretics, saying that only the baptism of the Holy Spirit, through the imposition of the bishop's hand, was required.[30] Basing his argument on the baptisms of the Samaritans in Acts 8, the author distinguishes between water and Spirit baptism and insists that no one can be saved without the baptism of the Holy Spirit. Thus, while the treatise acknowledges the validity of baptism by schismatics, those who returned to the fold still needed to receive the baptism of the Holy Spirit from the hands of a bishop within the "true" church. This necessary baptism could also be given directly by God before or after baptism in water or blood.[31]

Drawing on the story of the baptism of Cornelius and the gentiles (Acts 10:44–48; 11:15–17), in which the Holy Spirit descended prior to their receiving the bath, the treatise's author maintains that converts may be baptized by the

---

28. See Jensen, "With Pomp, Apparatus, Novelty, and Avarice."

29. Tertullian, *Bapt.* 1.3.

30. Anon., *Rebapt.* 3.

31. Anon., *Rebapt.* 10. This had to have been the case in the baptism of the Ethiopian eunuch, as the author points out. See *Rebapt.* 2.

Holy Spirit without water. The only benefit given by the bath, he says, is that in it Christians follow the example of Christ. He concludes that the baptism of water is of less account than the baptism of the Spirit. To be baptized in water alone would signify an imperfect faith and an incomplete ritual.[32]

In some places, where baptism in the Holy Spirit was deemed more essential than baptism in water, water might have even been eliminated altogether. According to Irenaeus, certain gnostic sects believed the water useless, perhaps on the basis of John's promise about future baptisms or possibly because they judged material elements incapable of conveying anything from the divine realm. Among these were groups who anointed with scented oil or incorporated fire or light as a means to express the Spirit's ineffability, its utter distinction from the world of physical matter, and its gift of illumination (special, mystical knowledge).[33] Such practices were repudiated by those in the mainstream tradition who, though they held the gift of the Spirit to be as central as the cleansing bath, would not have considered washing in water preliminary or dispensable. Tertullian is adamant about this, proclaiming that the liquid element is essential in the sacrament of "our water."[34]

Gnostic Baptism, Anointing, and Waterless Baptism

The use of oil and anointing in the baptismal rite may have arisen first within gnostic sects. Tertullian's condemnation of those who would "take the little fishes out of the water" zealously asserts the primacy and necessity of the water bath over against a group who offered a competing ritual of "waterless baptism." Several groups were associated with such practices, including the Cainites, the Marcosians, and the followers of Marcion. The *Gospel of Thomas* and the *Gospel of Philip* also mention baptismal practices that arose within the circle of the Alexandrian teacher Valentinus.

MARCIONITE, CAINITE, MARCOSIAN, AND ARCHONTIC BAPTISM

Tertullian's heretical baptizers may have been followers of Marcion, who would have disparaged water since it was a part of the material creation.[35] However, since he refers to them, it is more likely that they were so-called

---

32. Anon., *Rebapt.* 5–6. John Chrysostom makes a similar argument a century or so later in a homily on Acts 1, explaining that since there was no water in the upper room, the apostles must have received water baptism earlier (from John the Baptist). He claims, though, that the more *essential* baptism is of the Spirit. *Hom. Act.* 1.

33. See Irenaeus, *Haer.* 1.21.3–4; also the *Book of Jeu* 46, which describes a baptism of fire and a sealing with myrrh oil. A longer discussion of gnostic baptism follows in the next section. Fire at baptism also was reported by Justin Martyr, *Dial.* 88; and anon., *Rebapt.* 16. See Jensen, "With Pomp, Apparatus, Novelty, and Avarice," 77–83.

34. Tertullian, *Bapt.* 1.1 (*de sacramento aquae nostrae*).

35. Tertullian, *Marc.* 1.14. See also Ferguson, *Baptism in the Early Church*, 276–78.

Cainites. According to Tertullian, the "viper" who had recently carried off a fair number of converts and attempted to destroy baptism by "her exceptionally poisonous teaching" (*venenatissima doctrina sua*), was a member of this group.[36] The Cainites also figure in Irenaeus's polemical treatise *Against Heresies*, which describes them as a licentious sect that credited Cain and the Sodomites with having their origin from "the power above." According to Irenaeus, these Cainites venerated Judas, who understood "the mystery of betrayal" and underwent "sinful and abominable actions" in order to attain perfect knowledge in the name of an angel who attended and incited them.[37] Yet Irenaeus says nothing specific about Cainite baptismal practices, nor does he, like Tertullian, mention their preference for dry and waterless places.

Tertullian's concern may have been based on an actual, and not just hypothetical, case. Some surviving documentary evidence suggests that certain gnostic groups practiced "waterless baptisms" or at least emphasized the use of oil and the action of anointing as a rite superior to immersion in water. The importance of scented or perfumed oil also seems to have been stressed in some of these rites. Irenaeus identifies a group he calls the Marcosians, whose initiatory practice, he says, was both invisible and incomprehensible. They supposedly denied that the baptism instituted by the human Jesus for the remission of sins was sufficient. Instead they offered a ritual that was meant to accomplish spiritual perfection—a ritual instituted by the invisible Christ, who had descended upon Jesus, a mere, mortal creature.[38]

In other sections of his treatise, Irenaeus describes other groups who led their initiates to the water and baptized them into the name of the unknown Father of the Universe, into Truth (the Mother of all things), into the One who descended upon Jesus, into union and redemption, and into communion with the Powers. According to Irenaeus, following this water baptism, the neophytes were anointed with balsam because its fragrance was a type of sweet odor that transcended others. Moreover, he adds, some even asserted that it was superfluous to bring persons to the water, "but mixing oil and water together, they place[d] their mixture on the heads of those who [were] to be initiated, with the use of some such expressions as we have already mentioned . . . [since they] maintain[ed] that the mystery of the unspeakable and invisible power ought not to be performed by visible and corruptible creatures."[39]

In his dubiously regarded catalog of heresies, Epiphanius of Salamis includes a group he calls the Archontics, who, he claims, condemned baptism even though some of them had been baptized. According to Epiphanius, these

---

36. Tertullian, *Bapt.* 1.5–7.
37. Irenaeus, *Haer.* 1.31.1–2. The Cainites also were mentioned in Epiphanius's catalog of heresies, *Pan.* 38.2.4.
38. Irenaeus, *Haer.* 1.21.2.
39. Irenaeus, *Haer.* 1.21.3–4, *ANF*, 1.346–47.

Archontics believed that participation in baptism and other sacraments was given in the name of Sabaoth, the autocrat of the seventh heaven and father of the devil.[40] Scholars have doubted the existence of this group, however, since Epiphanius is their only witness. Despite the difficulty of evaluating evidence provided by obvious detractors, it seems that gnostic practices generally avoided material elements as sacramental signs.

BAPTISM IN THE ACTS OF THOMAS

As noted above, the baptisms described in the second-century *Acts of Thomas* are inconsistent. They are, also, not necessarily understood to be from a heterodox sect; rather, they are set within a narrative of the apostles' evangelical mission to India. Nevertheless, as described, the baptismal rituals suggest a preference for oil over water. When India's King Gundaphorus and his brother Gad ask to receive the seal from the missionary apostle, Thomas entreats God to unite the king and his brother with the flock, cleanse them by baptism, and anoint them with oil to release them from the error that has surrounded them. In the end, the men seek to receive the "seal of the word," and Thomas pours oil over their heads while chanting a hymn that includes an invocation of the Holy Spirit.[41]

Later, when Mygdonia, wife of Charisius and relative of King Misdaues, requests this seal, the apostle first pours oil over her head and prays: "Holy oil, given to us for sanctification; hidden mystery, in which the cross was shown to us; you are the straightener of bent limbs; you are the humbler of hard works; you point out the hidden treasures; you are the sprout of goodness. Let your power come and rest on your servant Mygdonia and heal her by this liberty."[42] After her anointing, Mygdonia is robed in white linen, and Thomas leads her to a spring to be baptized in the triune name. The ritual concludes with Mygdonia's receiving her first Eucharist.[43] Toward the end of the narrative, Mygdonia then assists Thomas at the sealing and baptism of more members of the royal family. This ritual opens with a consecratory prayer, recited over the cup of oil and addressed to the olive:

> Fruit, more beautiful than the other fruits, with which no other can be compared; most compassionate; you who burn with the power of the word; power of the wood, which if men put on they overcome their enemies; you who crown the victors; symbol and joy of the weary; who have brought to men the good news of their salvation; who show light to those in darkness; whose leaves are bitter but whose fruit is most sweet; who are rough in appearance, but tender to use; who seem weak, but carry the all-seeing power by the extraordinariness of your

40. Epiphanius, *Pan.* 40.5.6.
41. *Acts Thom.* 25–26.
42. *Acts Thom.* 121, trans. Elliott, *ANT*, 494
43. *Acts Thom.* 121 cont. See a similar account at paras. 132–33.

power. . . . Jesus, let your victorious power come and rest upon this oil as it once rested upon the wood related to it—and your crucifiers could not endure its word; let also the gift come by which you breathed upon your enemies and thereby made them retreat and fall headlong, and may it dwell in this oil over which we name your holy name![44]

When the anointing is complete, the apostle makes the candidates go down into the water, where he invokes the triune name over them. After they emerge, they celebrate the sacred meal.[45]

VALENTINIAN BAPTISM

A purely spiritual form of baptism would have been suited to the gnostic Valentinians' rejection of material creation, demonstrated their status as pneumatic Christians, and been deemed superior to water baptism, which conveyed forgiveness only of bodily sin. Presumably, the promise of John that Jesus would baptize with the Holy Spirit and fire (rather than with water) had particular appeal for this circle of Christian gnostics. Several documents associated with Valentinian gnosticism offer some evidence for this. For instance, the *Gospel of Truth* includes a short section devoted to the identification of the elect through anointing: "See that those that are disturbed will receive restoration, and he will anoint them with ointment. The anointment is the mercy of the father, who will be merciful to them; and those whom he has anointed are the perfected."[46]

In another Valentinian text, the *Reality of the Rulers*, the true human being teaches the last generation about everything and "will anoint them with the ointment of eternal life, given unto that being from the undominated race . . . and they will ascend into the limitless light, where this posterity belongs."[47]

The respective roles of water and oil are, arguably, most clearly delineated in the *Gospel of Philip*, a Valentinian text that probably dates to the second century.[48] Found among the Nag Hammadi documents, it speaks of the five mysteries, one of which is baptism; the other four are anointing with chrism, Eucharist, ransom/redemption, and bridal chamber. These appear to comprise stages of initiation, each a little more advanced than the previous one. Thus baptism lies at the beginning of a process of sacramentally achieved perfection. Whether this was a ritual that incorporated material elements as signs or was a spiritual (and invisible) transformation is unclear.

---

44. *Acts Thom.* 157, trans. M. James, edited and updated by Elliott, *ANT*, 504–5.

45. *Acts Thom.* 158.

46. *Gospel of Truth*, 3613–33, trans. Layton, *Gnostic Scriptures*, 261–62. Discussion of many of these documents can be found in Lampe, *Seal of the Spirit*, 120–28.

47. *Reality of the Rulers*, 971–77, trans. Layton, *Gnostic Scriptures*, 76. See also the *Ap. John* 6.18–28.

48. On gnostic baptism in water, see also the *Trim. Prot.* 47.35–49.11.

It is possible that some gnostic groups observed two distinct baptismal rites, the first of which was imperfect and bodily, associated with the baptism of the earthly Jesus by John the Baptist (for the remission of sins), and the second, a perfecting spiritual baptism that was only for those who had been recognized as true gnostics.

In any case, the *Gospel of Philip* treats baptism and chrism together as sanctifying. It regards as soul and spirit to be constituted of water, fire, and light. It compares God with a dyer of textiles who imparts the imperishable colors through a dipping in water. Yet an emphasis on the sanctifying role of the chrism and the Spirit is apparent when the text says, "If one goes down into the water and comes up without having received anything and says, 'I am a Christian,' he has borrowed the name at interest. But if he receives the Holy Spirit, he has the name as a gift. He who has received a gift does not have to give it back, but of him who has borrowed it at interest, payment is demanded. This is the way [it happens] when he experiences a mystery."[49]

Even more vividly, the *Gospel of Philip* includes the motifs of light and fragrance, and although water has its role, this last element is imparted only through the act of anointing. "Through the Holy Spirit we are indeed begotten again, but we are begotten through Christ in the two. We are anointed through the spirit. When we were begotten we were united. No one can see himself either in water or in a mirror without light. Nor again can you see in light without water or mirror. For this reason it is fitting to baptize in the two, in the light and in the water. Now the light is the chrism."[50] This gospel also mentions the chrism's aroma, remarking that "all those who anoint themselves with it take pleasure in it," and noting that "while those who are anointed are present, those nearby also profit (from the fragrance)."[51]

Thus, the conclusion G. W. H. Lampe offered more than fifty years ago still seems reasonable. He locates the distinction between water and Spirit baptism either within the gnostic movement or as advanced by it: "It is in all probability, then, to these curious sects that we must go in order to find the source of the separation of the Spirit-baptism from water-baptism which we meet from time to time in the third century, and it is to these circles that we probably ought to look for the introduction of subsidiary ceremonies such as post-baptismal unction; even if these rites did not originate with the Gnostic or semi-Gnostic sects, they probably acquired a new and greatly enhanced significance at their hands."[52]

49. *Gos. Phil.* 64, trans. Wesley Isenberg, in *NHL*, 148.

50. *Gos. Phil.* 68, trans. Isenberg, in *NHL*, 141.

51. *Gos. Phil.* 78, trans. Isenberg, in *NHL*, 146. Fragrance and Spirit are associated also in Cyril of Jerusalem, *Procat.* 1.

52. Lampe, *Seal of the Spirit*, 127.

Anointing and the Spirit's Gift in the Fourth Century

According to the surviving documentary evidence, the gift of the Holy Spirit and the act of anointing with oil were firmly linked in the liturgy of baptism by the fourth century. The development, as Lampe argues, was not a conscious borrowing from sectarian practice; rather, it was a natural answer to the need to symbolize the transmission of the Holy Spirit with some kind of visible action and material symbol. The Gospels provided the language of anointing, and the need for a distinct sign or gesture (the imposition of hands) was given clear justification in the canonical Acts of the Apostles.

To this end, the baptismal ritual was elaborated to include one or any combination of other actions: the imposition of hands, an anointing with oil, and the sealing with the sign of the cross. Depending on date and locale, these actions occurred in different order and at different points in the ceremony. And although signing or marking also symbolized the joining to the new family, and prebaptismal anointing could be exorcistic or strengthening, these acts also conveyed the gifts of the Holy Spirit, especially if they took place while candidates stood in the font or immediately after they emerged from the font.

The variations in baptismal anointing practices evident in this period appear to be regionally specific. Many attempts to identify the origins, significance, and meaning of these different practices have grouped them geographically in the interest of finding common patterns.[53] In general, three distinct forms are discernible. The first form, associated with the Eastern, Syrian rites (e.g., the rite described in the *Didascalia Apostolorum*), includes a two-stage prebaptismal anointing, initially on the candidate's forehead in the sign of the cross, and subsequently over the whole body. The anointing on the forehead marked the candidate for Christ, while the anointing of the body was for exorcism and strengthening of candidates prior to their bath. The second form includes North African practices, which, as described by Tertullian and Augustine, appear not to have incorporated a prebaptismal anointing. While neither Tertullian nor Augustine refers to a prebaptismal anointing, both describe a postbaptismal chrismation, followed by the imposition of hands. The third form, as found in the rituals from Rome, Milan, and Jerusalem (e.g., those described in the *Apostolic Tradition* and in the fourth-century catecheses of Ambrose and Cyril), included both prebaptismal (exorcistic) anointing and postbaptismal chrismation.[54]

---

53. Articles on the significance of the prebaptismal anointing in the East include Spinks, "Baptismal Patterns in Early Syria"; Brock, "Transition to a Post-Baptismal Anointing"; Winkler, "Syriac Prebaptismal Anointing"; and idem, "Original Meaning of the Prebaptismal Anointing."

54. On the prebaptismal anointing, see above discussion and Hippolytus, *Trad. ap.* 21; Ambrose, *Sacr.* 1.4; Cyril of Jerusalem, *Myst.* 2.2; John Chrysostom, *Catech.* 2.24 (Stav. 2); Theodore of Mopsuestia, *Bapt. hom.* 3.8.

The consequence of this variability means that even well into the fourth century the distinctions between baptism by water and the baptism of the Holy Spirit were not consistently understood or practiced across the Christian world. Some earlier documents, like Tertullian's treatise *On Baptism*, regard the Spirit as given both in the water and in the anointing with oil. This understanding also describes certain teachings from the Greek and Syrian churches. For example, John Chrysostom's baptismal homilies present the Holy Spirit as fully descending upon the candidates while in the water.[55]

Nevertheless, the two aspects of the ritual gradually became more and more distinct. Citing the story of Nicodemus (John 3:1–10), Gregory of Nyssa reminds his congregation that Jesus insisted a person must be born of both water and the Spirit to enter the kingdom of God. According to Gregory, this pericope demonstrates that the gift of the Spirit alone cannot be sufficient for baptism. The need for both, he says, is due to humanity's composite nature (visible body and invisible soul), which requires two distinct kinds of medicines (or sacramental elements): sensible water for the flesh and invisible Spirit for the soul. Thus, he insists that no one should despise the water bath, nor should anyone think of it as merely common or ordinary.[56]

Basil of Caesarea identifies the baptism in water with the death and burial of the old person, and the giving of the Spirit as the raising of the new one from that death. He argues against those who stressed the importance of water over against the necessity of the Spirit at baptism not, he insists, to disparage the water, but rather to uphold the role of the Spirit. The water, he says, receives the body as if in a tomb, while the Spirit pours in the life-giving power, renewing souls from the deadness of sin. This is, he explains, what Scripture means by needing to be born of both water and the Spirit. It is in the giving of the Spirit that the neophyte is restored to paradise.[57] This idea of the twofold action is also apparent in the West. For example, Pacian of Barcelona plainly calls the ritual a double blessing, comprised of the bath, which purifies from sin, and the holy anointing, which pours out the Holy Spirit on the baptized.[58]

Anointing in the Eastern Churches

Scholars have argued that baptism in the East was modeled primarily on Jesus's baptism by John rather than on any other New Testament baptism. Thus it would follow that the prebaptismal "christic" anointing was even more important than the subsequent water bath, which explains the absence

55. See John Chrysostom, *Catech.* 2.25 (Stav. 2), for example.
56. Gregory of Nyssa, *Diem lum.* Gregory of Nazianzus, in *Or.* 40.8, makes a similar argument.
57. Basil of Caesarea, *Spir. Sanct.* 15.35–36.
58. Pacian of Barcelona, *Bapt.* 1.6.

of postbaptismal chrismation in certain regions. The prebaptismal anointing of the head was thus the key ritual action that conferred the gifts of the Spirit prior to the candidate's descent into the water.[59] This order of actions is presented in the *Acts of Thomas*, discussed above.

Another instance of such a ritual (lacking a postbaptismal anointing) comes from John Chrysostom's catechetical homilies, delivered in Antioch at the end of the fourth century. Here the transmission of the Holy Spirit is accomplished through an imposition of hands while the candidate stands in the water. Prior to their entering the water, candidates are anointed on the forehead with scented chrism to deter the devil and are then anointed over their whole bodies with olive oil as a strengthening agent. Accompanied by the priest's words and hand gesture, the Holy Spirit descends upon the candidates once they step into the font.[60]

By contrast, the baptism ritual described in the Syriac *Apostolic Constitutions* begins with the bishop anointing the candidates with holy oil as a form of spiritual baptism. Candidates are then dipped in water and given a second anointing at the ritual's conclusion. This document probably dates to the late fourth century but, reflecting earlier practices, explains that the water bath points to Christ's death and burial, while the oil is for the Holy Spirit.[61] Significantly, the text adds that if oil or chrism should be lacking, water alone could suffice for anointing, sealing, and washing away sins.[62] Yet a little further on, when it prescribes a prayer for the consecration of the oil, the text implies that without the anointing, the ritual's efficacy is vacated: "This is the efficacy of the laying on of hands on every one; for unless there be such a recital made by a pious priest over every one of these, the candidate for baptism does only descend into the water as do the Jews, and only puts off the filth of the soul."[63]

Cyril of Jerusalem likewise describes a prebaptismal anointing of the whole body for exorcism. But regarding the relationship of water and Spirit, Cyril (like Gregory of Nyssa) cites the twofold nature of humans, yet asserts that the water, although it cleanses the body, also contains the power of sanctification because of the invocation of the Holy Spirit over it: "Therefore, when about to enter the water, regard it not as mere water, but look for its saving power by the efficacy of the Holy Spirit, for without both you cannot be made perfect." Cyril adds that a person who does not receive the "seal by water" does not enter the kingdom of heaven and praises water as a grace-imparting element in itself.[64]

---

59. See Winkler, "Original Meaning of the Prebaptismal Anointing."
60. John Chrysostom, *Catech.* 2.5 (Stav. 2).
61. *Const. ap.* 3.16–17; 7.22.
62. *Const. ap.* 7.22, ANF, 7:469.
63. *Const. ap.* 7.44, ANF, 7:477, slightly adapted by author.
64. Cyril of Jerusalem, *Cat.* 3.3–5.

Nevertheless, Cyril's *Mystagogical Lectures*, delivered to the newly baptized during Easter week, also describes a postbaptismal anointing and gives the Holy Spirit's descent upon Jesus as its model:

> He bathed in the river Jordan and, after imparting the fragrance of his godhead to the waters, came up from them. Him the Holy Spirit visited in essential presence, like resting upon like. Similarly for you, after you had ascended from the sacred streams, there was an anointing with chrism, the antitype of that with which Christ was anointed, that is of the Holy Spirit. . . . Beware of supposing that this ointment is mere ointment. . . . With this ointment your forehead and sense organs are sacramentally anointed, thus while your body is anointed with the visible oil, your soul is sanctified by the holy, quickening Spirit.[65]

Theodore of Mopsuestia outlines initial ritual actions like those described by John Chrysostom. He likewise refers to a preliminary signing with oil on the forehead (the mark of the cross), which seems to have been both strengthening and apotropaic.[66] This is followed by a full-body anointing before entering the font; however, after candidates emerge from the font and put on their white garments, they receive a postbaptismal anointing (sealing) on the forehead, again with oil. Theodore explicitly connects this postbaptismal anointing to the descent of the Holy Spirit at Jesus's baptism, and he cites the text from Luke 4:18, "the Spirit of the Lord is upon me, and therefore the Lord has anointed me."[67]

Anointing in the Western Churches

Ambrose's summary of the rite in Milan includes one prebaptismal anointing over the whole body, followed by the renunciation of Satan, the consecration of the font, and the baptism. According to Ambrose, after the candidates leave the font, the priest anoints them a second time into "eternal life." Then, after the bishop washes their feet, they are "spiritually sealed." Although Ambrose does not specify the use of unction in this final step, his reference to "sealing" suggests making the sign of a cross on the forehead with chrism. In any case, Ambrose is most explicit about the nature of the Spirit's benefits and the purpose of the rite. He explains that the baptized are anointed on their heads because the intellectual faculties are within the head.[68] He also names the seven distinct virtues of the Spirit given at this point: the spirit of wisdom and understanding, of counsel and strength, of knowledge and piety, and of "holy fear."[69]

65. Cyril of Jerusalem, *Myst.* 3.1–3, trans. McCauley and Stephenson, *Works of Saint Cyril of Jerusalem*, 2:169–71.
66. See chap. 2, under the heading "Marking with the Sign of the Cross."
67. Theodore of Mopsuestia, *Bapt. hom.* 3.27.
68. Ambrose, *Sacr.* 3.1.
69. Ambrose, *Sacr.* 3.8–10; cf. *Myst.* 7.42.

Although Augustine's surviving writings lack any detailed outline of the baptismal rite in Hippo (or anywhere), his sermons, treatises, and letters offer enough information for a hypothetical reconstruction of the ritual. Like Tertullian, he specifies no prebaptismal anointing, although in one place, he compares candidates to wrestlers approaching their contest with Satan, a possible allusion to a prebaptismal anointing.[70] Moreover, Augustine's treatise *On the Trinity* emphasizes the descent of the Holy Spirit like a dove upon Christ (an invisible anointing) as signifying the chrism given after neophytes emerged from the font.[71] Elsewhere, Augustine refers to the postbaptismal anointing with chrism, which, when joined with the imposition of hands, imparts the sevenfold gifts of the Spirit.[72] In a powerfully vivid passage from an Easter sermon, he reminds the newly baptized of their recent ordeal: "Then came baptism, and you were, in a manner of speaking, moistened with water in order to be shaped into bread. But it's not yet bread without fire to bake it. So what does fire represent? That's the chrism, the anointing. Oil, the fire-feeder, you see, is the sacrament of the Holy Spirit."[73]

The eventual move toward a consistent identification of the gift of the Spirit with the rites (anointing and imposition of hands) that follow immersion seems logically tied to the continuing emphasis on the baptism of Jesus in the Jordan as both the type and the model of Christian baptism. Jesus first went down into the water and then, emerging, saw the dove descending. To the extent that these are viewed as two chronologically distinct moments in the baptism of Jesus (and to the extent that they make Jesus's baptism different from all previous baptisms), these two ritual actions can be correlated with those moments. The order of the acts, therefore, is determined by the Gospel accounts, for the event is meant to be a reenactment of the baptism of Jesus. This also means that the two actions should not constitute two separate sacraments or ceremonies, although the latter (the giving of the Spirit) may be subsequent to and dependent on the other.[74]

Anointing's Signification

Anointing as a sign of the gift of the Holy Spirit at baptism bore meanings beyond the broad understanding of the Spirit's gifts (cf. 1 Cor. 12:8–13). One of these gifts was the joining of the anointed person to Christ and thus his

70. Augustine, *Tract. Ev. Jo.* 33.3.

71. Augustine, *Trin.* 15.36.

72. Augustine, *Tract. Ev. Jo.* 118.5; *C. litt. Petil.* 2.104.237 and 2.105.238; *Serm.* 229M.2; 248.5; 249.3.

73. Augustine, *Serm.* 227, trans. Hill, *Works of Saint Augustine*, 254. See also *Tract. ep. Jo.* 3.5.3.

74. Johnson, *Rites of Christian Initiation*, 108–12, summarizes other arguments about the shift.

or her becoming a "christ." This dimension of chrismation also conveyed the idea of joining the priesthood, a theme discussed above, but here with an emphasis on the spiritual rather than the social dimension of the gift.[75] The second significance is the imparting of spiritual knowledge or wisdom (*gnōsis*). The one baptized is illumined and granted special insight or understanding.

Anointing as Messianic

According to the biblical narratives, the descent of the Spirit was the moment at which Jesus was proclaimed the Son of God, although only the Gospel of John clearly makes this proclamation a public one (John the Baptist announces that he saw and heard the dove and voice from heaven himself [1:32–34]). According to the Gospel of Luke, Jesus returned from his baptism "full of the Holy Spirit" (4:1). Shortly after his forty days in the wilderness, Jesus went to his synagogue in Nazareth and proclaimed that Isaiah 61:1–2 had been fulfilled, that the Spirit of the Lord had "anointed [him] to bring good news" (Luke 4:16–21). Thus, possession of the Holy Spirit became a particularly Christian mark of authority (cf. John 20:22–23). Nevertheless, the Gospels make almost no claim that Jesus was actually anointed (as Messiah). Matthew uses a form of the verb "anoint" (*aleiphō*) only in the instructions for fasting (6:17). The woman who pours pure, fragrant nard over Jesus's head or feet in the other three Gospels does this act either as a preparation for his burial or as a display of her love (cf. Mark 14:3–8; Luke 7:37–38; John 12:3–8).

Acts specifically identifies Jesus as the Lord's anointed one (4:27) and in 10:38 directly connects the descent of the dove with the anointing of Jesus. However, forms of the verb "anoint" (*chriō*) occur only in 2 Corinthians 1:21 (cited above), Hebrews 1:9 (a quote from Ps. 45:7), and 1 John 2:20 and 27, which refer to the Holy Spirit's anointing of individual Christians. From this, the apostolic church equated the descent of the Spirit with an anointing, thereby expanding the meaning of anointing itself to include the gift or possession of the Spirit, with or without the sign of oil. In the baptismal ritual, the anointing of the newly baptized brings each one into union with Christ, and so they share in that title of "christ."[76]

Still, as noted above, ritual anointing in the Jewish scriptures especially evokes the identification (and divine authorization) of priests and kings. Pouring oil over the heads of certain chosen ones (e.g., Aaron, Saul, and David) supplied the prototype of baptism anointing as granting sacerdotal and royal status. The action thus demonstrates the continuity between the priests and kings of Israel and the followers of Jesus.

Tertullian explicitly links the ancient Israelite rituals, the descent of the Spirit on Christ, and the chrismation of the newly baptized:

75. See chap. 2, under the heading "Priests, Prophets, and Kings."
76. See, for example, Cyril of Jerusalem, *Myst.* 3.1, or Augustine, *Civ.* 17.4.9 and 20.10.

After that, emerging from the bath, we are anointed with the blessed unction. This is according to the ancient practice by which priests were customarily anointed with oil from a horn, just as Aaron was anointed by Moses [Exod. 30:30; Lev. 8:12]. That is why he [the priest] is called a Christ, from the word "chrism," which means "anointing." And from this the Lord also obtained his title, though it had become a spiritual anointing, in that he was anointed with the Spirit of God the Father. . . . So also in our case, the unction flows upon the flesh, but its purpose is a spiritual benefit.[77]

Here Tertullian justifies the use of oil in the Christian ceremony, despite its omission in accounts of Christ's own baptism.

These associations are even more evident in fourth- and fifth-century documents. Ambrose cites the anointing of Aaron to make the case that the newly baptized were incorporated into the sacerdotal state, "for we are all anointed into the kingdom of God and unto the priesthood with spiritual grace."[78] John the Deacon adds a regal dimension to the priestly status imparted through anointing, saying that in this action, a royal and a priestly mystery are conjoined, each of them granting their distinct character and authority to their recipients.[79] Augustine expressly maintains that Old Testament instances of anointing were prefigurations of the coming of Christ, the anointed one, and argues that even the Jews should recognize this:

Who, then, is the God who was anointed by God? Let the Jews tell us that. After all, these scriptures are theirs as well as ours. God was anointed by God, and when you hear the word, "anointed," understand that it means Christ, for "Christ" is derived from "chrism," and the name "Christ" means "anointed one." Nowhere else were kings and priests anointed; it was done only in that kingdom where Christ's coming was prophesied, where he was anointed, and from where the name Christ was to come. . . . So God was anointed by God, and with what kind of oil? Spiritual, obviously. Visible oil is a sign; invisible oil is a sacramental mystery, for the spiritual oil is within.[80]

Cyril of Jerusalem adds an element to this typology, asserting that Old Testament figures were anointed after being bathed. Thus, their chrismation is linked with an action that even more vividly prefigures baptism. The former anointing and bath signify a future (perfected) sacrament: "You must know that this chrism is prefigured in the Old Testament. When Moses, conferring on his brother the divine appointment, was ordering him high priest, he anointed him after he had bathed in water, and thenceforward he was called 'Christ,' clearly

77. Tertullian, *Bapt.* 7 (CCSL 1:282), trans. author.
78. Ambrose, *Myst* 6.30; and see the discussion of the sacerdotal or royal status as a mark of membership in chap. 2, under the heading "Priests, Prophets, and Kings."
79. John the Deacon, *Ep. Sen.* 6.
80. Augustine, *Enarrat. Ps.* 44.19, trans. Boulding, *Works of Saint Augustine*, 297.

after the figurative chrism. Again, the high priest, when installing Solomon as king, anointed him after he had bathed in Gihon."[81] Cyril concludes his analysis of these parallels by claiming that Aaron's and Solomon's anointings were merely types, while baptismal anointing is complete and "truthful" insofar as it inaugurates salvation in the one who was anointed by the Holy Spirit "in truth."[82]

Anointing as Illuminative

The First Epistle of John addresses its readers as those who "have been anointed by the Holy One" and who "have knowledge" (2:20). A few verses later, the author says, "The anointing that you received from him abides in you, and so you do not need anyone to teach you. But as his anointing teaches you about all things, and is true and is not a lie, and just as it has taught you, abide in him" (2:27).

This, one of the earliest testimonies to the tradition that the gift of the Spirit is enlightenment or knowledge, was not unique. The Epistle to the Hebrews twice refers to enlightenment (*phōtismos*) through the Holy Spirit, and its author may refer to baptism when he writes: "For it is impossible to restore again to repentance those who have once been enlightened, and have tasted the heavenly gift, and have shared in the Holy Spirit" (6:4; cf. also 10:32). In addition to these New Testament documents, the enumeration of the Spirit's sevenfold gifts as outlined in Isaiah (11:2–3) finds its way into early commentaries on baptism, which associate the gift of the Spirit with the gift of knowledge or illumination.[83]

Justin Martyr speaks of baptism as a means to transform Christians into children of choice and knowledge (rather than of necessity and ignorance), and he goes on to explain that "this washing is called illumination [*phōtisma*], because they who learn these things are illuminated in their understanding, ... the one who is illuminated is washed."[84] Similarly, Tertullian claims that the sacred significance of the water is that in it the "sins of our original blindness" (*delictis pristinae caecitatis*) are washed away. Here Tertullian conflates sin with lack of sight, by which he means understanding.[85]

Writing also at the beginning of the third century, Clement of Alexandria likewise refers to baptism as illumination or enlightenment, which is, for him, the ritual's significant benefit. He begins his discussion on the subject by saying

81. Cyril of Jerusalem, *Myst.* 3.6, trans. McCauley and Stephenson, *Works of Saint Cyril of Jerusalem*, 2:172–73.

82. Cyril of Jerusalem, *Myst.* 3.6, trans. McCauley and Stephenson, *Works of Saint Cyril of Jerusalem*, 2:172–73.

83. See, e.g., Ambrose, *Myst.* 7. 42, and *Sacr.* 2.8.

84. Justin Martyr, *1 Apol.* 61, ANF, 1:183.

85. Tertullian, *Bapt.* 1.1.

that the very instant of Christian regeneration (baptism) was also the moment of illumination. He also comments that Jesus (while baptized) had no need of illumination: "for him to make any addition to his knowledge is absurd, since he is God." In this instance, Christ was the source, not the recipient, of the enlightenment effected in baptism. Clement sums up his idea of the graces offered by the rite: "Becoming baptized, we are illuminated; illuminated, we become sons; being made sons, we are made perfect; being made perfect, we are made immortal. . . . This work is variously called grace, and illumination, and perfection, and washing; washing by which we cleanse away our sins; grace by which the penalties accruing to transgressions are remitted; and illumination, by which that holy light of salvation is beheld, that is, by which we see God clearly."[86] Clement believes that one of the effects or gifts of baptism is special knowledge (*gnōsis*). He compares baptism to waking from sleep, removing a sight-obscuring cataract, moving from darkness into light, advancing from childishness to maturity or from perplexity to understanding. He clarifies that by "knowledge" he means the illumination imparted by the Spirit; such illumination banishes ignorance and grants clear vision or wisdom. Clement also gives a special name to those catechumens undergoing the final stages of preparation. Like many Greek writers to follow him, he calls them "the ones being enlightened" (*phōtizomenoi*).

In the fourth century, Cyril of Jerusalem also addressed the catechumens as "dear candidates for enlightenment," and as noted above, in his lectures to them, he mentions the fragrance of the Holy Spirit that was already wafting about them.[87] Although the scented chrism must have instantiated this, many Christian writers emphasize the sweet fragrance of sanctity.[88] For example, the *Apostolic Constitutions* offers a prayer for the mystical ointment, giving thanks for its fragrance and for the immortality that it signifies (made known through the person of Christ).[89]

John Chrysostom also addresses the newly illumined with symbolic references to light and darkness, noting that if they so chose, their light (like Christ's) would never be extinguished. He further differentiates the eyes of the body from the eyes of faith, saying that at baptism bodily eyes see only water, but the eyes of the spirit see the soul being washed and the new person emerging—a sight invisible to those who do not believe.[90] He is also explicit about the nature of the bestowed knowledge:

> Whenever grace comes and drives out the darkness from our mind, we learn the exact nature of things; what frightened us before, now becomes contemptible

86. Clement of Alexandria, *Paed.* 1.6, *ANF*, 2:215.

87. Cyril of Jerusalem, *Procat.* 1. See also *Procat.* 2, the discussion of Simon, who, though he was dipped, was not enlightened.

88. See Harvey, *Scenting Salvation*, 71–73.

89. *Const. ap.* 7.27.

90. John Chrysostom, *Catech.* 11.11–13 (Pk. 3); 12.10 (Montf. 2).

in our eyes. We no longer fear death after we have learned carefully from this holy initiation that death is not death but a sleep and repose that lasts but for a time. Nor are we afraid of poverty or disease or any such misfortune, because we know that we are on our way to a better life, which is impervious to death and destruction and is free from all such inequality.[91]

John affirms that one of the benefits of baptism is the grace-given sacred knowledge or insight that comes from outside the individual, since "illumination" implies a sudden awareness or awakening rather than the results of long study.

Christians thought of themselves as "children of light" over against children of darkness and ignorance—a contrast that resonates with earlier anti-Jewish or anti-pagan polemic.[92] Such identifying terminology clearly draws on the many scriptural references to Jesus as a bringer of light (e.g., John 1:4–9; 12:36, 46) and to his followers as both recipients and transmitters of that light (cf. Matt. 5:14–16). A particularly emphatic use of this imagery comes from a sermon of Gregory of Nazianzus, preached on the "Day of Lights" (Epiphany), in which he urges the unbaptized in the audience to stop procrastinating. "Therefore," he says, "since you have heard these words, come forward to it, and be enlightened, and your faces shall not be ashamed through missing the grace. Receive then the enlightenment in due season, that darkness pursue you not, and catch you and sever you from the illumining."[93]

Symbols of the Holy Spirit's Gifts

The most obvious symbol of the Holy Spirit at baptism is the dove that descended upon Jesus. However, other symbols and their related ritual actions were used to point to the Spirit's gifts, including the cup of milk mixed with honey that was given to the neophytes as part of their first Eucharist and carried by the newly baptized as they entered the congregation for the first time as new members of the flock. These symbols appear not only in the texts and recorded practices but also in visual art and the décor of baptismal chambers.

91. John Chrysostom, *Catech.* 12.12 (Montf. 2), trans. Harkins, *St. John Chrysostom*, 176.
92. The use of the oppositional metaphors of light and darkness is particularly associated with gnostic or Manichaean sects in the early Christian centuries. However, the Gospel of John uses this theme frequently and specifically differentiates the children of light from the children of darkness (12:35–36). Qumran's *War Scroll* also opens with a clash between children of light and children of darkness, indicating that this theme was used not only in Christian polemic. The *Didache* opens with a contrast between the two ways—of life and of death (*Did.* 1). See also Ps. Dionysius, *Ecc. hier.* 2.1–3 (where he refers to the rite of baptism simply as "illumination"). This is also addressed in *Barn.* 18.1.
93. Gregory of Nazianzus, *Or.* 40.24, NPNF[2], 7:368. See also *Or.* 40.5–6 (a discourse on divine light and illumination).

The Dove

The canonical Gospels describe the Holy Spirit descending upon Jesus at his baptism in the form of a dove. This image is so visually inscribed in Christian art and imagination that the depiction of the Holy Spirit as a dove is hardly ever questioned. It rarely is given another symbolic form in early Christian art, which indicates that early Christians found the imagery completely understandable and acceptable; yet the choice, significance, and implication of a dove as the sign of the Holy Spirit deserves some consideration.

Imaging the Spirit of God as a bird occurs in scriptural references beyond the narratives of Jesus's baptism. The Spirit hovers over the waters in Genesis and therefore would seem to have wings. Eagles appear in biblical imagery (Exod. 19:4; Deut. 32:11; Ps. 103), as do other birds, including hens (Matt. 23:37). Flying and soaring are obvious metaphors for ascent, both intellectual and spiritual, and nests symbolize safety. The dove, however, has a special place in Christian symbolism.

In addition to being the symbol of the Holy Spirit, doves also signify beauty, innocence, and chastity. Tertullian maintains that the Holy Spirit appeared in the form of a dove at Jesus's baptism in order to show Christians that a dove was a "creature of simplicity and innocence," and then he cites Jesus's admonition that the disciples should be as guileless as doves (Matt. 10:16). Their white color associates them with purity, and the belief that they mated for life made them a symbol of faithfulness. In pre-Christian traditions the dove symbolized erotic love; doves were associated with both Aphrodite and Astarte. The dove of the Song of Songs (2:14; 5:2; 6:9) is the object of desire, and it comes to be identified with both the church and the soul in Christian allegory. The dove of the Song also may be the source of certain images in the *Protevangelium of James*, which presents the young Virgin as being nurtured in the temple "like a dove" and describes doves flying out of Joseph's rod and landing on his head (revealing him as Mary's divinely selected spouse).[94] In medieval and Renaissance iconography, a dove-like Holy Spirit appears to Mary at the annunciation.

The dove also symbolizes the soul as it makes its ascent to heaven. In the *Martyrdom of Polycarp*, a dove flies out of the saint's body when the guard lands the dagger's deathly blow.[95] In nearly countless Christian epitaphs, a dove appears next to an orant, probably to represent the soul (fig. 3.1). Sometimes these images include an olive branch and the phrase *in pace*. The funerary associations of the dove are reinforced by the Roman practice of referring to stacked niches for cremation urns as columbaria (dovecotes), perhaps because they were roosting places for the souls (*columbae*) of the departed.

---

94. *Prot. Jas.* 8–9.
95. *Mart. Pol.*, 16. See also Prudentius, *Carm.* 3.33. St. Benedict also saw the soul of St. Scholastica fly up to heaven in the shape of a dove.

Doves also were sacrificial animals. According to the Gospel of Luke (2:24), when the time came for the purification according to the Jewish law, Mary and Joseph came to the temple and offered a pair of turtledoves or two young pigeons as a thank offering. Such birds were sold in the courtyard of the temple (cf. Matt. 21:12; John 2:13–16). The pair of doves was a fitting offering for a poor family: one for a sin offering and the other for a burnt offering (Lev. 5:7–10).

The dove in the story of Noah probably has the strongest baptismal associations. Tertullian recalls the dove of Genesis, who brought the olive branch to Noah after the flood waters had receded (Gen. 8:8–9). Here again the ark typifies the church, the flood the purifying font, and the dove the Holy Spirit who descends upon neophyte emerging from the font. The dove brings the message of God's

Figure 3.1. Funerary plaque of Priscus. Museo Nazionale, Rome. Late fourth century. (Photo by author.)

peace to the earth (symbolized by the baptized and now-cleansed human body).[96]

Like Tertullian, Ambrose connects the dove of the Holy Spirit at Jesus's baptism with the dove in the flood narrative, and he took the opportunity to teach a lesson in the ways symbols point to truth yet remain imperfect in themselves:

> Why did the Spirit here descend like a dove, except that you might see, except that you might know that this dove, which the just Noah sent forth from the ark, was the image of this dove, so that you might recognize the type of the sacrament. Perhaps you may say: "While this was a true dove which was sent forth and that one only descended like a dove," how can we say that it was a likeness in one place, and truth in another, since according to the Greeks it is written that the Spirit descended "in the likeness of a dove"?

Ambrose answers his own posed question, arguing that through likeness one may approach the truth as well as gain wisdom. For, he says, the Lord admonished us to be "as blameless as doves" (Matt. 10:16).[97]

Peter Chrysologus, in a sermon for Epiphany, likewise draws on the story of Noah and makes a parallel between the dove's olive branch and the olive oil of anointing:

---

96. Tertullian, *Bapt.* 8.4. For contrast, see the anonymous treatise *Adv. Novatian 5.*
97. Ambrose, *Myst.* 4.24–25 (SC 23:168), trans. author.

Today the Holy Spirit hovers over the water under the appearance of a dove, so that just as that dove announced to Noah that the flood that inundated the world had subsided, so too by this sign it would be known that the unremitting shipwreck of the world had come to an end. But it did not carry a branch from the old olive tree, as that one did, but pours out rich, new chrism all over his head, as Parent, in order to fulfill what the prophet said: "God, your God, has anointed you with the oil of gladness before your fellows."[98]

Finally, in addition to citing the dove in the story of Noah and Jesus's admonition that his followers be as innocent as doves, Ambrose reminds his audience of the beloved in the Song of Songs, whose eyes are doves (4:1). These doves are the newly baptized who are washed in the font and garbed in white, like the doves in the Song.[99] Drawing the parallel between the beloved dove and the soul of the faithful Christian, Ambrose elaborates: "Moreover, it [the soul] is praiseworthy because it is faithful, powerful in the word, fertile in producing various fruits; because it is one like a dove, having a unity of spirit by which peace may exist. . . . That soul, therefore, is a dove, and perfect, which is to say simple and spiritual, not disturbed by the passions of the body, which fights external battles and harbors internal fears."[100]

One of Narsai's fifth-century Epiphany sermons on Christ's baptism speaks of the dove as a sign: "By the dove, he showed that he has received the entire wealth of the Spirit. . . . Through this peace-loving bird, he depicted the manifestation of that one in whom the peace of the universe will remain unshaken." A little further on, the text portrays John the Baptist (alone deemed worthy to see the dove descend upon Jesus) describing his vision, saying, "I saw the Spirit, a hidden nature, under the mystery of a bird descend [and] abide hidden in a visible one in perfect love."[101]

The Dove in Early Christian Art

Clement of Alexandria lists the dove as one of the acceptable symbols for a Christian person's signet ring, along with the fish, the ship, and the anchor.[102] All these figures are common in Christian art and iconography, especially on simple tomb epitaphs that often combine one or more of these popular signs, perhaps to indicate the deceased's status as a baptized member of the community (figs. 3.1, 3.2).

The dove as a favored image for burial monuments has prototypes and parallels in both Roman and Jewish iconography.[103] In those contexts, it was

98. Peter Chrysologus, *Serm.* 160.4, trans. Palardy, *St. Peter Chrysologus*, 3:279–80.
99. Ambrose, *Myst.* 7.37.
100. Ambrose, *Isaac* 7.59 (CSEL 32:683.1–15), trans. author.
101. Narsai, *Hom. Epiph.* 300–320, trans. McLeod, in Graffin, ed., *Narsai's Metrical Homilies*, 89–91.
102. Clement of Alexandria, *Paed.* 3.11. See Finney, "Images on Finger Rings."
103. Goodenough, *Jewish Symbols*, 8:22–46; Sühling, "Die Taube als religiöses Symbol."

Figure 3.2. Funerary inscription. Catacombs of San Lorenzo fuori le Mura. Fourth century. (Photo by author.)

probably intended as a general symbol of peace and blessing. Both in Christian and non-Christian imagery, the dove usually carries an olive branch and appears with the legend *in pace*. The olive branch may refer specifically to the flood narrative (cf. figs. 1.3, 1.4), but it was also a simple Roman sign for peace and in Christian art sometimes occurs with the Greek word for peace (*eirēnē*). The dove often accompanies an orant figure (fig. 3.1), which itself may have been a generic figure meant to point to the soul of the deceased, or it could refer to that person's piety. These standard images also appear in catacomb paintings and on sarcophagus reliefs (cf. fig. 1.1).[104] The fifth-century baptistery of Albenga in northwestern Italy contains a mosaic that shows twelve doves surrounding a tripled image of the chi-rho monogram (fig. 3.3).

Given their number, the doves in the mosaic probably refer to the apostles, but they may also symbolize the newly baptized, who have been made newly innocent. Paulinus of Nola describes a similar composition, in the apse of his basilica (which no longer exists). Here the Trinity was represented by a lamb for Christ, a dove for the Holy Spirit, and the voice of God (probably depicted as a hand). The apostles were shown as a circle of doves surrounding a wreath mounted upon the cross.[105]

Baptism scenes in early Christian art almost always depict the dove descending into the scene, particularly when the image is intended to show John baptizing Jesus (see discussion above and figs. 1.1, 1.2, 1.7, 2.1, 5.1). These images occur in both catacomb frescoes and sarcophagus reliefs from the third and fourth centuries; they also appear on ivories and monumental mosaics of the fifth century forward, extending through the history of Christian art to the present. The dove also appears in a rare image of an ordinary Christian

104. Sühling, "Taube und Orante."
105. Paulinus of Nola, *Ep.* 32.10, 14. See also his description of the basilica at Fundi, with a dove (the bird of peace) representing the Holy Spirit, *Ep.* 32.17.

Figure 3.3. Mosaic. Baptistery in Albenga, Liguria. Sixth century. (Photo by author.)

baptism, a grave inscription from Aquileia, which depicts a young girl baptized by a figure dressed as a shepherd, who lays his right hand on her head (fig. 3.4). To the left, another male gestures toward the scene. He has a halo, indicating that he is probably a saintly witness, and wears the tunic and pallium. The dove descends within a starry orb that spills water over the neophyte from a crescent at its base.

In some baptism images, the dove appears to be spewing water (perhaps breath or oil) from its mouth. The most impressive and famous example is in the medallion mosaic the Arian baptisteries in Ravenna (fig. 2.1). Here the dove descends from the heavens, right above Jesus's head, beak down and emitting a substance that has a faint blue tint. Interpreters have suggested that the substance is water, oil, breath, or light, none of which are directly supported by the Gospel narratives of Jesus's baptism, but all of which could be explained by reference to liturgical actions in the baptismal liturgy.[106] Thus, because early Christians associated the descent of the dove with the moment of Jesus's anointing, the dove could be understood as providing one of the material elements of the ritual: water for affusion, oil for anointing, or breath for exsufflation. Because of its alignment with the font, the descending dove in the Ravenna baptistery could be interpreted as descending on Christ as well as on the recipient of the baptism, thus uniting him or her with Jesus in the iconography overhead. Each candidate then became a "christ" and received the Spirit just as Christ did. This idea is perfectly expressed in Ephrem of Syria's sixth hymn for the Epiphany:

> The Spirit descended from the heights and sanctified the water as it hovered.
> When John baptized Jesus, it left all others and settled on one,
> but now it has come down and settled upon all
> who are reborn in the water of baptism.

106. See Sühling, "Die Taube als religiöses Symbol," 150–54; and Deichmann, *Ravenna*, 1:210 and 2:257. See also Stryzgowsky, *Iconographie der Taufe Christi*, 11–13.

Figure 3.4. Marble grave marker. Aquileia, Museo Archeologico Nazionale. Fourth century. (Photo by author.)

> Of all those that John baptized the Spirit dwelt on one alone,
> but now it has flown down to dwell upon many.
> Running to meet the First who went up from the Jordan
> it embraced and dwelt upon him.[107]

The Man Born Blind

The story of Jesus healing the man born blind (John 9) serves as a type of baptism, not only because of its healing aspect but also by virtue of the transformation of its recipient from blindness to sightedness. Certain narrative details in the text help to make the connections by allowing the metaphor of blindness to mean ignorance. Jesus anoints the man's eyes with a mixture of spittle and clay and tells him to wash in the pool of Siloam (both actions later taken to prefigure aspects of the baptismal rite). Once the man's blindness is cured, he recognizes who Jesus is and worships him. Jesus's concluding lines make the point: "I came into this world for judgment so that those who do not see may see, and those who do see may become blind" (John 9:39).[108]

The use of spittle and clay in the blind man's story figures in the controversy over the role or value of matter. Refuting gnostic denigration of material creation, Irenaeus prefers to argue that the main purpose of the healing of the blind man was to show forth God's will to remake the physical world.

---

107. Ephrem, *Epiph.* 6. 1–2; Finn, *Early Christian Baptism*, 166. An early Byzantine document records Joannes Diakrinomenos criticizing those who were so childish as to portray the Holy Spirit as a dove, saying that the Gospels said only that the Holy Spirit was seen in the form of a dove—not as an actual dove; see Mango, *Art of the Byzantine Empire*, 43–44.

108. See discussion of this type in chap. 1, under the heading "The Paralytic and the Man Born Blind."

Just as Adam was first made of dust and mist, Jesus healed this man with clay and spit, in order to teach that the hand of God, which formed us in the beginning, and which likewise forms us in the womb, also seeks to win us back from sin to eternal life.[109]

Different interpretations of the story focus on the contrast between blindness and sightedness, but not always in predictable ways. For example, Cyril of Jerusalem uses the metaphor of blindness versus sightedness, but he muses that the splendor of God could be blinding to those who do not believe; that is, the gospel's radiance would have no impact on those who cannot bear to look directly on its brilliance.[110] Ambrose compares the healing of the man's eyes to the healing of the eyes of the neophytes' hearts. They receive the spiritual sight of faith and so perceive the light emitted by the sacraments.[111]

Augustine regards the story of Jesus healing the blind man as an allegory of sin and salvation, interpreting the man as signifying the fallen human race and his healing as enlightenment through baptism. Accordingly, he views the blind man as anointed and made into a catechumen when Jesus takes spittle, makes clay, and places it on his eyes. He then instructs the man to wash, a sign of his baptism. His return to sightedness is proof of his illumination through this ritual. Wishing his catechumens to be similarly anointed with spittle and clay (the Word made flesh), Augustine urges, "Let them hurry to the font if they seek light."[112]

Early Christian iconography of Christ healing the man born blind is discussed above as a symbol of baptismal healing.[113] This image might have referred to the illumination at baptism in addition to baptismal healing and so should be considered here as well. Just as images may signify multiple ideas, this one in particular may point simultaneously to these two primary aspects of the baptismal ritual: cleansing from sin and receipt of the Holy Spirit.

Milk and Honey

In a hymn addressed to Christ, attributed to Clement of Alexandria, Christ is presented as a shepherd of royal lambs, a fisher of men, an unwavering helm of ships, and a secure bridle of untamed foals. One line of the prayer addresses Christ as "heavenly milk pressed from the sweet breasts of the bride, gracious gifts of your wisdom." The hymn continues: "Tiny infants with tender mouths suckled at the nipple of the *Logos* and were filled with the dewy Spirit."[114]

---

109. Irenaeus, *Haer.* 5.15.2. On Irenaeus's fear about the gnostic implications of the term "illumination," see *Haer.* 2.17.9 (which also cites this text of the man born blind).

110. Cyril of Jerusalem, *Cat.* 6.28–29.

111. Ambrose, *Sacr.* 3.11–15.

112. Augustine, *Tract. Ev. Jo.* 44, passim, but esp. 2 (CCSL 36:382), trans. author.

113. See discussion in chap. 1, under the heading "The Paralytic and the Man Born Blind."

114. Clement of Alexandria, *Paed. Hymn* 40–50, trans. Hoek, "Hymn of the Holy Clement," 301.

The images of the Good Shepherd carrying a bucket of milk might reflect this symbolic milk of wisdom, given by the Shepherd to his flock (fig. 2.7).

This language echoes phrases found in one of the *Odes of Solomon*, a collection of early Christian hymns probably composed in Syriac, whose date is disputed, although scholars usually place them in the second or third century. The image of milk occurs in several places in these hymns, but most vividly in Ode 19:

> A cup of milk was offered to me,
> and I drank it in the sweetness of the Lord's kindness.
> The Son is the cup,
> and the Father is He who was milked;
> and the Holy Spirit is She who milked Him;
> because His breasts were full,
> and it was undesirable that His milk should be ineffectually released.
> The Holy Spirit opened Her bosom,
> and mixed the milk of the two breasts of the Father.
> Then She gave the mixture to the generation without their knowing,
> and those who have received it are in the perfection of the right hand.[115]

A wide variety of ancient religions, including certain Greco-Roman cults, viewed milk as a divine fluid. For example, Apuleius's account of the mysteries of Isis in the *Metamorphoses* describes a priest carrying a golden, breast-shaped vase from which he pours a libation of milk.[116] Isis was depicted seated with the child Horus on her lap and a breast bared for nursing (fig. 3.5). Historians have proposed this as a prototype for the iconography of Mary, "seat of wisdom," who holds the child Jesus on her lap and in late medieval and Renaissance art often nurses her son or offers him her breast.[117]

A miracle involving milk also appears in an early Christian legend. According to the apocryphal *Acts of Paul*, when the Roman soldiers beheaded Paul, milk, rather than blood, spurted on their clothing. This amazed the soldiers and led to their conversion.[118]

Milk is more than simple food; it provides spiritual wisdom and perfection. It is described, moreover, as sweet. Another of the *Odes of Solomon* compares this milk to honey dripping from the honeycomb of bees.[119] The connections

115. *Odes Sol.* 19.1–5, trans. *OTP*, 2:752–53. Compare Ode 8.14: "I fashioned their members, and my own breasts I prepared for them, that they might drink my holy milk and live by it." See also *Odes Sol.* 14.2; 35.3; and 40.1.

116. Apuleius, *Metam.* 11.10. See commentary with other examples in Griffiths, *Isis-Book*, 208–11.

117. Recently published in the catalog for the exhibition *Cradle of Christianity*, ed. Israeli and Mevorah, 52–53.

118. *Acts of Paul* 2.5.

119. *Odes Sol.* 40.1.

Figure 3.5. Harpocrates on Isis's lap. Painting from a house in Karanis, Egypt. Third century. (Photo from the Kelsey Museum Archives, University of Michigan.)

between drinking milk and attaining wisdom are associated with the image of the church as a mother who suckles her children, a theme prominent in some Syrian texts.[120] As in Clement's hymn, the Word/Logos also is associated with milk. He is the cup or the milk itself, and as the ode quoted above proclaims, the Father's breasts are engorged with holy milk for nourishing his children. In his treatise *Against Heresies*, Irenaeus compares Christ to a mother who does not give adult food to her babies but rather gives the food appropriate to their maturity. Thus Christ came in a form that humans were capable of receiving and offered himself to them (infants) as milk. "He did this when he appeared as a man," Irenaeus writes, "that we, being nourished, as it were, from the breast of his flesh, and having, by such a course of milk-nourishment, become accustomed to eat and drink the Word of God, may be able also to contain in ourselves the Bread of immortality, which is the Spirit of the Father."[121]

The symbolism of milk is well established in the New Testament Epistles, where milk is contrasted with solid food. In 1 Corinthians 3:1–2, Paul says that he can address his readers not as "spiritual" but as still children of the flesh, babes in Christ: "I fed you with milk, not solid food, for you were not ready for solid food." The author of 1 Peter urges his audience to be "like newborn infants" and "long for the pure, spiritual milk, so that by it you may grow into salvation" (2:2). The author of the Epistle to the Hebrews maintains, "You

120. See, e.g., Murray, *Symbols of the Church and Kingdom*, 127, 265–67.
121. Irenaeus, *Haer.* 4.38.1, *ANF*, 1:521.

need milk, not solid food; for everyone who lives on milk, being still an infant, is unskilled in the word of righteousness" (5:12–13).

Clement of Alexandria probably had these passages in mind as he wrote the section of his treatise *The Instructor* that attends to the symbolism of milk. Diverging slightly from Paul, Clement interprets the milk as a source of perfect spiritual nutriment rather than as food for infants in the faith, noting that childhood in Christ is relative maturity when compared to living under the law. Clement further associates the divine Word with milk in a lengthy discourse on human biology, pregnancy, parturition, and bodily fluids. He writes, "You will certainly find nothing else more nourishing, or sweeter, or whiter than milk. In every respect, accordingly, it is like spiritual sustenance, which is sweet through grace, nourishing as life, and bright as the day of Christ." In Clement's imagistic text, God is the nourisher and Christ is the care-soothing breast of the Father. Christ alone, according to Clement, "supplies us children with the milk of love, and those only are blessed who suck this breast."[122]

Clement also connects milk with the water of baptism, and in language quite similar to Tertullian's discussion of the mixing of the Holy Spirit with the water, he compares the mixing of milk and water with the mixing of the divine Logos with the water in the font:

> Further, milk has a most natural affinity for water, as assuredly the spiritual washing has for the spiritual nutriment. Those, therefore, that swallow a little cold water, in addition to the above-mentioned milk, straightway feel benefit; for the milk is prevented from souring by its combination with water. . . . Such is the union of the Word with baptism, is the agreement of milk with water; for it receives it alone of all liquids, and admits of mixture with water, for the purpose of cleansing, as baptism for the remission of sins.[123]

Clement even refers to a drink of milk mixed with honey, calling it a sweet nutriment: "the Word blended with Love." This may allude to the first drink of the newly baptized, a cup of milk mixed with honey, which symbolizes their status both as newly born children and as ones entering the promised land.[124]

Clement concludes by extending the milk symbolism to include butter (the fat of the milk) that was used to light lamps and to anoint the body, thus representing the role of the milk for illumination and spiritual sealing. Here he cites Isaiah 7:14–15, which describes the sign of the child, Immanuel, eating honey-sweetened curds "by the time he knows how to refuse the evil and choose the good." Clement's citation of the Isaiah text may indicate that

122. Clement of Alexandria, *Paed.* 1.6, *ANF*, 2:219–20. Compare Augustine, *Conf.* 1.6.7, where Augustine credits God for filling his nurse's breasts with milk, which provides his first spiritual awareness of God's providence in his life. For more discussion, see Bunt, "Milk and Honey."
123. Clement of Alexandria, *Paed.* 1.6, *ANF*, 2:222.
124. See *Barn.* 6.8–17.

eating sweetened milk at baptism had an eschatological dimension (a figure of Christ's return).[125] Beneath these images lies the scriptural description of the promised land as flowing with milk and honey (Exod. 3:8; Deut. 31:20; etc.).

As just noted, Clement's reference to the Isaiah text might have had a ritual connection or context. Milk and honey were fed to the newly baptized, according to a number of documents. Origen, commenting on the passage from Matthew in which Jesus commands the disciples not to despise the "little ones" (Matt. 18:10), notes that all who are born in the regenerative font are like newly born babies, being assigned guardian angels and longing for spiritual milk.[126] Tertullian refers to this as the food of newly born infants and notes that it was given to the neophytes before their first Eucharist.[127] A canon from the Council of Carthage (397) comments on this practice as well, specifying that it should not be mistaken for the sacrament of the Lord's body and blood.[128] The *Apostolic Tradition* also describes a meal of milk and honey as part of the initial eucharistic meal of the newly baptized. In this instance the mixture points to the fulfillment of the promise, given to the patriarchs, of a land flowing with milk and honey; only now that land is understood as Christ's flesh, by which he nourishes infant believers and makes bitter things sweet by the gentleness of his word.[129]

The custom of giving a mixed drink of milk and honey to the newly baptized continued in the West, at least through the sixth century and possibly even later. The *Verona Sacramentary* (attributed to Leo I) records the practice and includes a blessing over the elements of water, milk, and honey, asking God to nourish the newly baptized through them and bring them into the land of promise—a land flowing with milk and honey—like the patriarchs Abraham, Isaac, and Jacob.[130] Similarly, John the Deacon, writing from Rome in about the year 500, explains the symbolism of this first eucharistic food:

> You ask why milk and honey are placed in a most sacred chalice and offered with the sacrifice at the Paschal Sabbath. The reason is that it is written in the Old Testament and figuratively promised to the new people: "I will lead you into the promised land, a land flowing with milk and honey." . . . Therefore this kind of sacrament is offered to the newly baptized so that they should know that they and no others but themselves who partake in the body and blood of the Lord shall be received into that promised land, and as they commence their journey, they are nourished like little children with milk and honey . . . so that they, who in their first birth were nourished with the milk of corruption and

125. Pacian of Barcelona also quotes this Isaiah text, *Bapt.* 1.3. On the paradisiacal image of milk and honey, see Tertullian, *Marc.* 3.16.4; *Scorp.* 1.12; *Res.* 26.

126. Origen, *Comm. Matt.* 13.27.

127. Tertullian, *Cor.* 3; *Marc.* 1.14.

128. *Brev. Hipp.* 23.

129. Hippolytus, *Trad. ap.* 23.

130. Leo I, *Verona Sac.* 10.1.205.

wept tears of bitterness, in their second birth might taste the sweetness of honey in the Church's womb.[131]

The Isaiah 7:15 text (instead of the Exodus and Deuteronomy references) probably prompted the vision of the third-century African martyr Perpetua, who saw herself arriving in paradise and meeting a white-haired man dressed as a shepherd who offered her sweetened milk curds to eat.[132] In a sermon preached on the Feast of Saints Perpetua and Felicity (March 7), Augustine interprets this vision as demonstrating that the Good Shepherd had found plenty of milk in his sheep and was showing off the overflowing pails to prove that the milk came from hearts purified by acts of charity. Augustine adds that Perpetua and her companions received some of this fresh milk as a sacramental meal prior to shedding their blood, which is why she awoke from her visionary sleep with a sweet taste in her mouth.[133]

Milk or cheese is known to have been included in earthly Eucharists as well. The *Apostolic Tradition* records a prayer, offered over cheese. Describing it as milk congealed into a single mass, the prayer asks that the members of the community be likewise congealed in love.[134] Several early communities seem to have offered cheese or yogurt along with (or in place of) bread and wine at the Eucharist. Epiphanius described a group—the Artotyrites—who ate a sacramental meal of bread and cheese.[135] According to Hippolytus, milk and honey were eaten by the heretical Naassenians, who believed it was the proper food of those who were perfect and shared in the Pleroma.[136]

Clement's association of milk and water (along with his highly feminized imagery) has an echo in a later Italian liturgical source: the late fourth-century bishop of Verona, Zeno, who in one of his invitations to the baptismal font urged his hearers to "run to the milky fluid of the generative font," a fluid he also describes as sweet nectar.[137] The juxtaposition of nectar and milk points, again, to the gift of milk and honey, here in the church's womb (the font) rather than on its table (the altar). The image of a spring of water, milk, and honey points to the promise of wisdom and nurture, more than to cleansing. Such an image also occurs in the earlier *Odes of Solomon*, in a hymn that prays that God would open bountiful springs to supply copious amounts of milk and honey.[138]

131. John the Deacon, *Ep. Sen.* 12, trans. author, cf. text in Wilmart, *Analecta reginensia*, 177.
132. *Passio Perp. et Fel.* 4. Note that in Gen. 18:8 Abraham serves curds to his three visitors at the Oak of Mamre. This is depicted in the fifth-century mosaic of the scene in the basilica of Sta. Maria Maggiore in Rome.
133. Augustine, *Serm.* 394.
134. Hippolytus, *Trad. ap.* 6.
135. Epiphanius, *Pan.* 49.1. Their name is literally translated "bread and cheese eaters."
136. Hippolytus, *Haer.* 5.3. See McGowan, *Ascetic Eucharists*, 106.
137. Zeno of Verona, *Tract.* 1.12 (CCSL 22:51), trans. author.
138. *Odes Sol.* 4.10; compare with the living fountain in *Odes Sol.* 30.4.

Candles, Torches, and Fire

In addition to the postbaptismal chrismation to impart the gift of the Holy Spirit, one other ritual practice alluded to the illumination of the newly baptized. This was their presentation with lit tapers or torches as they processed from the baptistery to the church.

Interestingly, this ritual is often cited (and incorporated into modern liturgies), but it is not actually well attested in literature that predates the early Middle Ages.[139] Cyril of Jerusalem addresses his catechetical lectures to his "dear candidates for enlightenment" and notes that they had already walked in procession with the tapers of brides in their hands, presumably referring to the ceremony of enrollment.[140] Proclus, bishop of Constantinople (d. 446 or 447), mentions lamps in the hands of the neophytes at the Easter vigil and says that the lamps symbolize the illumination of the neophytes' souls.[141] Generally, however, the importance of candles or lamps in the baptismal ritual is hypothesized, based on the imagery of light so often used by writers with reference to baptism. For example, John Chrysostom, commenting on the brightness of the neophytes' white garments, explains that being zealous for good works and praise of God is like being a light for the world. Citing Matthew 5:16, he exhorts:

> It was on this account that Christ said: "Let your light shine before others, in order that all may see your good works and give glory to your Father who is in heaven." Did you see how he urges us to let the light within us shine forth, not by garments but by deeds? . . . This light does not stop with your bodily senses but illumines the soul and understanding of those who see it; after it dispels the darkness of evil, it draws those who find it to shine with their own light and to imitate the life of virtue.[142]

Gregory of Nazianzus's comparison of the neophytes carrying their lamps into the main church with the brides in the parable of the wise and foolish virgins (Matt. 25:1–13) is a convincing witness to this practice. Telling the candidates that they will presently stand before the altar in the great sanctuary, he admonishes them to think of themselves as brides waiting for their bridegroom. The lamps they kindle are a "sacrament of the illumination" and

---

139. For example, Johnson asserts this with no specific reference in *Rites of Christian Initiation*, 31. Finn seems to assume this as well in *Death to Rebirth*, 182. See also Whitaker, *Baptismal Liturgy*, 57, 79.

140. Cyril of Jerusalem, *Procat.* 1, trans. McCauley and Stephenson, *Works of Saint Cyril of Jerusalem*, 1:69–70.

141. For text and translation, see Riley, *Christian Initiation*, 417n180: "how the lamps in your hands symbolize the illumination of your soul."

142. John Chrysostom, *Catech.* 4.19–20 (Stav. 4), trans. Harkins, *St. John Chrysostom*, 73.

symbolize their shining souls and faith.[143] An image of the five wise brides with their lamps also appears in the paintings of the Dura Europos baptistery (fig. 3.6), which suggests the importance of this parable to the liturgy of baptism.[144]

Certain other aspects of the ritual incorporate lights. Cyril of Jerusalem, for example, explains that candidates turned toward the west to renounce Satan because that was the direction of darkness.[145] When he speaks about the move down into the font, he describes it as descending into night. As they come out, he adds, they find themselves in bright daylight.[146] In his *Procatechesis*, delivered to catechumens preparing for baptism at the Easter vigil, Cyril likens emerging from the font to entering paradise and offers this wish:

> May God one day show you that night whose darkness is daylight, the dark of which it is said: "Darkness shall not be dark to thee, and night shall be light as the day" [Ps. 139:12]. Then may the gate of paradise be opened to every man and woman of you. Then, may you enjoy the fragrant, Christ-bearing waters. Then may you receive Christ's name and the power of things divine . . . on the day when, like new stars of the Church, you will enter, your bodies bright, your souls shining.[147]

Cyril may have been referring to the brightly lit shrine of the Holy Sepulchre where he would preside over the baptism of these catechumens during the paschal vigil. According to Egeria, the congregation waited in the large church (the Martyrium) while the bishop led the newly baptized from the font to the Anastasis for a special prayer and then into the church to join the congregation for the eucharistic celebration.[148] This procession, from the baptistery to the Anastasis to the great church, must have been torch-lit as the event would have taken place at night.

Finally, the association of fire with baptism is attested in various places, including Justin Martyr's *Dialogue with Trypho*, which mentions that a fire was kindled on the Jordan at the time of Jesus's baptism.[149] Perhaps the warning given by the Baptist that the one coming after him would baptize with the Holy Spirit and with fire (Matt. 3:11; Luke 3:16) seemed to call for the presence of actual fire in or near the font in later ritual practices. The *Sibylline Oracles* insist Jesus escaped from a fire that appeared on the Jordan after he

143. Gregory of Nazianzus, *Or.* 40.46. The bridal motif is considered below in chap. 5, under the heading "Bridal Motifs in Baptismal Catecheses."

144. This image is often identified as the women coming to Christ's tomb. See the discussion below, chap. 5, under the heading "Bridal Motifs in Baptismal Catecheses."

145. Cyril of Jerusalem, *Myst.* 1.4.

146. Cyril of Jerusalem, *Myst.* 2.4.

147. Cyril of Jerusalem, *Procat.* 5, trans. McCauley and Stephenson, *Works of Saint Cyril of Jerusalem*, 1:81–82.

148. Egeria, *Itin.* 38.1–2.

149. Justin Martyr, *Dial.* 88.

Figure 3.6. Five wise brides or women coming to Christ's tomb. Painting, Dura Europos baptistery. Mid-third century. (Photo from Yale University Art Gallery, Dura Europos Collection.)

was baptized and was the "first to see delightful God, coming in the spirit on the white wings of a dove."[150]

The *Treatise on Rebaptism*, written in North Africa sometime in the third century, describes a liturgical practice of kindling fire at baptism. Apparently, citing John's words about being baptized both in the Holy Spirit and in fire, certain persons were administering baptisms that they deemed more perfect because fire appeared on the water. The text suggests that this was done by some trick, magic potion, or malignant creature that could force fire from the water.[151]

Gregory of Nyssa may have known some practice of kindling fire at baptism. His sermon delivered on the Feast of Christ's Baptism (Epiphany) refers to Elijah's contest with the priests of Baal (1 Kings 18:20–40) in which the prophet kindled (rather than quenched) fire with water. Noting the juxtaposition of water and fire, Gregory claims that the miracle of the fire on the altar was a figure of the fiery Holy Spirit at baptism: "Now herein, by that wondrous sacrifice, Elijah clearly proclaimed to us the sacramental rite of baptism that should afterwards be instituted. For the fire was kindled by the water thrice poured upon it, so that it is clearly shown that where the mystic water is, there is the kindling, warm, and fiery Spirit, that burns up the ungodly and illuminates the faithful."[152]

150. *Sib. Or.* 6, trans. OTP, 1:407.
151. Anon., *Rebapt.* 16.
152. Gregory of Nyssa, *Diem lum.*, NPNF[2], 5:522. Slightly earlier he spoke about the four fundamental elements (earth, air, fire, and water) to show how they all belong to baptism. See, for comparison, Basil of Caesarea, *Spir. Sanct.* 15.36, which cites John's proclamation of a baptism of fire and explains that it indicates the trial at the final judgment.

The appearance of fire, or at least a blazing light, at baptism also appears in the East, especially in the Syrian and Armenian traditions. Ephrem, among others, testifies to it at Christ's baptism. In his hymn "Christ as Light in Mary and the Jordan," Ephrem writes that Christ was as dazzling as a daystar as he went up from the river.[153] This is clearly illustrated in the image of Christ's baptism found in the Syriac *Gospels of Rabbula* (ca. 586; fig. 3.7). Other documents that refer to fire or light at baptism include the *Acts of John*, the *Rituale Armenorum*, and Tatian's *Diatesseron*.[154]

The symbolic significance of flame or light at baptism could explain the appearance of candles, lamps, and torches in certain early Christian images of baptism as well as in the decoration of early Christian baptisteries. As noted above, the paintings on the walls of the Dura Europos baptistery include a representation of the wise brides carrying their torches and approaching the bridegroom's tent (fig. 3.6). An ivory, now in the British Museum, shows a scene of Jesus (as a youth) being baptized by John the Baptist. An angel looks on, and the water falls from the beak of a descending dove. Two tall candles stand to either side (fig. 3.8). Candles also appear in the fresco of the baptistery in the Ponzianus Catacomb in Rome, in a pavement from the African baptistery of La Skhira (fig. 3.9), and in the decoration of the font from Kélibia, now in Tunis's Bardo Museum (fig. 5.4).

Candles also have a particular place in the iconography of the saints, where two candles are often shown on either side of the holy person who stands in the posture of prayer (fig. 3.10). This iconography may have been based on the actual practice of lighting candles in saints' shrines.[155] The occurrence of candles in baptismal iconography reinforced the association of baptism with martyrdom or the joining of the neophytes to the community of the saints.

Baptism at Pentecost and Epiphany

The presence of fire and the Holy Spirit at Christ's baptism also has implications for the practice of baptizing at Pentecost. Considering the liturgical importance of the reception of the gifts of the Spirit at baptism and the drama in the Acts narrative of the Spirit's descent upon the apostles as tongues of flame (2:1–4) followed by the subsequent baptism of three thousand persons (2:41), Pentecost would seem to be an especially auspicious feast on which to administer the rite, and good evidence shows that it was so.[156]

153. Ephrem, *Eccl.* 36.5.
154. See Winkler, "Appearance of the Light." Winkler's essay includes translations of many of the pertinent texts.
155. See Jerome, *Vigil.* 4.7; and Augustine, *Mir. sanct. Steph.* 2.2.4.
156. See Johnson's essay "Tertullian's '*Diem Baptismo Sollemniorem*' Revisited." Johnson argues that the evidence is scantier than this author would argue.

Figure 3.7. Detail of John baptizing Jesus. *Gospels of Rabbula*, folio 4v., Syria. Late sixth century. (Photo from Wikimedia Commons.)

Tertullian states that after Passover (i.e., Easter), Pentecost was the second most suitable season for baptism.[157] Gregory of Nazianzus asserts that the three most popular days for baptism were Easter, Epiphany, and Pentecost, but urges that any unbaptized hearers on that day after Epiphany delay no longer.[158] John Chrysostom does not oppose the idea of Pentecost because it was at that feast that the apostles received the grace of the Holy Spirit and three thousand were then baptized. He worries, nevertheless, that candidates receiving baptism at Pentecost would not be able to undertake the preparatory fast (since it was Eastertide).[159] However, both Pope Siricius and Pope Leo wrote letters to fellow bishops urging that they cease baptizing on Epiphany and baptize only on Easter and Pentecost. Leo especially insists that Pentecost was the day to baptize all those who missed Easter baptism due to ill health or travel delays.[160] The surviving sections of the sixth-century *Verona Sacramentary* include a baptismal mass for Pentecost.[161]

157. Tertullian, *Bapt.* 19.1–2. After that, he says, any day, hour, or season is appropriate.

158. Gregory of Nazianzus, *Or.* 40.24.

159. John Chrysostom, *Hom. Act.* 1. On the cessation of fasting and kneeling in prayer during the Easter season, see Tertullian, *Or.* 23.2; *Cor.* 3.4.

160. Siricius, *Epistole ad Himerium* (i.e., Himerius of Tarragona, who seems to have been baptizing also on Christmas); Leo I, *Ep.* 16.2–5 (to all the bishops of Sicily). See Cabié, *La Pentecôte*.

161. Leo I, *Verona Sac.* 10. Note that this includes a blessing for the milk and honey, served to the newly baptized (cited above).

Figure 3.8. Baptism of Jesus and Jesus in the temple with the elders. Ivory plaque from Egypt or Syria. Mid-sixth century. (Photo by author with permission from the Trustees of the British Museum.)

Figure 3.9. Lamps, birds, and crosses. Mosaic, baptistery of La Skhira, Tunisia. Sfax Archaeological Museum. Sixth century. (Photo by author.)

Epiphany was the day that early Christians, especially those in the East, commemorated Jesus's baptism by John.[162] It was also a solemn occasion for administering baptism in many communities, although it may also have been a day on which catechumens enrolled for Easter baptism and began their preparation.[163] The name "Epiphany" points to the manifestation of Christ, and its placement on the feast of his baptism offered a rich opportunity for homilists and catechists to reflect on the theme of divine manifestation and

162. This is especially noted in Syria and Armenia; see Johnson, *Rites of Christian Initiation*, 47.

163. Gregory of Nazianzus's two sermons on the feast (*Or.* 39–40) suggest a two-day festival, with baptism on the second day. Ambrose, however, says that Epiphany was a day for enrollment, *Exp. Luc.* 4.76. Talley argues that the day after Epiphany was an enrollment day and the beginning of a fast in preparation for baptism in Alexandria, *Origins of the Liturgical Year*, 189–214.

Figure 3.10. The Theotechnus family. Painting, arcosolium of the Theotechnus Family. Catacomb of San Gennaro, Naples. Fourth century. (Photo from Scala/Art Resource, New York.)

spiritual enlightenment.[164] The title of one of Gregory of Nazianzus's surviving sermons, *On the Holy Lights* (*eis ta hagia phōta*), as well as one of Gregory of Nyssa's, *On the Day of Lights* (*hēmera tōn phōton*), refers to the lit tapers carried by the faithful to symbolize the illumination that came through baptism.[165] Finally, Ephrem the Syrian composed a hymn that called forth the metaphors of light and knowledge, appropriate for baptism at the Feast of Epiphany:

> When it is associated with a source of light
> an eye becomes clear,
> it shines with the light that provisions it.
> It gleams with its brightness,
> it becomes glorious with its splendor,
> adorned by its beauty.[166]

The gift of the Holy Spirit at baptism was multivalent. It shared in many aspects of baptismal incorporation: it sealed the neophytes to Christ and marked them as members of the community. Because of its association with

164. Gregory of Nyssa's sermon, preached on Epiphany, *Diem lum.* (also *Bapt. Christ*), is an excellent example. See Ferguson, "Preaching at Epiphany." See also Hippolytus, *Serm. Epiph.*

165. Gregory of Nazianzus, *Or.* 39. See also *Or.* 40.

166. Ephrem, *Eccl.* 36.1, trans. Brock, "St. Ephrem on Christ."

anointing with holy unction, it also joined them to the company of priests and kings. Yet perhaps most of all, it transmitted those unique gifts—of wisdom and knowledge—that were associated specifically with the Spirit. This gift was delivered through either the bishop's imposition of hands or anointing, or both. In some cases it was given through the water alone. Nevertheless, many groups perceived the gift of the Spirit as the confirmation and perfection of the baptismal ritual that begins, but is not finished, in the water. Certain other communities, believing this to be the true element of initiation, appear to have dispensed altogether with the water bath, seeking only the outpouring of the Spirit as the salvific act.

The spiritual transformation through baptism was represented in such ritual actions as the drinking of honeyed milk or receiving a lit candle. It was symbolized in art and architecture by images of the descending dove or the use of lamps and torches, which also illuminated the baptismal chamber. As the newly baptized processed from the font in their white garments, their faces would have shone, the oil that had anointed their heads reflecting the light from their tapers. The scent of the chrism would have added another sensory dimension to the glow, wafting the sweet fragrance of knowledge and the odor of sanctity into the company of the gathered faithful.

4

Baptism as Dying and Rising

Although it diverges in significant ways from the paradigmatic events of John's baptism of Jesus or the Holy Spirit's Pentecostal descent upon the apostles, the theme of baptismal death and rebirth appears in the earliest strands of Christian teaching and is, arguably, the most transformative dimension of early Christian initiation. Through the rite of baptism, an individual dies and is reborn; this relates to his or her cleansing and incorporation insofar as it depends on setting aside the old, sinful self and joining a new "birth family." Such rebirth also relies on the gift of the Holy Spirit, which is expressed in the claim that it is a spiritual rather than simply a bodily renewal.

Two key New Testament passages are crucial for understanding this aspect of baptism, but relate to somewhat different dimensions of it. On the one hand, the Pauline claim in Romans 6:5 that a Christian participates in Christ's death and resurrection through the ritual of baptism sets the ritual in a paschal context. On the other hand, the Johannine declaration that one must be born again "from above" in both water and the spirit (John 3:3–5) introduces the idea of spiritual rebirth. Both passages suggest that baptism is a new birth in this world as well as in the next and bears the promise of resurrection for both present and future. Yet while the former is directly linked with Christ's death and resurrection, the latter appears within a discussion of mortal birth from a mother's womb.

Along with these two Scripture texts (Rom. 6 and John 3), early interpreters viewed several Old and New Testament narratives as prefiguring the power of baptism to effect spiritual death and rebirth. Old Testament figures who were miraculously rescued or preserved from the danger of death (e.g., Jonah and Daniel) were especially potent, along with New Testament figures who were resuscitated (e.g., Lazarus and Jairus's daughter). The stories of these miracles appear in baptismal sermons and catecheses as well as in the programs of early Christian art, often adjacent to other baptismal motifs (e.g., Jesus's baptism, Noah, or the healing of the blind man and of the paralytic; see figs. 1.1, 1.4, 1.6, 1.7, 4.4). This baptismal motif was concretely expressed through both architectural design and ritual actions. The spaces of baptism were constructed to allude to the grave and the maternal womb. The ritual practices of triple immersion, the stripping of candidates, and the reclothing of neophytes instantiated the idea of shedding the old person and putting on Christ. Baptism at Easter emphasized the initiates' participation in Christ's passion while also symbolizing their rebirth and future resurrection.

Scriptural Sources for Baptismal Rebirth

Of the two primary scriptural texts that lay the foundation for the theme of regeneration, one of them (Rom. 6:3–11) explicitly associates baptism with Christ's passion. In this passage, Paul describes baptism as participation in the paschal mystery and presents it as both a model and an invitation for each Christian to undergo symbolic death to sin (or the old self) and rebirth to new life. The former, sinful self is symbolically crucified and buried in this baptismal water. Although Paul does not explain how the ritual actually dramatizes (or enacts) this transformation, he insists that it is the means by which a Christian is united to Christ's passion and resurrection.

The second key text recounts the conversation between the Pharisee and Jesus in John's Gospel (3:1–10). The Pharisee, Nicodemus, asks Jesus how someone could be "born from above." Presumably, Nicodemus has heard the followers of Jesus speak in these terms. Nicodemus is confused, since, as he notes, no one can actually reenter his or her mother's womb a second time in order to be born again. Jesus does not answer his question. Instead, he reiterates the point: no one enters the kingdom of God unless born of both water and the Spirit. Although it lacks an explicit reference to baptism, the passage resonates with the themes of death and rebirth, which led early Christians to interpret it as an allusion to baptism's two parts: the water bath and the descent of the Spirit. Moreover, the point that Jesus makes to Nicodemus suggests a conversion of life as well as faith. Being born of the Spirit (or "from above") has its outcome in actual deeds. Unlike those who love darkness and do evil, those who are reborn do what is true, and their deeds are "done in God."

Paschal Aspects of Baptism in Early Christian Thought

These two texts are important for understanding the ways the early exegetes linked the baptism of John the Baptist with the Pauline theology of baptism as death to sin and rebirth to new life. As discussed previously, John's baptism of Jesus is the model and source of Christian baptism. It was administered to sinners who wished to repent and change their lives.

In Mark 1:5, those who came to John for baptism were baptized while confessing their sins. The Baptist proclaims that his baptism is preparatory; it prepares those who receive it for the time when the one coming after him will bring them something different. His baptism in water is supplemented or completed by the one who brings a baptism with the Holy Spirit (and with fire—Matt. 3:11//Luke 3:16). This promise resonates with Jesus's insistence in John 3 that those who wish to enter the kingdom of God must be born of both water and the Spirit. Yet in an earlier Johannine passage, the Baptist announces that the coming one is the Lamb of God who will take away the sins of the world (John 1:29). He is, John says, the one who baptizes with the Holy Spirit, while he, John, baptizes only with water. The close juxtaposition of Jesus's identity as sacrificial lamb and as the bringer of Spirit baptism implies that Spirit baptism transmits the benefits of Christ's redemptive death. That idea is paralleled in Paul's Epistle to the Romans, which insists that through baptism Christians are united to Christ's death and resurrection and undergo a type of the crucifixion themselves: "For if we have been united to him in a death like his, we will certainly be united to him in a resurrection like his. We know that our old self was crucified with him so that the body of sin might be destroyed, and we might no longer be enslaved to sin" (6:5–6).

Although the earliest Christian writers do not emphasize the theme of being buried with Christ, some make subtle references to the text of Romans 6. Explaining the mystery of the cross, Ignatius of Antioch claims that Christ was born and baptized so that by his suffering he could cleanse water for the rite.[1] When Origen reflects on the baptismal use of visible water and oil, he argues that true baptism consists of receiving the invisible Holy Spirit from above. This, he says, is given only to those who have already died to sin. Then, in an indirect reference to Romans 6, he adds that someone still living in sin cannot be buried with Christ or be wrapped in clean, fresh linens and interred in a new tomb.[2]

Although Tertullian never describes baptism as participating in Christ's death and resurrection, he asserts that Christ witnessed to baptism throughout his life, especially at his crucifixion: "Water is evident when he is given up to the cross (as Pilate's hands know); when he is wounded water gushes from his side (as the soldier's lance knows)."[3] Later, when Cyprian of Carthage specifies that any biblical reference to water is a prophetic testimony to bap-

---

1. Ign. *Eph*. 18.2.
2. Origen, *Comm. Rom*. 5.8; *Cels*. 2.69. See Buchinger, "Towards the Origins of Paschal Baptism." Buchinger here considers Origen's *Peri Pascha* and suggests that Origen's reference to paschal anointing with blood might be a baptismal reference.
3. Tertullian, *Bapt*. 9.4 (CCSL 1:284), trans. author.

tism, he says that Moses's striking the rock in the wilderness (Exod. 17:5–6) is a type of Christ at his crucifixion. Both the rock and the Savior were split open (a reference to the side wound Jesus received), and both blows brought forth water. To support this Cyprian quotes John 7:38, which itself claims prophetic authority: "As the Scripture says, 'out of his belly will flow streams of living water.'"[4] Thus, even though baptism's paschal dimensions were not fully developed in the early period, Christ's death and resurrection were never completely absent from the theology of baptism.

In the fourth century, just as Pauline theology generally became more prominent in Christian thought, the paschal significance of the baptismal ritual became central. Because of this, the paschal season became the preeminent time for baptism. Candidates were prepared in the period of the pre-paschal fast and initiated at the Easter vigil. The pilgrim, Egeria, remarks on their enrollment, formation, and baptism in Jerusalem during this season, which included seven weeks of catechesis and daily exorcism. After their baptism (during the week of Easter), she reports that the bishop explained the mysteries of baptism to the neophytes. These lessons took place within the shrine of the Anastasis, a venue that concretized the connection between Christ's resurrection and baptismal rebirth.[5]

Cyril of Jerusalem, the bishop who may have delivered these very lessons, stresses the paschal symbolism of baptism. He assures his hearers that while Jesus needed to die on the cross in order to slay sin, they had only to enter the font to destroy their former, sinful selves. They did not really die, nor were they actually buried. The action was figurative and symbolic, but the salvation was real.[6] In his second mystagogical lecture, Cyril draws attention to the ways that recipients imitate Christ's passion in the baptismal ritual. First, by entering the baptistery chamber and removing their clothing they replicate Christ's nakedness when he was on the cross.[7] Then, as they are led to the pool they enact Christ's being laid in the sepulcher. Finally, with each confession of faith and dunking in water, they symbolically share Christ's three days in the tomb. Cyril completes this idea with a quote from Ecclesiastes (3:2): "In that same moment you were dying and being born, and that saving water was at once your grave and your mother. What Solomon said in another context is applicable to you: 'A time for giving birth, a time for dying'; although for you it is a case of a 'time for dying and a time for being born.' One time brought both, and your death coincided with your birth."[8] Cyril, urging his listeners to meditate on the meaning of this, insists that baptism is

---

4. Cyprian, *Ep.* 63.8.3. This discussion takes place within an argument for the use of wine at the Eucharist. John's source is unclear but probably is a version of Isa. 44:3.

5. Egeria, *Itin.* 45–47.

6. Cyril of Jerusalem, *Cat.* 3.12; *Myst.* 3.5.

7. Cyril of Jerusalem, *Myst.* 2.1.

8. Cyril of Jerusalem, *Myst.* 2.4–5, slightly adapted by author.

more than the remission of sins, adoption, or receiving the gift of the Holy Spirit. It is all these things and more; it is the emulation of Christ's passion, as Paul proclaimed in Romans 6.[9]

Basil of Caesarea similarly urges the unbaptized among his flock to accept burial with Christ in baptism. Citing Romans 6, he insists that if they do not accept the burial, they cannot be raised with Christ.[10] In a treatise on the Holy Spirit, he reiterates this same idea but urges them to become like Christ in his death so that they might attain resurrection from the dead (here citing Phil. 3:10–11). Baptism, he asserts, is the manner of this death and burial that puts an end to the old life and inaugurates the new one. Bodies, he says, are buried in the water—the water becomes their temporary tomb.[11]

John Chrysostom likewise claims that the way Christians die, are buried, and resurrected with Christ is through their baptism. He declares that baptism is for the Christian what the cross and tomb are for Christ. Even though baptismal death and burial are not actually in the flesh (as was Christ's), it is a true death to sin and the old self.[12] Furthermore, Chrysostom extols the particular suitability of Easter as a baptismal time on two counts: first, because it is a season for celebrating victory over sin and death, and second, because it allows Christians to participate in the passion of Christ. To support this, he specifically quotes the passage in Romans: "St. Paul says 'He was crucified on the wood.' Be crucified yourself through your baptism. For, he says, baptism is a cross and a death."[13]

In another sermon, Chrysostom is even more explicit about the paschal and sacrificial associations of baptism. Asserting that baptism is a kind of cross, he remarks that even Christ used the terms interchangeably. This happened first when he said that he had a baptism to be baptized with (Luke 12:50) and again when he asked the sons of Zebedee whether they were prepared to be baptized with the baptism with which he would be baptized (Mark 10:38). Chrysostom assures his listeners, lest they be frightened, that baptism is not a bodily (physical) death but the death of sin that, as such, bears the likeness of death. By sharing death and burial with Christ in this symbolic way, the newly baptized also share in the outcome of Christ's passion (the resurrection). He concludes by declaring that baptism is simultaneously burial and resurrection.[14]

9. Cyril of Jerusalem, *Myst.* 2.6.

10. Basil of Caesarea, *Bapt.* 2.

11. Basil of Caesarea, *Spir. Sanct.* 15.35.

12. John Chrysostom, *Hom. Rom.* 10.4; 11.1. See also John Chrysostom, *Catech.* 10.8–11 (Pk. 2), cited below (which quotes Rom. 6 directly).

13. John Chrysostom, *Catech.* 10.7 (Pk. 2), trans. Harkins, *St. John Chrysostom*, 150.

14. John Chrysostom, *Catech.* 10.8–11 (Pk. 2). On the Mark text, see also Cyril of Jerusalem, *Cat.* 3.10. See also *Const. ap.* 7.22, 43, in which baptism is described as being crucified and buried with Christ in order to rise with him in adoption, being dead to sin and living in righteousness.

Chrysostom's homily on Romans 6 further elaborates the significance of the Romans passage for the baptized Christian and explains the difference between symbolic and literal participation. Again he insists that Christians do not actually suffer crucifixion, nor are they immediately resurrected after baptism. Although prebaptismal sins are buried in the font, remaining dead to sin after baptism is still the work of human effort. Just as Christ's body, buried in the earth for three days, brought forth the fruit of righteousness, so Christian bodies being buried in baptism (a likeness of Christ's death) bear the fruits of righteousness, sanctification, and adoption. This leads to their participation in a resurrection like Christ's, but one still in the future.[15]

Ambrose, Chrysostom's counterpart in Milan, also cites Romans 6 to proclaim that just as Christ tasted death, so also the candidates die, but that baptism is death to sin and not cessation of bodily life. This different kind of death is, in his terms, a "sacrament of the cross" (*sacramentum crucis*), which those being baptized receive as they are immersed. Ambrose describes the neophytes as fastened to Christ just as Christ was fastened to the cross, and he offers a prayer that Christ's nails should continue to hold them, lest the devil try to pull them back into human sinfulness.[16] Later he reminds the newly baptized that the seal they received after they emerged from the water was the sign of the cross, a mark that enabled them to emulate the life of the crucified one.[17] Ambrose also compares the baptismal font to the grave but stresses that this grave is of water rather than of earth; it is a means for a living person to die and yet become alive. By dying in the font, the candidate still serves the heavenly sentence imposed by sin (death). Yet this sentence includes both heavenly remedy and gift.[18]

Ambrose's contemporary in Rome, Ambrosiaster, correspondingly describes baptism as the way Christians appropriate the benefits of Christ's sacrificial death and the expectation of sharing his resurrection. He asserts that baptism kills sin and destroys death, which gives the recipient hope of rising again to new life. He also reasons that as the baptismal water washes dirt from the physical body, the invisible and incorporeal body is spiritually cleansed and renewed. Baptism, he concludes, is both the image and the pledge of resurrection.[19]

Another fourth-century catechist-bishop, Theodore of Mopsuestia, incorporates the Romans passage into his third baptismal homily and, after recounting the text, explains it to his audience: "Believing this we come to him for baptism, because we now wish to share in his death so as to share, like him, in the resurrection of the dead. So when I am baptized and put my head under the water, I

---

15. John Chrysostom, *Hom. Rom.* 11.5–6.

16. Ambrose, *Sacr.* 2.23 (SC 25:88).

17. Ambrose, *Sacr.* 6.7. See also Basil of Caesarea, *Spir. Sanct.* 15.

18. Ambrose, *Sacr.* 2.19 and 2.23. Additional associations of baptism with Christ's passion are in Augustine, *Serm.* 229A.1; and Paulinus of Nola, *Ep.* 23.18.

19. Ambrosiaster, *Comm. Rom.* 6.1–6.

wish to receive the death and burial of Christ our Lord, and I solemnly profess my faith in his resurrection when I come up out of the water—this is a sign that I believe that I am already risen."[20] Here Theodore offers one of the most convincing descriptions of baptism as a submersion of the candidates. Putting the head under water is the means of enacting death and burial.

Augustine, like the others, interprets Romans 6 so as to link Christ's crucifixion with the baptismal death of the old self, just as Christ's resurrection points to the baptismal rebirth. He adds that, while Christ bore no sin of his own, his death was a symbol of sin and a way to destroy sin's consequent mortality. Human sin, however, dies and is buried in baptism. Following Christ's actual death on the cross, real human sins—even those of infants—are washed away in baptism.[21] Thus the cleansing aspects of baptism are joined to the idea that on the cross Christ redeemed human sin. By figuratively dying in the font, the initiate receives the benefit of Christ's saving sacrifice and ensures that they will also one day be resurrected from death (the punishment for sin). Just as one death overthrew the grasp of Satan and the wages of sin (death), a second death will do the same and, like that first one, promises a future resurrection from the tomb.

Baptism as Rebirth in Early Christian Thought

The conversation between Jesus and Nicodemus in John 3 introduces the idea that a person must be "born anew" (or "born from above," *gennēthē anōthen*) in order to see the kingdom of God. Nicodemus, misunderstanding, asks how any person could be born a second time. Jesus does not exactly correct this misperception, but merely reiterates that those who are not born from water and Spirit cannot enter the kingdom.

This story had both symbolic and practical implications for early Christian baptism and, perhaps ironically, Nicodemus's literalism became accepted as a baptismal ideal from at least the mid-second century.[22] John 3:5 was cited by Justin Martyr, who describes how candidates for baptism were brought to a place of water for the purpose of what he terms their "regeneration" (*anagennēsis*), and he directly quotes the text: "Unless you be born again, you shall not enter the kingdom of heaven." Acknowledging Nicodemus's confusion, Justin adds that this is a spiritual rebirth, not another earthly birth from a human mother's womb. Earthly birth is of necessity and takes place in ignorance; the second spiritual birth is by choice and grants knowledge, which is why it is called "illumination."[23] Although Justin disparages earthly conception as the union

20. Theodore of Mopsuestia, *Bapt. hom.* 3.5, trans. Yarnold, *Awe-Inspiring Rites of Initiation*, 182–83.

21. Augustine, *C. Jul. op. imp.* 6.7.

22. See Jensen, "*Mater Ecclesia* and *Fons Aeterna*"; and Plumpe, *Mater Ecclesia*.

23. Justin Martyr, *1 Apol.* 61.

of fluid seed and maternal womb, he does not propose an alternative, "spiritual" mother figure. An alternative mother emerged very quickly, nevertheless.

In his refutation of the gnostic heresies (and their female mother figures), Irenaeus employs maternal imagery to describe both the church and Christ. The church becomes the repository of living waters, which are the "entrance to life." Those who are not within the church never approach the "shining fountain" that issues from Christ's body, nor do they receive the nourishment that comes from the mother's breasts. This true mother is a virgin, since her regenerative act is spiritual and not bodily, and she grieves for her lost children.[24]

In his *Treatise on Baptism*, Tertullian twice quotes John 3 directly: "Except a person be born again of water and of the Holy Spirit he cannot enter the Kingdom of heaven."[25] When he contrasts pagan lustrations with Christian baptism, he specifies the former as being performed with barren or "widowed" waters (*viduis aquis*), rather than water that has been both penetrated and inhabited (*et penetrare et insidere*) by the Holy Spirit.[26] Such barren water is more than useless. Because of its associations with idolatry and its deliberate use by the deceptive demon, it is actually death-dealing. The water of Christian baptism is generative amniotic fluid. At the end of his treatise, Tertullian describes the neophytes coming from the washing of new birth and gathering in their mother's house (*apud matrem*) to offer prayers to their common father.[27]

Cyprian, concerned more with schismatic than pagan baptisms in the middle of the third century, uses this symbolism as a way to contrast legitimate with illegitimate birth. Only children born from the true spouse/mother could inherit. Thus, Cyprian portrays the church simultaneously as fecund and nurturing as well as chaste and faithful. The church has only one home (*domus*) and one bedroom (*cubiculum*). Other mothers (e.g., rival Christian groups) thereby are rendered adulterous and their offspring illicit. "They cannot be heirs to the kingdom since one cannot have God for a father who does not have the [true] church for a mother."[28] Cyprian describes the church in metaphors that could have described a pagan earth goddess: "She spreads her branches in generous growth over all the earth, she extends her abundant streams ever further; yet one is the head-spring, one the source, one the mother who is prolific in her offspring, generation after generation. Of her womb we are born, of her milk we are fed, of her Spirit our souls draw their life-breath."[29] Being born, through baptism, to this mother brings spiritual benefit, nurture, and security. Once delivered from the womb, the newborn children are nourished,

---

24. Irenaeus, *Haer.* 3.4.1; 4.33.4, *ANF*, 1:415, 507.
25. Tertullian, *Bapt.* 12.1; 13.3.
26. Tertullian, *Bapt.* 4.1; 5.1.
27. Tertullian, *Bapt.* 20.5.
28. Cyprian, *Unit. eccl.* 6 (a famous line): "Habere iam non potest Deum patrem qui ecclesiam non habet matrem."
29. Cyprian, *Unit. eccl.* 5; cf. 19, 23 (CCSL 3:253), trans. author.

safe within the house of a loving father, and surrounded by siblings. As long as they remain within the walls of this home (the church), they are protected from the onslaughts of the evil one.

NICODEMUS AND MOTHER CHURCH IN FOURTH-CENTURY CHRISTIAN WRITINGS

In a sermon delivered on Epiphany, Gregory of Nyssa refers to the story of Nicodemus to argue that baptism not only purifies from sin but also brings about rebirth. Then he warns his listeners not to make Nicodemus's mistake in thinking that this rebirth would be visible or bodily: "For we shall not, according to the Jew Nicodemus and his somewhat dull intelligence, change the old person into a child, nor shall we form anew the one who is wrinkled and gray-headed to tenderness and youth by restoring that one to her mother's womb. But we do bring back, by royal grace, the one who bears the scars of sin, and has grown old in evil habits, to the innocence of the babe."[30] Urging the unbaptized to seize the opportunity to be renewed, he assures them that such royal grace brings them bounteous liberation from all penalties, just as the newborn child cannot be held accountable for or accused of any misdemeanors.

Theodore of Mopsuestia also found the Nicodemus story extremely useful in his instruction to catechumens. Explaining the consecration of the font as its spiritual fertilization, Theodore asserts that this is the way the font is made capable of being a womb for sacramental birth. Theodore explains that when Jesus told Nicodemus that he must be born of water and the Spirit, Jesus meant that while in a natural birth God's hand creates and forms the seed that the mother's womb receives, so too in spiritual birth "the one baptized settles in the water as in a kind of womb, like a seed showing no sign of an immortal nature; but once baptized and endowed with the divine grace of the Spirit, that one's nature is reshaped completely."[31]

Ambrose likewise invokes Nicodemus in the conclusion to his postbaptismal instruction of neophytes. He admonishes them to recognize that they have been born again, but not by entering their mothers' wombs a second time. Rather, he explains, the course of nature has been transformed by the excellence of grace. Thus conception is not always "natural" just as in the Virgin's conception of Christ: "If then, the Holy Spirit, coming down upon the Virgin, brought about conception and effected the benefit of generation, surely we should not doubt that the Spirit coming down upon the font, or upon those who receive baptism, consequently effects the reality of the new birth."[32]

Ambrose's comparing the conception of new Christians (by the Holy Spirit descending upon the water in the womb-like font) to the Virgin Mary's

---

30. Gregory of Nyssa, *Diem lum.*, NPNF², 5:519, slightly adapted by author.
31. Theodore of Mopsuestia, *Bapt. hom.* 3.9, trans. Yarnold, *Awe-Inspiring Rites of Initiation*, 186. See also *Bapt. hom.* 3.3–4.
32. Ambrose, *Myst.* 9.59 (SC 25:192), trans. author.

conception of Christ leads him to view the Virgin as the prototype of the church. As he elaborates his parallels, he draws on the long-standing claims that Mary was a virgin before, during, and after the birth of Jesus. Both mothers are ever-virgins, both bring forth their children without pain, and both remain physically intact during and after delivery.[33] In his treatise *On Virginity*, Ambrose extols the church as being "immaculate in intercourse" and "fertile in childbirth." She is also a "virgin in virtue of her chastity," and mother by virtue of having borne children. She gives birth without painfully breaking her hymen (*parit non cum dolore membrorum*). In a moment of contrast, he notes that the church nourishes her children, not by the milk of her body (*nutrit non corporis lacte*), but by the teaching of the apostles.[34]

Perhaps more than any of the other fourth-century writers, John Chrysostom emphasizes the fecundity of this mother more than her virginity. In one of his postbaptismal homilies, he tells the neophytes that they are the "joy of their mother" and describes the church's maternal happiness as she gathers her children around her. Likening her to a fertile field that produces a lush, spiritual (rather than earthly) crop, he offers these poetic words of praise: "Consider, my beloved, the excellence of her love. See how many children this spiritual mother has brought forth suddenly and in a single night! But we must not be surprised. Spiritual child-bearing is such that it needs neither time nor a period of months."[35] This elaboration of gendered, maternal imagery for the church demonstrates how willing these writers were to employ bodily—even sexual—analogies. They were not reticent to speak in graphic terms about the processes of impregnation and birth. In many of these discussions, these processes were their source metaphors; human procreative activity became the model for the heavenly coupling of Spirit and church.

Nevertheless, in a different context (a series of homilies on the Gospel of John), Chrysostom refers explicitly to Christ's admonishing Nicodemus to distinguish between that which is born from the flesh and that which is born from the Spirit (John 3:6). Chrysostom uses this Scripture passage as an opportunity to expand on the distinction between spiritual and fleshly childbirth and to downplay the role of Mother Church, replacing the mother with the water in the font: "There is no longer a mother, or pangs, or sleep, or coming together and embracings of bodies; henceforth all the fabric of our nature is framed above, of the Holy Spirit and water. The water is employed, being made the birth to the one who is born; what the womb is to the embryo, the water is to the believer."[36] In these lines, John regards the water as the source of rebirth

33. See the excellent study of Ofrasio, "The Baptismal Font."
34. Ambrose, *Virg.* 1.6.31.
35. John Chrysostom, *Catech.* 4.1 (Stav. 4), trans. Harkins, *St. John Chrysostom: Baptismal Instructions*, 66, slightly adapted by author.
36. John Chrysostom, *Hom. Jo.* 26.1, NPNF[1], 14:90, slightly adapted by author. Augustine's interpretation of the baptismal significance of the Nicodemus story focuses on the unrepeatability

as well as the base material for the new life, shaped and enlivened by the Holy Spirit. This imagery echoes the story of the first creation, which describes God breathing life into the nostrils of a mist-moistened creature (Gen. 2:7).

BIRTHING METAPHORS IN FOURTH-CENTURY SERMONS ON BAPTISM

Just as the fourth-century writers described the church as a mother with a watery womb (the font), the heavenly impregnation of that font by the invocation of the Holy Spirit, and the neophytes as newly born and innocent babies, they described the actual birthing process in terms of human labor and delivery.

Zeno of Verona is especially explicit in his description of baptism as a birthing process. In his *Invitations to the Font*, he portrays the font as inviting and warm. It was, he says, the sweet, milky womb of an ever-virgin mother.[37] He contrasts birth from this font with earthly birth, accompanied by groaning, travail, and sordid rags. Babies born into this world, he added, are nourished at filthy cradles. Babies born for the heavenly kingdom are joy-filled, nourished at fragrant altars, and their cries are sweet rather than bitter.[38]

Ephrem, the fourth-century Syrian hymnographer, also describes the church as a mother who, like Mary, gives birth without pain: "O womb that gives birth without pangs to the children of the kingdom!" He further compares the officiating priest to a midwife, who "ministers to this womb as it gives birth." Ephrem is more specific about the most appropriate food for the newborn babes. Referring to the first eucharistic meal after the neophytes emerge from the font, he says, "Once this womb has given birth, the altar suckles and nurtures them: her children eat straight away not milk, but perfect bread."[39]

In the Latin-speaking West, Augustine preached several sermons to both catechumens and the newly baptized in which he spoke about baptism in birthing terms. In one, addressed to candidates in the final week before their baptism, he explicates the Lord's Prayer. Taking up the opening address to God as "our Father," he tells his listeners that they are just beginning to have God for a father. They have been conceived from God's "seed" (*illius semine concepti estis*) and will be duly brought forth from the church's womb (*utero ecclesiae*), but for the moment they are still in the gestational stage.[40] In a different sermon, Augustine urges these gestating fetuses to take care lest they be miscarried. Citing Paul's Epistle to the Romans, he admonishes them to think of their mother (the church) as groaning in labor, striving to bring them forth into the light of faith (Rom. 8:22–23). He warns them not to agitate the maternal womb with their impatience to be born, lest they constrict the

---

of baptism—just as there is no repeating birth from the womb, there is no repeating of baptism: *Tract. Ev. Jo.* 11.6.

37. Zeno of Verona, *Tract.* 1.55.
38. Zeno of Verona, *Tract.* 1.32.
39. Ephrem, *Virg.* 7.7–8, trans. Brock, *Harp of the Spirit*, 49.
40. Augustine, *Serm.* 56.

birth canal (*viscera*).[41] Yet in another sermon, Augustine tells the candidates that they are called "petitioners" (*competentes*) because they are agitating in their mother's womb, begging to be born. Once delivered, they will be called *infantes*.[42]

Most of Augustine's sermons in Easter week were addressed to the newly baptized. In these he reminds them that, no matter how old they are, they are now newly born of God. He also identifies their heavenly mother's womb with the waters of baptism. Like Zeno (and in similar terms), Augustine contrasts their first (earthly) and second (spiritual) births. Their first was a birth of misery, initiated by mingling male and female bodies. Their second is the result of a union between God and the virginal church. Like most of his counterparts, Augustine was pessimistic about the possibility of remaining free of sin after baptism. This newborn innocence is only briefly restored in this world, and even after the second birth the struggle continues until death and final resurrection into the promised safe haven.[43]

Possibly because of their particular vulnerability as well as their fresh purity, in the first week after their Easter baptisms neophytes stood with the clergy in the chancel area of the church when they received the Eucharist, an area Augustine called their "cradle" (*cunabulum*). Referred to as "infants," they wore their baptismal robes for the full eight days, kept their heads veiled, and wore special sandals so that their feet should not come into contact with the earth.[44] At the end of the Easter octave, they received the final mark of their new status: they set aside their robes, veils, and special sandals and joined the rest of the congregation. Augustine compares them to fledgling sparrows preparing for their first flight from the nest, himself with the mother bird anxiously circling them, offering last-minute instructions.[45] In a burst of filial affection, he then exhorts them to pay frequent visits to the mother who bore them, to be ever grateful to her for all that she does, and to frequently come to her table for those spiritual meals she prepares, which nourish both bodies and souls. He urges that they "never desert such a mother" who devotedly nurtures and guides her worthy children "safe and free into eternal life."[46]

Augustine's fellow bishop and friend Paulinus of Nola also thought of baptism as a birthing from a spiritual mother's womb. In a poetic inscription written for the baptistery built by his friend Sulpicius Severus at Primuliacum, Paulinus compares the town's twin basilicas to the two breasts of the mother and the baptistery set between them to her womb. Noting that the priest will deliver newborn babies from the watery font, he writes:

41. Augustine, *Serm.* 216.7.
42. Augustine, *Serm.* 228.1.
43. See, e.g., Augustine, *Serm.* 353.2.
44. Augustine, *Serm.* 223.2; 121.4; 229P.4; 253.1; 376A.1; *Ep.* 55.19.35.
45. Augustine, *Serm.* 376A.1–2.
46. Augustine, *Serm.* 255A, trans. author, cf. *Misc. Agos.* 1.333.2–9.

This font begets souls in need of restoration;
it brings forth living water by divine light.
The Holy Spirit descends from heaven into this river
and marries the sacred water in the heavenly font.
The water receives God into itself, and by this fertile fluid
a consecrated progeny is brought forth from an eternal seed.
God's compassion is wonderful; the sinner is plunged into the flow
and soon emerges justified by the water.
Thus a person undergoes a blessed death and birth,
dying to earthly life and being born to everlasting life.
Guilt dies, but life returns; the old Adam perishes,
and the new one is born for the eternal kingdom.[47]

Typological Figures of Baptismal Rebirth

Although Jesus's own death and resurrection were the ultimate prototypes of Christian death and rebirth, many early Christian writers saw other biblical figures (or their stories) as figures of resurrection from death. These included Noah, Elijah, Enoch, Jonah, Daniel, the three youths in the fiery furnace, Ezekiel (raising the dry bones), Lazarus, Jairus's daughter, and the widow's son.[48]

Several of these Christian symbols or visual images point to the idea of rebirth or resurrection in baptism. Some figures, like Lazarus, are specifically mentioned in the surviving documents as baptismal types. Others not mentioned as baptismal types (e.g., Daniel and the man born blind) might be reasonably seen as baptismal symbols in light of certain attributes or characteristics they bear, such as their nudity (Daniel) or their diminutive size (the man born blind). Like the candidates preparing to enter the font, Daniel professes his allegiance to God and prepares for combat with the forces of evil. That he is rescued from death and freed from his tomb at daybreak contributes to his potential for signifying the (baptismal) rebirth. The man born blind symbolizes the sin-forgiven and healed, but also enlightened, neophyte.

Despite their symbolic associations with baptismal rebirth and their frequent appearance in funereal iconography (e.g., catacomb paintings and sarcophagus reliefs), Lazarus, Jonah, and Daniel rarely, if ever, appear in surviving decoration of early Christian baptisteries.[49] Instead, most extant baptisteries' iconographic schemes include images of fish, deer, or the shepherd with his flock.

47. Paulinus of Nola, *Ep.* 32.5 (CSEL 29:279–80), trans. author. Similar themes appear in the baptismal sermon of Pacian of Barcelona (*Bapt.*, PL 13:1989–1994), trans. Thomas P. Halton in Hamman, *Baptism*, 71.

48. See, e.g., the list in *Const. ap.* 5.7.

49. The exception is the Orthodox Baptistery in Ravenna, which includes stucco decoration that shows Jonah and Daniel.

These themes allude to the Christian community and often are surrounded by paradisiacal motifs (birds, flowers, fruit-bearing trees).[50]

Lazarus and Other Resurrected Figures

The raising of Lazarus from the dead (John 11:1–45) foreshadows the Easter narrative in many details. Stones seal tombs; women mourn; and the raised cast off their linen winding sheets. Early Christian writers saw these parallels and interpreted the raising of Lazarus as an assurance of bodily resurrection. The biblical story itself suggests this reading. Jesus tells Martha: "I am the resurrection and the life. Those who believe in me, even though they die, will live, and everyone who lives and believes in me will never die" (John 11:25–26).

For example, Irenaeus viewed Lazarus's raising as evidence that although the body decays after death, even decomposing flesh can be restored and glorified at God's command. Lazarus undoubtedly emerged from the tomb with the same body, or he could not have been the same person. To this analysis Irenaeus adds an extra idea: Jesus's command to the bystanders that they should unbind his friend signifies Lazarus's being released from the bondage of sin. While Irenaeus does not mention baptism in this context, he emphasizes the parallels between being released from death and being forgiven of sin. Each leads to resurrection, either here and now or in the future. The one who heals and raises the dead thereby offers a sign or a surety, so that his promise may be believed.[51]

Tertullian similarly sees Christ's restoring Lazarus's decaying flesh to wholeness as the preeminent sign and promise of bodily resurrection. In his treatise *On the Resurrection of the Flesh*, he acknowledges that Lazarus's soul was resurrected along with his body, but he insists (against those who would deny the resurrection of the flesh) that it was Lazarus's body that had decayed and not his soul. Thus, he contends, it is the physical or animate body that Paul declares is sown perishable and raised imperishable (1 Cor. 15:42–43).[52]

This interpretation continued into the fourth and fifth centuries. Ambrose and Augustine both also explored the allegorical possibilities of Lazarus's story. Reading the story as having a penitential application, Ambrose elaborates on the stench of Lazarus's dead body, explaining that it symbolizes the state of sin. As soon as forgiveness is granted, the foul odor disappears.[53] Augustine similarly draws out the moral implications of the narrative, seeing Lazarus's

---

50. See discussion, chap. 5, under the heading "The Jordan River, the Rivers of Paradise, and the Fountain."

51. Irenaeus, *Haer.* 5.13.1.

52. Tertullian, *Res.* 53.

53. Ambrose, *Paen.* 2.7.58.

Figure 4.1. Peter striking the rock, Peter being arrested, Jesus raising the dead, Jesus healing the blind man, multiplication of the loaves, Jesus entering Jerusalem. Sarcophagus, Museo Pio Cristiano, Vatican. Mid-fourth century. (Photo by author with permission from the Vatican Museum.)

tomb as a symbol of his alienation from God and the stone across its entrance as sin weighing on the human soul.[54]

Although he too sees the moral implications, Gregory of Nazianzus also explicitly perceives the baptismal symbolism in the Lazarus story. He admonishes the yet-unbaptized members of his congregation to listen, like Lazarus, to the voice telling them to come out of their tombs and to be released from the bindings of their sins.[55] Cyril of Jerusalem likewise makes a direct link between Lazarus's story and baptismal regeneration, comparing the newly baptized to Lazarus since they also had been raised from death.[56] Lazarus's tomb itself is a symbol for the old life, and his burial wrappings signify the bonds of sin that keep a person attached to death and the lifestyle that leads to it.

In his final pre-Easter catechetical lecture, Cyril delivered a long discourse on the resurrection of the body, referring to biblical figures who were raised from the dead: Elijah, the widow's son, the daughter of Jairus, and the saints coming from their tombs at Christ's death (Matt. 27:52–53; cf. fig. 1.7, 1.9, 4.1). He reminds his hearers that the apostles also brought the dead to life: Peter raised Tabitha, and Paul raised Eutychus. Cyril also notes the prototypes of Christ's raising the dead, especially Ezekiel, who opened the graves in the Valley of the Dry Bones (Ezek. 37).[57] This connection between Ezekiel and Christ appears in early Christian iconography. In these scenes Jesus, like Ezekiel, raises the dead, who often are depicted as childlike, nude figures (fig. 4.1). This scene may be based on Jesus's proclamation: "Just as the Father raises the dead and gives them life, so also the Son gives life to whomever he wishes" (John 5:21).

54. Augustine, *Tract. Ev. Jo.* 49.20–5.
55. Gregory of Nazianzus, *Or.* 40, 33.
56. Cyril of Jerusalem, *Cat.* 2.5; 5.9.
57. Cyril of Jerusalem, *Cat.* 18.1–21.

In most early Christian portrayals of Jesus raising Lazarus, Christ points toward the tomb, where a small, mummy-like figure stands in an aedicule-type tomb awaiting his instruction to "come forth" (figs. 4.2, 4.4). The composition of this scene in early Christian art is notably consistent. A popular image in fourth-century catacomb paintings and sarcophagus reliefs, as well as on gold glasses, fifth-century ivories, silver reliquaries, and liturgical boxes (pyxides), its figures include Jesus, Lazarus, and one or both sisters, with Mary often kneeling at Jesus's feet (cf. John 11:32). Sometimes one or more witnesses also appear.

In these images Jesus usually points at Lazarus with a staff. This detail has drawn much scholarly comment, since it appears that Christ wields this tool in order to perform the miracle of Lazarus's resuscitation.[58] Jesus also holds a staff in depictions of his working wonders (e.g., the miracle at Cana, the multiplication of loaves, or other resurrection scenes). It rarely appears in healing miracles, where he usually cures by the touch of his hand (e.g., the healing of the paralytic or the man born blind). Although some commentators have seen this as a device aligning Jesus with ancient wonder-workers or magicians, recent analysis has argued that Jesus is here depicted as a new Moses, who also performed miracles (e.g., the parting of the sea, bringing water from a rock) with a staff.[59]

In some presentations, an additional figure, a small, nude male child, also stands at Christ's feet (fig. 4.2). This figure is almost certainly meant to be the resurrected Lazarus, who is represented here as restored to the innocence of a young child. In this regard, he is a type of baptismal rebirth. Lazarus is nude, not only because he has lost his linen burial clothes but also because he has been reborn. In this respect he appears like Jesus, also shown as a small, nude child at his baptism in early Christian art (see figs. 1.1, 1.2, 1.7, 2.4, 3.8), or like Adam, newly created and about to receive God's blessing (fig. 4.3).[60] Thus, here Lazarus's representation recalls the newly baptized Christ and the newly-created Adam, as well as the resurrected ones in the Jesus-as-Ezekiel images.

Some compositions juxtapose Jesus's raising of Lazarus with Abraham's offering of Isaac. One exceptional example of this is a fifth-century ivory pyx (a box for the consecrated host) from Syria on which the Lazarus and Isaac scenes appear on opposite sides of the object. In this instance, Abraham's knife echoes Jesus's staff. Lazarus and Isaac are both small figures, and both could be seen to symbolize Christ, first, in his voluntary and sacrificial death (Isaac) and, second, at his resurrection (Lazarus).

---

58. See, e.g., Mathews, *Clash of the Gods*, 54–89; and Finney, "Do You Think God Is a Magician?"

59. Jefferson, "Image of Christ," PhD diss.

60. See discussion below, under the heading "Nudes and Small Figures in Early Christian Art."

Figure 4.2. Jesus raising Lazarus; arrest of Peter. Sarcophagus, Museo Pio Cristiano, Vatican. Mid-fourth century. (Photo by author with permission from the Vatican Museum.)

Jonah

The precedent for reading Jonah as a type of baptismal rebirth is derived from the New Testament words of Christ himself: Jesus refers to the "sign of the prophet Jonah" (Matt. 12:39–40) as a figure of the three days in which the

Figure 4.3. Detail of the Trinity creating Adam and Eve; Adam and Eve receiving the symbols of their labor. Sarcophagus, Museo Pio Cristiano, Vatican. Early fourth century. (Photo by author with permission from the Vatican Museum.)

Son of Man was in the tomb. Both Irenaeus and Tertullian regard the "sign of Jonah" as a reference both to Christ's resurrection and to the Christian's raising from death. Irenaeus, moreover, uses the story as a rebuttal to gnostic antimaterialism. If Jonah could be trapped in the sea creature's belly for three days and still be regurgitated whole, God certainly could raise dead bodies from their graves.[61] Likewise arguing for the reality of fleshly resurrection against those who would deny it, Tertullian compares Jonah's preservation to the three youths who remain untouched by the flames of the furnace. To these examples of incorruptible flesh, Tertullian adds the bodily ascents of Enoch and Elijah, who were exempted from physical decay.[62]

Because Jonah plunges into the water, then into the belly of the sea creature, and finally reemerges alive, his story would seem to be an obvious figure of Christian baptism. Nevertheless, this connection is rare in the surviving literature. Basil of Caesarea, however, notes the parallel. Basil sees Jonah's three days in the fish's belly as symbolizing the triple immersion of the neophyte and identifies Jonah's font with the belly of the sea creature.[63] This alignment of belly or womb and font is re-created in the baptistery. The place of burial is also the vessel of birth.

Scenes of Jonah being swallowed by the big fish, being spat out, and reclining on land were among the most popular images in early Christian art. Often presented in distinct, sequential episodes, especially in catacomb painting, Jonah vastly outnumbers most other biblical characters in pre-Constantinian funerary iconography.[64] One of the most effective renderings of this is on the so-called Jonah Sarcophagus in the Museo Pio Cristiano of the Vatican Museum (fig. 4.4). The sequence is also well represented on the sarcophagus of Sta. Maria Antiqua (fig. 1.1).

Jonah usually appears nude, a significant detail here. He is naked as he goes into the sea creature's mouth and naked as he comes out. Returned to dry land under his gourd vine, he does not stand heroically or even in a posture of prayer, but rather he reclines, a recumbent figure in a blissful state, much like the figure of Endymion on earlier Roman sarcophagi. Jonah's posture was likely based on Endymion's, whose pose suggests a state of sexual availability, which in Endymion's case is to the goddess Selene (the moon).[65] However, Jonah has no apparent consort, and his nude state may allude to the paradisiacal promise of a blissful afterlife. Like Adam's nudity before his fall,

61. Irenaeus, *Haer.* 5.5.2.
62. Tertullian, *Res.* 58.
63. Basil of Caesarea, *Spir. Sanct.* 14.32.
64. Jonah may almost equal the Good Shepherd in a number of early occurrences.
65. On the parallels between the figures of Jonah and Endymion, see Lawrence, "Three Pagan Themes in Christian Art."

Figure 4.4. Scenes from the story of Jonah, with Noah, and a fisherman; Moses striking the rock; Jesus raising Lazarus. Sarcophagus, Museo Pio Cristiano, Vatican. (Photo by author.)

Jonah's nudity suggests innocence, specifically an innocence restored through the sacrament of baptism.[66]

A well-known early Christian monument, the Jonah Sarcophagus (fig. 4.4), may be interpreted as thoroughly expressive of the idea of rebirth through baptism. This sarcophagus, usually dated to the late third century, was discovered in excavations of the cemetery beneath St. Peter's Basilica. The central images of Jonah being fed to the sea creature from the boat, being regurgitated, and then reclining on the shore are surrounded by scenes of Jesus's raising of Lazarus (upper left), Moses striking the rock for the thirsty Israelites (upper center), and Noah in his ark (lower center).[67] Fishing scenes frame the lower right and left, and a shepherd guards his flock in the upper right. At the top center is an image that has puzzled interpreters. Usually identified as the arrest of Peter, it might also be an image of Mary Magdalene and Mary (the mother of James and Joseph), and perhaps Salome, lying prone and grasping at the heels of the resurrected Christ (Matt. 28:9).[68] If this identification is correct, the other two figures could be two other disciples, perhaps Cleopas and the unnamed disciple who met the resurrected Jesus on the road to Emmaus (Luke 24:23–27).

The composition of another late third-century Christian sarcophagus, the sarcophagus of Sta. Maria Antiqua (fig. 1.1), includes an image of John baptizing Jesus and prominently features scenes from the Jonah story. The figures on this single-register, tub-shaped sarcophagus all appear to be floating on a stream of water running across the bottom of the frieze. On the left end (the curved section), a river god (in what was perhaps meant to be the Jordan) holds a trident scepter and reed, his jug spilling forth the water that

66. See Mathews, "La nudità nel cristianesimo."

67. These images are identified as baptismal types elsewhere in this study: Noah in chap. 1 under the heading "Noah and the Flood," and Moses striking the rock in chap. 5 under the heading "Water from the Rock."

68. This identification has been proposed by Fuchs in "Jonah Sarcophagus."

feeds the stream. From left to right the main front frieze depicts the usual Jonah episodes (Jonah is going in and out of the sea monster's mouth and reclining again on dry land). The center features a large standing orant and a seated reader (perhaps representing the deceased wife and husband). To the right of the reader a shepherd stands with his sheep. On his right John baptizes a nude, childlike Jesus, who stands up to his ankles in water. John's right hand rests on Jesus's head, and a dove flies, beak downward, just above John's right shoulder. The right curved end depicts fishermen casting their nets.

Their iconographic programs viewed as entireties, both sarcophagi (figs. 1.1, 4.4) could be read as allegories of rebirth through baptismal water. They feature individual scenes that early Christian theologians interpreted as signifying aspects of Christian initiation, including being part of the catch of fish, joining the shepherd's flock, being safely delivered from the flood (Noah), receiving water in the wilderness (Moses striking the rock), and being freed from the tomb (Lazarus). The prominence of Jonah on both suggests that this particular story belongs to the group as a figure both of baptism and of bodily resurrection.

The Phoenix

According to ancient legends, the fabled phoenix dies in a conflagration every five hundred years. Three days later it rises again from its own ashes. The earliest known version of the myth is found in Hesiod, but it also occurs in the writings of Herodotus, Ovid, Pliny the Elder, and Tacitus.[69] The symbolism of the three days preceding its renewal leads Christian commentators, namely, Clement of Rome, Tertullian, and Eusebius, to adopt the phoenix as a symbol of Christ's resurrection.[70] Others give additional significance to the symbol. In his discussion of the Holy Spirit, Gregory of Nazianzus offers the phoenix as an example of a creature that is self-consumed and self-generated, while Augustine interprets the phoenix as a symbol of the resurrection of the gendered human body.[71]

A poem attributed to the fourth-century writer Lactantius extolls the phoenix as desiring nothing more than to die in order to be reborn, an idea that echoes the theme of baptismal regeneration, although indirectly. By the blessing of death, the poem asserts, the great bird gains her eternal life: "Her only pleasure is in death: that she may be born, she desires previously to die. . . . She

---

69. Hesiod, *Frag.* 163.3–4; Herodotus, *Hist.* 2.73; Ovid, *Am.* 2.6.54 and *Metam.* 15.392–407; Pliny the Elder, *Nat.* 10.2.3–5; Tacitus, *Ann.* 6.8.

70. *1 Clem.* 25; Tertullian, *Res.* 13.3; Eusebius, *Vit. Const.* 4.72; Gregory of Nazianzus, *Or.* 31.10. See also Gregory of Nazianzus, *Carm. th.* 1.2.2; Ps. Ambrose, *Trin.* 34; and Maximus the Confessor, *Ep.* 13. For a general survey, see Broek, *Myth of the Phoenix.*

71. Augustine, *Nat. orig.* 4.20.33 (against Vicentius Victor, who claimed that the soul—like the phoenix—had no gender).

is herself indeed, but not the same, since she is herself, and not herself, having gained eternal life by the blessing of death."[72] Cyril of Jerusalem, however, makes an explicit connection between the phoenix and baptism in one of his catechetical lectures. He asks the candidates whether resurrection from the dead had been granted to this irrational creature, which did not even know Christ, then how much more would God do for those who confess their faith and are joined through baptism to the company of the faithful?[73]

In Christian art, the phoenix appears with some frequency. It can be seen just above the hand of God in the decoration of the Naples baptistery (fig. 2.2) and also occurs in compositions showing Christ giving the law to Peter and Paul (the phoenix perched in a palm tree, usually on the left), as well as in later Christian apse programs (e.g., in Rome's basilica of Ss. Cosmas and Damiano).

Daniel

The story of Daniel in the lions' den (Dan. 6:16–24) has no overt references to resurrection, or any associations with water. Most early Christian writers interpreted Daniel as a type of the Christian martyr or as a prophet who foretold the coming of Christ.[74] Cyril of Jerusalem's fifth catechetical lecture presents Daniel as a model of faith.[75] Nevertheless, Daniel's having been sealed in a cave to die and found alive the next morning implies bodily resurrection, if not necessarily baptism. Hippolytus's commentary on Daniel imagines the prophet's words when he emerged from the den—a speech that compares his rescue from the lions to fleshy resurrection: "But while I was in this position, I was strengthened beyond my hope. For one unseen touched me and immediately my weakness was removed and I was restored to my former strength. For whenever all the strength of our life and its glory pass from us, then are we strengthened by Christ, who stretches forth his hand and raises the living from among the dead as it were from Hades itself, to the resurrection of life."[76] Here Daniel's role as both martyr and survivor may be linked to the idea of the saints' immediate resurrection from death, a resurrection also guaranteed by their baptism of blood.

Images of Daniel, like Jonah, are extremely frequent in early Christian art, and again like Jonah, Daniel normally appears naked, especially on Roman sarcophagi and catacomb paintings, where he stands in the *orans* position

---

72. Lactantius, *Ave phoen.*, ANF, 7:326.

73. Cyril of Jerusalem, *Cat.* 18.8–9.

74. See, e.g., Justin Martyr, *Dial.* 31–2; Irenaeus, *Haer.* 3.21.7; Origen, *Cels.* 6.45 and *Mart.* 3.3; Tertullian, *Scorp.* 8.7; Cyprian, *Laps.* 19, 31; Jerome, *Comm. Dan.*; and Gregory of Nazianzus, *Or.* 43.74.

75. Cyril of Jerusalem, *Cat.* 5.4.

76. Hippolytus, *Comm. Dan.* 10.16, ANF, 5:190, slightly adapted by author.

Figure 4.5. Daniel with lions. Mosaic, Borj El Yahoudi, Tunisia. Now in the Bardo Museum, Tunis. Fourth century. (Photo by author.)

(his hands stretched out in prayer), a lion on either side (fig. 1.4). The motif also is found on mosaics, gold glasses, and African red slipware (fig. 4.5). Daniel's nudity may signal its function as a baptismal reference, since it cannot be explained by any detail in the narrative of his being cast into the lions' den.[77] His nakedness may symbolize his miraculous survival as a resurrection or rebirth and may even be an allusion to Christ's resurrection. According to the Gospels of Luke and John, Jesus left his linen shroud behind in the tomb (Luke 24:12 and John 20:5–6).

Nudes and Small Figures in Early Christian Art

Adam, Eve, Lazarus, Jonah, and Daniel all appear as nudes in early Christian art. Adam and Eve are shown as small nudes at their creation (fig. 4.3) and as adult-sized nudes at the fall (fig. 4.6). Jonah and Daniel are represented as adults, while the (nude) Lazarus and the (nude) resurrected dead in the scenes where Christ is in the guise of Ezekiel are all depicted as children (figs. 1.9, 4.1, 4.2). Other figures in early Christian art are depicted as proportionally smaller than others around them, although not necessarily naked (e.g., the healed paralytic and the man born blind, fig. 1.8). Most surprising, perhaps, Christ himself is shown as a small, nude child (or youth) in iconography that depicts his baptism by John the Baptist (figs. 1.1, 1.2, 1.7, 2.4, 3.8).

77. This is argued by J. Z. Smith, "Garments of Shame." Daniel appears clothed in some early Christian art, for example in mosaic pavements from North Africa and in the stucco decoration of the Neonian (Orthodox) Baptistery of Ravenna.

Daniel's nudity might have been derived from classical conventions of showing certain gods or heroes as nudes (e.g., Hercules, Dionysus, and Apollo).[78] These were idealized figures, intended to extol the beauty of the young male body, especially those of the youthful gods or demigods. Certain Roman emperors were also depicted as heroic nudes, their veristic portrait heads often incongruously attached to bodies that clearly belonged to younger, more physically beautiful individuals.[79] Such preference for showing a god, hero, or prince as an idealized nude might account for Daniel's nudity as he too is heroic. Yet other Old Testament heroes (e.g., Noah and Moses) are not depicted as nude and the patriarchs (e.g.,

Figure 4.6. Adam and Eve. Painting, Via Latina Catacomb, Rome. Fourth century. (Photo © Estelle Brettmann, The International Catacomb Society.)

Abraham, Isaac, and Jacob) are always modestly covered. Moreover, the newly created or resurrected nudes depicted on many early Christian sarcophagi clearly are not heroes.

Thus it appears that nudity in Christian art carries a specific theological meaning rather than necessarily indicating heroic status or qualities. As noted above, the nudity and the diminutive size of certain figures (e.g., Lazarus, the raised dead) signifies their resuscitation, thereby making them figures of baptismal renewal. They are saved from death, healed from infirmities, and restored to life. These are also the effects of baptism, which is, not coincidentally, administered to nude candidates. Neophytes are like these rescued biblical characters. They are also returned to the state of childlike innocence, a transformation symbolized by the depiction of small, childlike figures in Christian visual art.

The way that Christ's own baptism appears in early Christian art bears echoes of these themes: rebirth and restored childlike innocence. As noted earlier, most early images of baptism found in Roman catacomb paintings and on sarcophagus reliefs depict Christ as a child-sized nude (figs. 1.1, 1.2, 1.7, 2.4, 3.8). This presentation is striking, especially since the biblical stories

78. See, for example, Leclercq, "Nu dans l'art chrétien," 1783; Swift, *Roman Sources of Christian Art*, 54; and Weitzmann, *Age of Spirituality*, 413.

79. See the excellent survey by Hallett, *Roman Nude*.

of Jesus's baptism presume that he is an adult, about to embark on his public ministry (Luke 3:23 even suggests that he was about thirty years old), and they do not specify that Jesus was baptized nude. That Jesus should be shown as significantly smaller than the baptizer also seems odd. Although it is possible that these images were meant to depict the baptism of a Christian child, child baptism was still relatively unusual in the third and fourth centuries, except in emergencies.

Jesus's identification with the small baptizand is made obvious by elements in the composition, including the baptizer's dress (in many cases an animal skin, which helps to identify him as John the Baptist), the outdoor context (flowing water and rocky banks), and the descending dove. One resolution to the problem of the iconography is that it alludes to the regenerative aspect of baptism: the return to the status of an innocent child. Jesus's baptism was the prototype for the ritual. Ergo, the iconography presents even Christ's baptism as an instance of rebirth. It also reflects the ordinary practice of baptizing in the nude.[80]

Iconography depicting Christ as nude in his baptism continues well after he is shown as a fully mature adult, as in the mosaics of the Orthodox and Arian baptisteries in Ravenna (fig. 2.1). These representations demonstrate that baptismal nudity was required, for it is difficult to imagine candidates wearing clothes (or even simple undergarments) directly below an image of the immersion of their naked Savior.

Architectural and Liturgical Evocations of Baptism as Death and Rebirth

The design of early Christian baptisteries underscores the understanding of baptism as a move from death to rebirth. The transition from outdoor baptism to indoor facilities probably began in the early third century, although the oldest surviving example, the baptismal chamber in the house church at Dura Europos, was built in the 240s (fig. 3.6). The move indoors was possibly motivated by a desire to keep the rite relatively private (witnessed only by the initiates themselves, their sponsors, and officiants) and to protect the modesty of those who were being stripped, anointed, and dipped in the font while nude.

Yet while indoor facilities offered both privacy and propriety, their architecture and decoration also reflected and reinforced the ritual's meaning. In other words, the design and interior decor of these spaces were never merely practical. Many freestanding baptisteries were centralized and vaulted structures, often built as round or octagonal buildings (cf. fig. 4.8). From the outside they would have looked like mausolea or martyrs' shrines. In addition to the

80. See discussion below, under the heading "Stripping and Nude Immersion."

mausoleum-like appearance of some of the baptistery buildings, many fonts were made to look like tombs or crosses. In this way they evoked the paschal symbolism of baptism. Others were round or vulva-like, perhaps intended to signify the rebirth from the church's womb.

The Baptistery and Font as Tomb or Cross

Freestanding baptistery buildings, like many in Italy and Gaul, sometimes resembled mausolea. Round or octagonal, centralized, and vaulted buildings were commonly used for tombs as well as shrines.[81] Candidates who entered such buildings may have sensed that they were entering a tomb. The parallels are sometimes striking. Rome's mausoleum of Constanza was, for a long time, assumed to have been an early Christian baptistery. Another prominent example, the Anastasis rotunda attached to the complex at the Holy Sepulchre in Jerusalem, is the prototypical tomb shrine. Although it probably was never a site for baptism, it was the place where the newly baptized received their mystagogical instruction during the week of Easter.[82]

The model of the martyr's shrine is also pertinent, given the understanding of martyrdom as a baptism in blood.[83] In fact, baptisteries were occasionally converted into martyrs' shrines and vice versa. Furthermore, baptisteries were sometimes added to large cemetery churches and remote monasteries, probably to serve pilgrims rather than the local population.[84] The enormous octagonal baptistery built at the entrance to the complex at the shrine of St. Simeon Stylites in northeastern Syria is an example. Rome's preeminent Lateran basilica baptistery may even have been upstaged by the font at St. Peter's, given the attention paid to the value of being baptized where the first bishop of Rome could preside (from his sacred tomb).[85]

Many scholars have argued that the appearance of centralized mausolea had a special influence on the design of early Christian baptisteries.[86] The contrast between the longitudinal basilica structure, with its terminating apse, and the centralized plan of a freestanding baptistery must have been deliberate. Baptisteries, like shrines or tombs, were not places for regular congregational worship but were designed for a single, specific purpose. Both were, in a sense, shelters for a transitional ritual: one that moved from death to the afterlife.

81. See, e.g., Styger, "Nymphäaen, Mausoleen, Baptisterien"; Grabar, *Martyrium*; and Krautheimer, "Introduction to an Iconography."

82. Egeria, *Itin.* 45–47.

83. See discussion above, chap. 2, under the heading "Saints."

84. Baptisteries that were also shrines include Jucundus's at Sufetula and Albenga in Italy. See chap. 2, note 60. On this practice of transforming shrines, or on baptism at holy sites, see Jensen, "Baptismal Practices."

85. See the collection of baptistery inscriptions related to St. Peter's, collected and translated in Jensen, "Poetry of the Font."

86. See, e.g., Grabar, *Martyrium*; or Krautheimer, "Introduction to an Iconography."

Their centralized form gave focus to their single purpose, and the vault drew the eye heavenward.

Baptismal fonts, both those inside the freestanding structures as well as those in more simple, attached rooms, concretely reflected the teaching that baptism was a kind of death and burial. Ambrose explicitly describes the baptismal font as having the shape and appearance of a tomb.[87] Although Ambrose's own font in Milan was an octagonal pool, his description demonstrates that he conceived of the font as a kind of coffin. In fact, rare surviving fonts do look like coffins, including the oldest surviving one at Dura Europos, which has a rectangular tub large enough to accommodate a recumbent adult body. Moreover, this font is covered by an *arcosolium*, much like the burial places in certain Roman hypogea (fig. 3.6).

Far more surviving fonts were cruciform-shaped, a design clearly meant to reinforce the idea that baptism was a participation in Christ's passion. Cross-shaped fonts are well represented elsewhere in Africa as well as in the East, from the Balkans to the Levant, including Ephesus and Alahan in Turkey. One of the best examples, a sixth-century font from Bulla Regia in northwestern Tunisia, has a long and deep central axis joined by two slightly shallower arms (fig. 4.7). In order to enact the transition from death to life, candidates presumably would enter from the western (sunset) side and descend five steps into a deep well where they were immersed. They ascended again on the eastern (sunrise) side.

Hexagonal fonts may have been intended to allude to the sixth day of the week (the day on which Christ was crucified), just as octagonal fonts were designed to symbolize the eighth day, the day of new creation. One hexagonal font, in Grado (Italy), is housed within an octagonal building (fig. 4.8). Perhaps the initiate was reminded of Christ's death on entering the font and of his resurrection on emerging from it.

The Font as Mother's Womb

The inscription in the Lateran basilica baptistery echoes some of Paulinus's poetic language, composed for Severus's baptistery at Primuliacum.[88] It speaks of the heavenly people about to be born from a fertile seed in the font, specifying, "By a virginal birth, the Mother Church bears the children she conceives by God's breathing." As already noted,[89] this inscription, added to the baptistery in the mid-fifth century, is usually ascribed to Leo I, prior to his election as bishop of Rome (while he was still archdeacon). The similarities in language between the inscription and several of Leo's sermons tend to confirm this at-

---

87. Ambrose, *Sacr.* 3.1. Since Ambrose's own cathedral font was octagonal, this comment may refer to the shape of the baptistery building rather than the water basin.

88. Paulinus of Nola, *Ep.* 32.5.

89. See chap. 2, introduction.

Figure 4.7. Baptismal font, Bulla Regia, Tunisia. Fifth century. (Photo by author.)

Figure 4.8. Baptistery, Grado, Italy. Fifth century. (Photo by author.)

tribution. For example, in a Christmas sermon, Leo tells his congregation that they had all participated in Christ's birth through their baptism. He writes, "Each person partakes of this spiritual origin in regeneration, and to everyone reborn, the baptismal water is an image of a virginal womb, for the same Holy Spirit fills the font who filled the Virgin, so that the sin, nullified by that sacred conception, might be removed by this mystical washing."[90] In a homily on Christ's passion, he speaks of an "innumerable multitude of children," born to the unpolluted church, fertilized by the Holy Spirit, and brought to life in baptism.[91]

The Lateran's original font was likely circular and set into the center of an octagonal building.[92] The font's shape might have underscored the idea that the font was the mother's womb.[93] Historians have argued that round fonts were

90. Leo I, *Serm.* 24.3, trans. author.
91. Leo I, *Serm.* 63.6.
92. On the Lateran font, see Brandt, "Ipotesi sulla struttura."
93. For a good summary of the building and the variations in theories of architectural historians, see Brandenburg, *Ancient Churches of Rome*, 37–54.

Figure 4.9. Baptismal font, Mustis, Tunisia. (Photo by author.)

Figure 4.10. Baptismal font, Church of Vitalis, Sbeïtla, Tunisia. Sixth century. (Photo by author.)

intended to mimic the shape of the womb, citing the fourth-century round font at Naples (San Giovanni in Fonte) and the original font in the Orthodox Baptistery in Ravenna as well as the font in the Lateran.[94] Some North African fonts were round, including those at Tebessa, Tipasa, and Mustis (fig. 4.9).

Other ancient fonts, especially two nearly identical ones in the North African site of Sufetula (modern Sbeïtla), appear to have been designed to represent a woman's vulva (fig. 4.10). These fonts' undulating and elongated shape allowed for entrance at one (probably the western) end, passage through the water, and emergence on the other side. The round center well with its Christogram may have been intended to symbolize either the womb or the birth canal. The font water was not only a cleansing substance but also a symbol of the amniotic fluid in the mother's womb. The newly baptized emerged from this womb wet and naked, just like infants coming out of their mother's body. Like those newly born children, they were immediately wrapped (swaddled) in white garments.[95]

Ritual Actions Signifying Death and Rebirth

Documents specify a number of particular ritual actions that would have signified baptismal regeneration. One of these, the triple immersion in the water of the font, specifically refers to Christ's three days in the tomb, but it also refers to the three persons of the Holy Trinity, whose names were invoked in the creedal affirmation of candidates as they stood in the font. Christians also believed that Christ's three days in the tomb were signified by Jonah's three days in the belly of the sea creature. At the end of these days, of course, came the ritual rebirth. In addition to the triple immersion, baptism in the nude not only allowed the entire body to be cleansed, but, more important, it symbolized the physical state and vulnerability of newly born babies emerging from their mother's womb. The ritual of clothing neophytes with new white garments after they came up from the water signified both their freshly restored purity and the swaddling of an infant. For the next seven days these garments indicated their change of status from catechumen to neophyte. The old person had drowned in the font; the new person (newly clothed in Christ) was ready to begin a new life.

Triple Immersion

Although the triple immersion of candidates in the font was usually associated with the creedal confession of the Triune Deity, Cyril of Jerusalem

---

94. See Davies, *Architectural Setting of Baptism*, 21–22, for other examples, along with the argument that the shape is intended to symbolize a womb. Other useful works include Stauffer, *On Baptismal Fonts*, 19–22; and Bedard, *Symbolism of the Baptismal Font*, 17–36.

95. This image is implied in Theodore of Mopsuestia, *Bapt. hom.* 4.1, when he refers to wrapping babies with swaddling cloths.

also claims that the three immersions symbolize Christ's three days in the tomb: "For as our Savior passed three days and three nights in the bowels of the earth, so you by your first rising out of the water represented Christ's first day in the earth, and by your descent the night."[96] The action of dunking thus enacted death, and the font was the body's tomb. Ambrose makes a similar assertion, saying that each time a candidate was immersed, he or she was symbolically buried. He explains that this death was not the reality of bodily death but only its likeness: "When you are immersed, you receive the likeness of death and burial, you receive the sacrament of his cross."[97]

Gregory of Nyssa likewise understood triple immersion as a symbolic participation in Christ's three days of entombment as well as an expression of the orthodox faith in the Holy Trinity. In the following text he also compares water to earth. Both are elements of burial.

> And we, in receiving baptism, in imitation of our Lord and teacher and guide, are not indeed buried in the earth (for this is the shelter of the body that is entirely dead, covering the infirmity and decay of our nature), but coming to the element akin to earth, to water, we conceal ourselves in that as the Savior did in the earth: and by doing this three times we represent for ourselves that grace of the resurrection which was accomplished in three days. And this we do, not receiving the sacrament in silence, but while there are spoken over us the three names of the three sacred persons in whom we believe, in whom we hope, and from whom we derive both our present and future existence.[98]

Gregory instructs neophytes to imagine themselves being buried as they descend into the water. As the three divine names are called out over them, they are, like Lazarus, released from the tombs of their old lives to join those who are reborn in this world and promised resurrection in the next.

Basil of Caesarea enunciated a quite different explanation of the triple immersion. He cited the story of Elijah's competing with the prophets of Baal to kindle fire on the altar at Mount Carmel. When Baal's prophets failed, Elijah poured water on the wood three times, a figure of the Trinity. This, to Basil, prophetically indicated the number of times water could be poured on a candidate for baptism.[99]

However, triple immersion was not universally practiced. Romano-Spanish Christians practiced a single immersion in order to assert the identity of the triune deity in contrast to their Visigothic, Arian neighbors, who practiced triple immersion, presumably to indicate the distinction of the three persons of

---

96. Cyril of Jerusalem, *Myst.* 2.4–5, trans. McCauley and Stephenson, *Works of Saint Cyril of Jerusalem*, 2:164. See also Ps. Dionysius, *Ecc. hier.* 2.3.

97. Ambrose, *Sacr.* 2.20–23, trans. Yarnold, *Awe-Inspiring Rites of Initiation*, 118–19.

98. Gregory of Nyssa, *Diem lum.*, NPNF², 5:520, slightly adapted by author. This same idea appears in Leo I, *Ep.* 16.4.

99. Basil of Caesarea, *Bapt.* 2.

the Trinity. The Nicenes' peculiar custom of a threefold creedal interrogation followed by the administration of only one immersion was intended to express that the three distinct persons of the Trinity were yet united and equal within the Godhead. The seventh-century bishop of Toledo, Ildephonsus, defended this practice, although he also allowed that the threefold immersion was not improper, since it symbolized the three days of the Lord's burial.[100]

To explain how a single immersion might be thoroughly trinitarian, Ildephonsus focused on the steps into and out of the font. Based on the work of an earlier Spaniard, Isidore of Seville, Ildephonsus interprets the candidates' descending three steps into the font as signifying their triple renunciation of Satan, all his angels, and all his works. Then, having reached the fourth step (the basin where they are fully immersed), they have arrived on solid ground and (in one immersion) are released from all sins. Their three steps up and out of the font signify their triple confession of faith in the Father, the Son, and the Holy Spirit.[101]

Stripping and Nude Immersion

Both documents and artwork attest to the practice of candidates being baptized nude.[102] The pictorial presentation of Jesus as a small, nude figure at his baptism can be explained almost no other way, and as discussed previously, the nudity of Jonah, Daniel, and the resurrected dead in early Christian iconography may be based on the actual practice of nude baptism. Furthermore, the two mosaic depictions of Jesus's baptism in the fifth-century Orthodox and Arian baptisteries at Ravenna show Jesus as an adult male, being baptized completely nude (fig. 2.1). As noted above, it seems impossible to imagine depicting Jesus as baptized nude above candidates who were not similarly disrobed. This depiction of Jesus as nude at his baptism is traditional in Eastern icons into modern times.[103]

Among the theological ideas baptismal nudity expressed was the concept of regeneration, being born again by shedding an old life with its sins and earthly vanities. It also signified participation in Christ's nakedness at crucifixion.

---

100. Ildephonsus, *Ecc. off.* 2.25.4.

101. Ildephonsus, *Cognit.* 110; cf. Isidore of Seville, *Eccl. off.* 2.25.

102. This assertion has its critics. At least one author has argued that the Greek and Latin terms for "nude" (*gymnos* and *nudus*) need not have implied stark nakedness, but rather may have included the wearing of minimal undergarments or even a short tunic. See Guy, "'Naked' Baptism in the Early Church."

103. According to Leonid Ouspensky, the nudity of Jesus in these icons "emphasizes the kenosis of His Divinity" and "shows the purpose of his kenosis, for, by stripping His body, He thereby clothes the nakedness of Adam, and with him that of the whole of mankind, in the garment of glory and incorruptibility." See Ouspensky and Lossky, *Meaning of Icons*, 164–65. Orthodox Christians still baptize nude.

Finally it symbolized the nudity (and innocence) of the newly born child emerging from the womb.[104]

One of the earliest documentary witnesses to this is the *Acts of Xanthippe and Polyxena* (ca. 250), which describes Paul's baptism of Probus: "Paul replied, 'See, my son, the water is ready for the cleansing of those that come to Christ.' Straightway then, eagerly stripping off his clothes, Paul holding his hand, he leapt into the water."[105] Similarly, in the *Acts of Paul and Thecla*, Thecla, wearing only a girdle as she entered the arena, threw herself in a vat of water filled with seals in an act of self-baptism. Then, according to the text, the seals died from a lightning flash and floated to the surface, and a cloud of fire appeared to hide Thecla's nakedness.[106]

The *Apostolic Tradition* specifies that candidates disrobe and requires women to loosen their hair and lay aside any jewelry (gold ornaments), lest they enter the font with alien objects that might interpose between their bodies and the water.[107] Although undoing a complicated hairdo or removing hair ornaments might have symbolized candidates' rejection of feminine adornment and artifice as well as a rejection of worldly vanity (cf. 1 Tim. 2:9), the rule probably had more to do with full nudity than with humility.[108] This concern is reflected in regulations for Jewish purificatory baths (*mikvaoth*), which prohibit wearing anything (even a hairpin) into the bath. According to the rabbis, the water must touch all parts of the body.[109]

Other documentary sources indicate that in some areas of the ancient Christian world, female deacons attended women candidates and administered their prebaptismal anointings for modesty's sake (although male clerics still performed the baptisms and confirmations of nude women candidates).[110]

The assignment of such roles to deaconesses raises the general question of sexual impropriety, that is, whether candidates were sexually segregated once inside the baptistery. Several documents specifically refer to the matter, providing evidence that mixed-sex, nude baptism typically was not practiced.

104. A discussion of nudity as symbolizing the restoration of Adam and Eve in the garden of Eden follows in chap. 5, under the heading "Adam and Eve's Nudity as Symbolizing Innocence." On the symbol of nakedness, see also Riley, *Christian Initiation*, 159–89; Leclercq, "Nudité baptismale"; idem, "Nu dans l'art chrétien."

105. *Acts of Xanthippe and Polyxena* 21; see *Apoc. Anec.* 1.43–85.

106. *Acts of Paul* 34.

107. Hippolytus, *Trad. ap.* 21.3, 5, 11.

108. On the demonic associations of hair ornaments or complex hairstyles, see Werblowsky, "On the Baptismal Rite."

109. *M. Miqw.* 9. See also *b. Pesaḥ.* 107a: "Nothing must interpose between flesh and the water."

110. As noted above, Jewish proselyte immersion separated the sexes and even assigned a same-sex attendant to those undergoing the ritual bath required for conversion: *m. Miqw.* 9 and *Gerim* 60a 1.4 clearly require the separation of the sexes and the assignment of same-sex attendants. See also *b. Yebam.* 47a–b and *b. Pesaḥ.* 107a.

For example, in the section regarding appointing deaconesses to assist women candidates, the *Apostolic Constitutions* assigns a woman deacon to assist in order to avoid scandal.[111] The *Apostolic Tradition* also directs that children be baptized first, then men, and women last.[112] Cyril of Jerusalem required the catechumens to wait in sex-segregated groups for prebaptismal exorcisms, reminding them that the good principle of seeking salvation should not become an opportunity for spiritual ruin.[113]

Such concern for preserving modesty and purity in prebaptismal rites suggests that something similar might have been in place for the actual immersion in the font. In fact, a need to protect privacy was probably a major reason for the building of set-off or stand alone baptismal chambers. These rooms may have been equipped as well with curtained cubicles for disrobing and waiting. They also could have been places to keep the discarded clothing as well as providing storage for the fresh robes to be given to the neophytes.[114]

One of the primary symbolic values of baptismal nudity was the representative stripping off of an old identity and old habits. This removal of clothing was an expressive gesture of taking off the old self so that a new one could be put on. Augustine, using Pauline language (Col. 3:9–14), exhorted the candidates to strip off the old nature (the old dirty clothes) and be clothed with the new.[115] Theodore of Mopsuestia referred to clothing as "proof of mortality, convincing evidence of the humiliating sentence, which made humanity need clothes."[116] Thus baptism was a life transition, ritually enacted in the removal of clothes, which symbolized the general repudiation of worldly possessions.[117]

Cyril of Jerusalem likewise viewed baptism as a stripping of the former self, but he also saw it as a means to identify with Christ on the cross: "Immediately, then, upon entering [the baptistery], you removed your tunics. This was a figure of the 'stripping off of the old self and deeds' (Col. 3:9). Having stripped, you were naked, in this also imitating Christ, who was naked on the cross, and by his nakedness 'throwing off the cosmic powers and authorities like a garment and publicly upon the cross leading them in triumphal

---

111. *Const. ap.* 3.2.15. See also *Did. Apos.* 3.12 in regard to deaconesses.

112. Hippolytus, *Trad. ap.* 21.5.

113. Cyril of Jerusalem, *Procat.* 14, trans. McCauley and Stephenson, *Works of Saint Cyril of Jerusalem*, 1:80.

114. See discussion below, chap. 5, under the heading "Stripping and Re-robing in White Garments."

115. Augustine, *Serm.* 216.2 (PL 38–39, 1077), "Exuite vos veterem hominem, ut induamini novo." Theodore of Mopsuestia also specifies that the candidates should strip prior to the first anointing all over the body as a sign that they will be "receiving the cover of immortality" through their baptism, *Bapt. hom.* 3.26.

116. Theodore of Mopsuestia, *Bapt. hom.* 3.8, trans. Yarnold, *Awe-Inspiring Rites of Initiation*, 185.

117. Hippolytus, *Trad. ap.* 21.5. See J. Z. Smith, "Garments of Shame," 235–36.

procession.'"[118] Cyril concluded by offering a prayer that those who took off the "old garment" might never put it on again and, like the bride in the Song of Songs (5:3), ask, "I have put off my garment; how could I put it on again?"

Nakedness also suggests the innocence of the sacramentally reborn. Just like newborn babies, the neophytes emerged naked from the heavenly mother's womb, as they were at their first birth. Theodore of Mopsuestia noted that when candidates presented themselves for baptism "in order to be born again and become immortal in anticipation," they needed, first of all, to take off their clothes.[119]

Finally, nude baptism also signifies the body's vulnerability. In that regard, the font serves as a place of safety. Nakedness ordinarily signifies exposure to external and environmental dangers, yet the waters of the font are a shelter from those dangers. In his letter to Senarius, John the Deacon reports that the candidates are "instructed to approach the font naked to their feet, so that, having set aside garments of mortality and carnality, they might recognize that they are embarking upon a road upon which nothing is harsh or able to do them harm."[120]

Reclothing with White Garments

The symbolism of baptismal nudity is heightened by the significance of candidates being reclothed in white garments once they have emerged from the font. In an invitation to the font, Zeno of Verona juxtaposes these two states and urges candidates to enter the living water, which has been tempered by the presence of both the Holy Spirit and fire: "Already the girded bath keeper awaits you, ready to do the work of anointing and drying and furnish the gold denarius with the triple effigy. Be happy then, for you will plunge naked into the font but soon emerge thence, white [*candidati*] and vested in a heavenly garment. The one who does not pollute [this robe] will enter the kingdom of heaven."[121] Although clothes generally indicate modesty, in the baptismal context, white garments symbolized the restored purity of the soul and the body. Zeno's text promises that after plunging naked into the font and then being dried off, the neophytes will emerge vested in a heavenly white garment that must remain "unsoiled" for entrance into the kingdom of heaven.[122]

118. Cyril of Jerusalem, *Myst.* 2.2, trans. McCauley and Stephenson, *Works of Saint Cyril of Jerusalem*, 2:161.

119. This connection is explicitly made by Ambrose, *Psal.* 61.32; and Theodore of Mopsuestia, *Bapt. hom.* 3.9–10.

120. John the Deacon, *Ep. Sen.* 6, trans. author, cf. text in Wilmart, *Analecta reginensia*, 50, 174.

121. Zeno of Verona, *Tract.* 1.23 (CCSL 22:70), trans. author. Notice here that Zeno transforms certain details of an actual Roman bath (e.g., the payment of a fee) into a symbol of faith in the Holy Trinity.

122. Zeno of Verona, *Tract.* 1.23.

Before the fourth century, Christian initiates probably brought their own clean clothing for the postbaptismal rites. For instance, the *Apostolic Tradition* speaks only of neophytes putting on robes before being brought for the final anointing.[123] However, extant literary evidence reveals that the re-robing ceremony had become an important symbol by the mid-fourth century, with neophytes receiving identifying new white garments known as *albata*, or albs. Ambrose describes the angels' marveling at the neophytes approaching the altar in their gleaming white robes as if having become angels themselves.[124] He describes the joy the church will feel as it sees its family all clothed in white and seated around its table.[125] The purity of their garments not only indicates their innocence but also recalls Jesus at his transfiguration:

> After this you received white garments to indicate that you had exchanged your covering of sins for the chaste robe of innocence, of which the prophet said: "Sprinkle me with hyssop and I shall be clean; wash me and I will be whiter than snow" [Ps. 51:7]. For the one baptized is seen to have been cleansed both according to the law and according to the Gospel; according to the law, because Moses sprinkled the blood of a lamb with a bunch of hyssop [Exod. 12:22] and according to the Gospel because the garments of Jesus were white as snow, when in the Gospel he showed the glory of his resurrection [Matt. 17:2]. As the Lord said through Isaiah: "Even though your sins are scarlet, I will make them as white as snow" [Isa. 1:18].[126]

The robes appear throughout the fourth-century literature on baptism. Theodore of Mopsuestia calls the alb "a dazzling garment of pure white."[127] Cyril of Jerusalem compares it to a bridal garment (cf. Isa. 61:10) and admonishes the newly baptized to "go always in white," meaning that they should remember their baptism at all times and keep their souls shining and pure.[128] John Chrysostom describes the alb as a royal robe, bearing the insignia of Christ.[129] Other relevant Scriptures include the mention of white robes worn by the martyrs as they rested under the heavenly altar or stood before the throne of the Lamb (Rev. 6:11; 7:9) and the clothes of the 144,000 "spotless" virgins (Rev. 3:4–5; 14:4–5). According to John the Deacon, white was also the color

123. Hippolytus, *Trad. ap.* 21.20.

124. Ambrose, *Sacr.* 4.5–8.

125. Ambrose, *Sacr.* 5.14.

126. Ambrose, *Myst.* 7.34 (SC 25:174.34), trans. author. These white robes are not depicted in any extant early Christian depiction of baptism, probably because the traditional image shows only the moment of the naked candidate in the font.

127. Theodore of Mopsuestia, *Bapt. hom.* 3.26, trans. Yarnold, *Awe-Inspiring Rites of Initiation*, 197.

128. Cyril of Jerusalem, *Myst.* 4.8 (and compare Ephrem, *Epiph.* 6.18); Zeno of Verona, *Tract.* 1.23.

129. Cyril of Jerusalem, *Cat.* 3.1; idem, *Myst.* 2.2; John Chrysostom, *Catech.* 4.17 (Stav. 4).

of priestly vestments. John asserts that the neophyte's head was arrayed in white linen to recall the mystic vesture of priests.[130]

Augustine likewise sees the robes as signifying innocence and compares their color to the brightness of the neophytes' cleansed souls. Seeing the neophytes entering the church following their initiation, he urges them to "walk as children of light" (cf. Eph. 5:8).[131] Thus the alb as seen in some of the iconography reflects an important concluding aspect of a complete baptismal ritual. In Hippo, the candidates wore these robes, covered their heads with veils, and wore special sandals on their feet for the first week of Easter.[132] These garments externally displayed their restored purity and innocence.

Baptism at Easter

Despite the emphasis on the paschal aspects of baptism, surviving documents do not indicate that Easter baptism was widely practiced prior to the fourth century. Nevertheless, two key documents witness to Easter as a baptismal day in the late second or early third century. The first is Tertullian's identifying Passover (*pascha*) as the most solemn day (*diem sollemniorem*) for observing the rite. After this, he suggests Pentecost as an appropriate occasion. Tertullian justified Easter's superiority over all other days on two counts: because Christians are baptized into the Lord's passion (without directly quoting Rom. 6:4) and because Jesus's last Passover was a type of baptism (he had told the disciples that they would know the place for the feast when they met a man carrying water; Mark 14:13; Luke 22:10).[133]

The second testimony comes from Hippolytus's *Commentary on Daniel*, in which he, like Tertullian, says that Pascha is an especially auspicious day for baptism. He claims this without any direct reference to Christ's death or resurrection, however. This may have been because of context, since his point is related to the story of Susanna: "What is an opportune day but that of the Pasch? On that day the bath is prepared in the garden for those who are burning, and the church, washed like Susanna, is presented to God as a pure bride; and faith and charity, like her two companions, prepare the oil and the unguents for those being washed."[134]

Some scholars argue that the *Apostolic Tradition* implies Easter baptism because it refers to ceremonies of fasting, exorcism, and all-night vigils on Thursday, Friday, and Saturday. In fact, some translations simply identify these

130. John the Deacon, *Ep. Sen.* 6, where he also compares the albs to bridal garments; see also below, chap. 5, under the heading "Bridal Motifs in Baptismal Catecheses." On the symbolism of the priestly vestments, see also Jerome, *Ep.* 64 (to Fabiola, PL 22:607–22).

131. Augustine, *Serm.* 223.

132. Augustine, *Ep.* 55.19.35.

133. Tertullian, *Bapt.* 19.

134. Hippolytus, *Comm. Dan.* 13.15 (SC 14:100), trans. author.

days as the Thursday, Friday, and Saturday of Holy Week.[135] Nevertheless, as others have pointed out, in addition to the problems of dating this text (sections may reflect fourth-century practices), nothing in the document specifically speaks of paschal observances. Three ceremonial days as preparatory to baptism could be observed on any week in the liturgical calendar.[136]

Evidence for a post-Epiphany, penitential season of preparation of catechumens for what would be, presumably, an Easter initiation has been compiled by a number of scholars, although the timing of the actual rite is not absolutely certain.[137] Thus observance of baptism at Easter is only implied prior to the mid-fourth century, when it almost suddenly emerges as one of the two preeminent occasions (along with Pentecost) for baptism, at least in the West.

Cyril of Jerusalem's final prebaptismal catechetical lecture, delivered on the last day of Lent, speaks clearly of Easter as the day of the candidates' salvation.[138] Egeria's pilgrimage diary provides a vivid description of enrollment for Easter baptism in late fourth-century Jerusalem. Her description probably reflects the practice that Cyril would have known when he was presbyter and then bishop, beginning in 349 or 350. She reports that the names of those to be baptized at the coming Easter are taken down on the first day of Lent, and that during the forty days the bishop goes through the entire Bible, beginning with Genesis, explaining the literal and spiritual meaning of the Holy Scriptures for three hours each day. After five weeks, the candidates received the creed, and the bishop explained it article by article for the next two weeks. In the eighth week (Great Week), they had no more classes, due to the number of services they were required to attend. Instead, at the beginning of the week (Palm Sunday) the bishop asked each of them to repeat the creed and told them that they must wait until after their baptism for further instruction in the mysteries that could not be shared while they were still catechumens. When Easter arrived, the candidates were baptized and joined the congregation. Once the services were over on that day, the bishop commenced the mystagogical lessons in the shrine of the Anastasis.[139]

John Chrysostom wrote at length about the special meaning of baptism at the season of Easter. Explaining why other seasons and feasts had been passed over, he says that while the grace is not diminished at other times, Easter was most associated with the mystery of initiation because it is the commemoration of Christ's victory over sin, death, and the devil.[140] In his homily on Acts 1 (noted previously), John adds that while baptism at Pentecost would be as

135. See Dix, ed., *Treatise on the Apostolic Tradition*, 31–32.
136. Hippolytus, *Trad. ap.* 17.20–21; Bradshaw, "*Diem baptismo sollemniorem.*"
137. See Bradshaw, "Baptismal Practice in the Alexandrian Tradition"; Talley, "Origin of Lent at Alexandria"; idem, *Origins of the Liturgical Year*, 189–215.
138. Cyril of Jerusalem, *Cat.* 18.32–33.
139. Egeria, *Itin.* 47.1.
140. John Chrysostom, *Catech.* 10.5 (Pk. 2).

efficacious, the candidates themselves would be better prepared to receive the sacrament after their preparatory Lenten fast.[141] John's mention of the Lenten fast shows that this pre-paschal season had become well established as a time for the preparation of those seeking baptism. However, whether the prebaptismal fast led to the establishment of the Lenten discipline (or vice versa) is ambiguous.

Ambrose argues for Easter baptism at Milan for different reasons. Rather than emphasizing the connection between Christ's resurrection from the dead and the candidate's rebirth, he observes that just as the high priest entered the holy of holies in Jerusalem's temple only once a year, on Passover, so the bishop enters the baptistery only once a year, at Easter. Elucidating this idea, Ambrose cites Hebrews 9, which describes the inner tabernacle as containing the ark of the covenant, the golden altar of incense, a golden urn containing incense, and Aaron's rod. Like Aaron's rod, he says, the baptized were once dry and dead. When they received water (from the font), they burst into bloom and began to bring forth fruit. Like the table of incense, the neophytes, cleansed of sin, became the sweet fragrance of Christ.[142]

Augustine's many sermons preached to the neophytes during the octave of Easter testify to the prominence of Easter as a baptismal day. The eight days of the Easter octave were his preferred occasion for reminding the newly baptized that they had been born again, and, for that special time, he addressed them as infants. At the conclusion of the week, he reminded them of the paschal nature of the ritual—that like the Israelites they had been brought safely out of slavery in Egypt and delivered into the promised land.[143] He referred to this (the eighth day) as the moment of their spiritual (rather than fleshly) circumcision, when their mortality would be finally and fully stripped away.[144] He seemed, moreover, to know no other particular or special day for baptism, although he acknowledged that baptism was permissible on other days, presumably for those who were in danger of dying unbaptized.[145]

In the mid-fifth century, Leo I addressed a letter to the bishops of Sicily specifically recommending baptism at Easter or Pentecost and prohibiting it at Epiphany. His letter explicitly cites the Romans text, saying that it had come to his attention (from a reliable source) that the Sicilian bishops had been baptizing at Epiphany rather than on Easter, thus confusing or conflating the sacred meaning of the two feasts. Claiming the authority of the See of Peter, he insists that they should conform to Rome's practice and administer baptism on the day when Christ rose from the dead. Leo adds that baptism at Pentecost should be administered only to holdovers who were unable to receive baptism

141. John Chrysostom, *Hom. Act.* 1.
142. Ambrose, *Sacr.* 4.1–2.
143. Augustine, *Serm.* 260B.
144. Augustine, *Serm.* 260A.4.
145. Augustine, *Serm.* 210.2. Augustine's sermons on Pentecost make no mention of baptism.

at Easter because of illness or travel delays. He also recognizes Pentecost's suitability for baptism as it closes out the paschal season, occurs on the same weekday as the celebration of the Lord's resurrection, and commemorates the descent of the Holy Spirit. In these respects, he concludes, the two feasts are closely related, with Pentecost being based on the former and sharing certain themes. Like Tertullian and Augustine, however, Leo also allowed that any day was permissible in emergencies—for those in mortal danger or desperately ill.[146]

The idea of baptismal death and resurrection has many aspects. It is the way that Christians participate in Christ's death and thus share in his resurrection; it is also the reversal of the human condition of sin and its resulting mortality. In baptism, Christians die to their former selves and are born anew as blameless children, from a virginal mother who cannot transfer the stain of original sin. In this respect all baptized Christians are generated through the joining of the divine Spirit with the water in that mother's marvelously fecund womb. They go into the water as if into a tomb and emerge from it like newborn babies: naked, wet, and vulnerable. Yet they are also protected from the onslaught of demons by the sealing with the sign of the cross and the new garment, which not only represents their newly established innocence but also indicates their immortality (the white alb).

The renewal is a total transformation of the self. John Chrysostom assures his candidates with characteristic verve: "This bath does not merely cleanse the vessel but melts the whole thing down again."[147] Gregory of Nazianzus, however, joins the idea of Christ's incarnation, death, and resurrection to the three births of a Christian: the natural birth, the birth of baptism, and the final birth of rising from death. Elaborating the differences, he explains that the first birth was by night and compounded with passion, while the second is by day and brings about the destruction of passion. The third birth, he continues, will be more terrible than the first and shorter than the second. This birth sets humans directly before the throne of God to account for their faith and actions on earth. Christ himself went through all three births: born of a human mother, he was baptized; in his resurrection he became the firstborn from the dead (Col. 1:18). As he deigned to share humanity's lot, so he deigned to be acknowledged and raised up as a faithful, obedient, and beloved child.[148]

146. Leo I, *Ep.* 16.2–5. See also Maximus of Turin, *Serm.* 44.4—Easter is when pagans are usually baptized, while Pentecost was when the apostles were baptized with the Holy Spirit.

147. John Chrysostom, *Catech.* 9.21 (Montf. 1, Pk. 1), trans. Harkins, *St. John Chrysostom,* 138.

148. Gregory of Nazianzus, *Or.* 40.3.

This is why baptism at Easter was so profoundly meaningful. The candidates participated in a ritual of death and resurrection, dying and rising. In this act they not only imitated Christ's own journey through the passion, but they also entered into it and became joined to the body of the community that was constituted in and through the rite.

5

Baptism as the Beginning of the New Creation

T
he ritual of Christian baptism not only effects the cleansing, incorporation, enlightenment, and regeneration of an individual; it also has a cosmic significance and benefit that transcends person and place. It recalls the moment when all creation began and foreshadows the unending moment when all creation will be transformed for, at least temporarily, the newly baptized are returned to Eden, the gates are opened, and paradise is restored. According to early Christian teachings, in their earthly birth humans are in exile (having inherited the state or sentence of their fallen first parents). Even as catechumens, they are still on the outside gazing at a promised future. However, through their baptismal cleansing neophytes are returned to the prelapsarian status of Adam and Eve—without shame. Baptism joins them to Christ, the new Adam. This union promises that they will one day share his bodily resurrection, just as he shared their physical death (Rom. 6:5). Moreover, through each individual's baptism, the divine image, which is humanity's glory and given at birth, is drawn toward perfection.[1] Thus recipients of the sacrament are given a glimpse of their personal future and the restoration of creation itself—as this fallen world passes and mortality is overcome by immortality.

That baptism is an eschatological event is symbolized in physical space, enacted in ritual practice, and elaborated in theological reflection. Preeminent

1. Tertullian, *Bapt.* 5.7.

among core Scriptures that underlie this idea are certain passages from Paul's Epistles: in particular, the two letters to the Corinthians, where Paul refers to Christ as the last Adam, a man from heaven and a life-giving spirit (1 Cor. 15:45), and to the passing of the old world at the advent of the new creation (1 Cor. 15:51–57; 2 Cor. 5:17–19).

For example, Cyril of Jerusalem's first lecture to those about to be baptized evokes the sensual beauty of paradise and promises that those who undergo the ritual will share the experience: "Already, my dear candidates for enlightenment, scents of paradise are wafted towards you; already you are culling mystic blossoms for the weaving of heavenly garlands."[2] A few lines later he continues: "Then may the gate of paradise be opened to every man and every woman of you; then may you enjoy the fragrant Christ-bearing waters. Then may you receive Christ's name."[3] In his second catechetical lecture, Cyril asks them to attend to the story of Adam's disobedience. Rather than condemning him to death at once, God set Adam outside Eden so that he could see the place from which he had been banished and thus be saved by a desire to repent and return.[4] At the beginning of his mystical catecheses, he even places himself in the story: "Now I am to be your guide to the brighter and more fragrant meadows of this second Eden."[5]

Similarly, in a sermon for the Feast of Epiphany, the Cappadocian father Gregory of Nyssa exhorts those who had deferred baptism to run to the font. While now they are outside paradise with Adam and Eve, they should see the gate beginning to open, so that they can return. He warns them not to dawdle, lest death should intervene to prevent their reentry.[6] He concludes his sermon with a prayer:

> You, O Lord, are the font of eternal goodness, who justly turned away from us and in loving kindness had mercy upon us. You hated us and were reconciled, you cursed and blessed, you banished us from Paradise and then recalled us; you stripped off the fig leaves, an unseemly covering, and put a costly garment on us instead. You opened the prison and released the condemned. You sprinkled us with clean water, and cleansed us from our filthiness. No longer shall Adam be confounded when called by you, nor hide himself, convicted by his conscience, cowering in the thicket of Paradise. Nor shall the flaming sword encircle Paradise and make the entrance inaccessible to those who draw near, but all is turned to joy for us, the heirs of sin. Paradise, yea, even heaven itself may be trodden by

2. Cyril of Jerusalem, *Procat.* 1, trans. McCauley and Stephenson, *Works of Saint Cyril of Jerusalem*, 1:69.

3. Cyril of Jerusalem, *Procat.* 15, trans. McCauley and Stephenson, *Works of Saint Cyril of Jerusalem*, 1:81.

4. Cyril of Jerusalem, *Cat.* 2.7.

5. Cyril of Jerusalem, *Myst.* 1.1, trans. McCauley and Stephenson, *Works of Saint Cyril of Jerusalem*, 2:153.

6. Gregory of Nyssa, *Diem lum.* (PG 46:417D).

humanity, and the creation both in the world and above the world, that once was at variance with itself, is knit together in friendship and we join in the angels' song, offering praise to God.[7]

Thus, the font is not only a place of personal cleansing or site of regeneration; it is Eden's door. Those who enter the water cross a time-space threshold into a new world. When they emerge, they will continue to live in that new place. Even though they continue to live in the fallen world, they are spiritual residents of the future, restored creation.

The Creation, Fall, and Restoration of Adam and Eve in Baptismal Catecheses

The baptismal restoration of creation may allude to an even more primordial setting than the garden of Eden: many early writers saw the Spirit's initial hovering over the water (Gen. 1:2) as prefiguring baptism. Tertullian, in particular, understood this text to signify water's natural ability to acquire and transmit sanctification. In his treatise *On Baptism*, he argues that the Spirit first was supported on the primeval waters, and because it transferred its power to them, water henceforth has the special ability to convey—or conduct—holiness. In regard to the Spirit, water becomes absorbent without dilution.[8]

Other early exegetes stress the life-giving properties of water as they appear elsewhere in the creation story. For example, Ambrose emphasizes the fifth day, when God commanded the water to bring forth living creatures (Gen. 1:20). For him this is proof of water's essential fertility and its ability to produce life as well as sustain it.[9] Cyril of Jerusalem focuses on the creation of the human from mist-moistened earth, enlivened by God's breath (Gen. 2:6–7). However, as sin impaired this original breathing, another infusion is required: the one given by Christ to the apostles (John 20:22–23) and transmitted through the ritual in the initial exorcistic breathing or the postbaptismal gift of the Holy Spirit.[10] Thus the candidate, dipped in the font and sealed with the Holy Spirit, is a re-creation of the first human being, once again a recipient of the divine breathing (*spirante deo*), as it is called in the Lateran baptistery inscription.[11]

7. Gregory of Nyssa, *Diem lum.*, NPNF[2], 5:524, slightly adapted by author.

8. Tertullian, *Bapt.* 4.1–2. This same idea is found in the early fourth-century Alexandrian Didymus the Blind, *Trin.* 14 (PG 39:692C); and Ephrem, *Epiph.* 1.1; 6.10.

9. Ambrose, *Sacr.* 3.3.

10. Cyril of Jerusalem, *Cat.* 17.12; 18.13. See also Tertullian, *Bapt.* 5.7; and Didymus the Blind, *Trin.* 2.12. On the exorcistic breathing see chap. 1 under the heading "Exsufflation" (cf. Hippolytus, *Trad. ap.* 20; Cyril of Jerusalem, *Cat.* 16.19).

11. See introduction to chap. 2.

Adam and Eve's Nudity as Symbolizing Innocence

Because of the profound bodiliness of the ritual and its proclaimed benefits to the individual Christian, the Genesis account of Adam and Eve's fall was a crucial source for the early Christian theology of baptism. Ambrose pays special attention to the story of Adam and Eve in his reflection on baptismal transformation. He reminds his catechumens that humanity was originally created to be immortal but because of sin became subject to death and cast out of paradise. Nevertheless, God found a remedy that would not contradict the justice of the sentence (that humans must die) and yet allow humans to rise again. This was manifest in Christ's resurrection, which signified that the devil's deceit would not be the last word, and death's bonds were overcome. Because baptism is a person's participation in Christ's resurrection it signifies a new beginning for all creation: the end of sin and a victory over death itself. In the font, the attributed sentence, "You are dust and to dust you shall return," is served and Satan's hold on an individual is broken. As Ambrose points out, water is from earth. Going down into the font is thus going into a grave, a grave that also releases its hold on the one who descends into it.[12] Each person's release signifies the time when all will be released and when Satan finally is vanquished.

Both Cyril of Jerusalem and Theodore of Mopsuestia refer to Adam's and Eve's original innocence but give it different emphases. Each argues that the candidates' nudity as they enter the water signifies their about-to-be-restored innocence, as it recalls the first pair's original lack of shame. Nude baptism even allows candidates of both sexes, at least theoretically, to be together in the baptistery (cf. Gen. 2:25). For Cyril, the baptistery is like paradise—a place without bodily shame or consciousness of nakedness around the opposite sex. Cyril saw a return to Edenic innocence in the ritual of stripping.[13] Theodore of Mopsuestia's interpretation of baptismal nudity incorporates the rest of the story: even though Adam was created naked and unashamed, once he became mortal he needed a covering (Gen. 3:7–10). Clothing is nothing more than evidence of the fallen state of humanity. The act of baptism, however, begins to reverse the process and offers renewal of innocence and immortality, so nakedness is the sign and proof of this return.[14]

John Chrysostom, who compares the baptistery itself to paradise, elaborates this same idea:

> After the anointing, then, it remains to go into the bath of sacred waters. After stripping you of your robe, the priest himself leads you down into the flowing

12. Ambrose, *Sacr.* 4.17–19.

13. Cyril of Jerusalem, *Myst.* 2.2. See Leclercq, "Nudité baptismale"; and idem, "Nu dans l'art chrétien."

14. Theodore of Mopsuestia, *Bapt. hom.* 3.8.

waters. But why naked? He reminds you of your former nakedness, when you were in Paradise and you were not ashamed. For Holy Writ says: "Adam and Eve were naked and were not ashamed," until they took up the garment of sin, a garment heavy with abundant shame. Do not then feel shame here, for the bath is much better than the garden of Paradise. There can be no serpent here, but Christ is here initiating you into the regeneration that comes from the water and the Spirit. You cannot see here beautiful trees and fruits, but you can see spiritual favors.[15]

Gregory of Nyssa similarly explains the first parents' attempts to cover their nudity. Gregory identifies the garments of skin with the irrational passions and other attributes of human life after the fall (e.g., false pride, vain desires, deceit, hypocrisy),[16] while Adam and Eve's original nudity is, for him, the sign of their original innocence before they were tempted and pridefully disobeyed God's edict.

This same idea appears in the fifth-century writing of the Syrian poet and homilist Narsai. In a sermon for Epiphany, he describes the coming of the second Adam. Because the feast commemorated the baptism of Jesus and was an occasion for baptism, Narsai connects the old Adam with the one seeking the sacrament as a means for renewing the original (created) image. He writes:

> The image, which was tarnished with the filth of iniquity
> > because of (Adam's) [desire for fruit]
> > is the very one that the Spirit molded in the crucible of baptism.
> The lowly vessel of soft clay the Potter took
> > and remade it (into) a vessel that is useful for glorious things.
> The nature of Adam's clay the Creator took
> > and fashioned it in water and heated it in the Spirit; and it acquired
> > beauty.[17]

Genderlessness in the Resurrection

The paradisiacal innocence symbolized by nude baptism alludes to the lack of bodily shame, and might also indicate an original genderlessness. Some Christian exegetes believed that in the first creation, God made no distinction between male and female, and this lack of distinction would be restored in

---

15. John Chrysostom, *Catech.* 11.28–29 (Pk. 3), trans. Harkins, *St. John Chrysostom*, 170. See John Chrysostom *Hom. Gen.* 6 (PG 62:342). See also John Chrysostom, *Catech.* 2.24 (Stav. 2), where he speaks of the candidates stripping off their garments prior to the first anointing, and *Ep. Innoc.* 3, which recounts an attack on a church that caused women to flee in terror from a baptistery while they were still naked.

16. This is characteristic of Gregory of Nyssa's thinking generally, but see, e.g., *Hom. op.* 18.

17. Narsai, *Hom. Epiph.* 367–72, trans. McLeod, *Narsai's Metrical Homilies*, no. 182. Ephrem's hymns also refer to baptism as the renewal of Adam's image: *Virg.* 7.5 and *Epiph.* 1.1.

the new creation. A postbaptismal community that overcomes or neutralizes gender classifications—as well as other social categories—also might be one way to interpret the line in Paul's Epistle to the Galatians: "As many of you as were baptized into Christ have clothed yourselves with Christ. There is no longer Jew or Greek, there is no longer slave or free, there is no longer male or female; for all of you are one in Christ Jesus" (3:27–28).

Such erasure of gender differences occurs in some gnostic writing; for example, the Coptic *Gospel of Thomas* maintains that there will be no sexual distinction in the new creation: "The two are made one; the male and female are the same."[18] The *Gospel of Philip* appears to describe an original androgynous creation: the differentiation of the sexes took place when Eve separated from Adam. The coming of Christ repaired the brokenness of male and female, and their primordial unity was restored through a ritual marriage in the sacrament of the bridal chamber.[19]

Gregory of Nyssa, in his treatise *On the Making of Man*, speaks of the consummation of corporeal existence; he looks back to the creation and argues that Adam's formation, although in God's image, was not a full likeness, as it had a created nature that included an irrational (animal) element and that was biased toward evil. This is why, Gregory explains, God gave humans the capability of generation, not according to the inherent and lofty nature of creation (or as God brings things into being), but instead according to sexual procreation. Yet, Gregory continues, the time will come when the predetermined number of souls is complete. Then humanity will be changed from being earthly and corruptible (and necessarily gendered) into impassible and eternal. Since there will no longer be need for generation, the eternal world will be beyond sexual difference.[20]

Other authors stress the loss of socially identifying markers in baptism (e.g., social class, ethnicity), but genderlessness is not as prominent in their thinking.[21] Augustine, for example, considers paradise a place where sexual differentiation will continue without sexual desire. The distinctions of gender in that instance are not for utility (i.e., procreation) but for their beauty.[22] Nude baptism does not eliminate physical differences between men and women; it merely neutralizes their social and sexual power.

18. *Gos. Thom.* Log. 23. See discussion of the Galatians text and the implications for genderlessness in the new creation in Meeks, "Image of the Androgyne," esp. 180–81. For an example of a lack of shame even when publicly nude as an indication of being "dead to the world," see the story of Serapion in Palladius, *Hist. Laus.* 37, trans. Meyer, *Palladius*, 105–14.

19. *Gos. Phil.* 70, and see discussion below, under the heading "Bridal Motifs in Baptismal Catecheses."

20. Gregory of Nyssa, *Hom. op.* 22.4–5. See also Karras, "Sex/Gender in Gregory of Nyssa's Eschatology," 363–68.

21. See discussion above, chap 2, under the heading "Church as Mother and God as Father"; noting Cyril of Jerusalem, *Procat.* 12; Zeno of Verona, *Tract.* 1.24.

22. Augustine, *Civ.* 22.24.

Genesis Themes in Baptismal Iconography

Adam and Eve commonly appear in early Christian art: in Roman cata-comb paintings and sarcophagus reliefs (figs. 1.9, 4.3, 4.6). They also appear in mosaics, gems, ivories, gold glasses, redware bowls, and terra-cotta tiles. Yet, they are not often found in existing baptistery décor, with the exception of the baptistery at Dura Europos, where they occupy a prominent place, appearing on the lunette directly behind the apse (fig. 2.8). The two figures are comparatively small in respect to the depiction of the Good Shepherd with his flock, which fills most of the area above them. But the juxtaposition of the images is significant nevertheless. It expresses the journey of the one in the font from a shared state with those first humans after their expulsion from paradise to their safe return into the flock of the divine Shepherd. The reconstruction of the badly damaged wall painting shows the two as nude with the tree between them and the serpent on the ground below their feet. With one hand each grasps the trunk of the tree; with the other they try to cover their nakedness with leaves. Their nudity is a reminder that all candidates are like Adam or Eve, anticipating the renewal of their original image and the restoration of their innocence. However, the neophytes' nudity is a sign, not of their sin, but of their restored innocence. It also alludes to that future time when they will exchange their garments of skin for robes of glory.

Adam and Eve appear most frequently in extant early Christian funerary art: catacomb paintings and sarcophagus reliefs (figs. 4.3, 4.6). These images are not revealed to expectant neophytes; rather, they symbolize the baptized Christian's hope for a return to paradise in the next life. As in the Dura bap-tistery, the features of Adam and Eve are not meant to remind viewers only of their fallen state. Their appearance also alludes to both the remedy for that state (baptism) and that remedy's further promise (resurrection). The newly baptized is a restored being; one who anticipates an Edenic home in the hereafter. In this sense, Adam and Eve are not only reminders of sin and exile; they are also reassuring symbols of human potential, a visual affirma-tion of eschatological hope.

The inclusion of Adam and Eve at the Syrian city of Dura is consistent with the theology of baptism characteristic of its region and time.[23] One of the *Odes of Solomon*, a text that is more or less contemporaneous with the baptistery's decoration, defines baptism as being taken back to paradise, the land of eternal life, where blooming and fruit-bearing trees are irrigated by rivers of gladness.[24] A century later, the Syrian father Ephrem continues to reflect on baptism as the means to restore humanity from its postlapsarian sin-ful state. The themes he includes in a hymn written for the Feast of Epiphany would have well suited the iconography of Dura's font:

23. See Dirven, "Paradise Lost, Paradise Regained."
24. *Odes Sol.* 11.

The baptized who have come up from the water are sanctified,
those who went down into it have been cleansed;
those who have come up have been robed in praise,
those who went down have stripped off sin.
Adam stripped off his glory all of a sudden,
you have put on glory all of a sudden.
A house made of mud bricks, when it gets old,
can be renovated by using water;
Adam's body, made of muddy earth,
Grew old and was renovated by water.
The priests are like builders, you see,
Making your bodies new once again.[25]

Later Syrian writers, including those cited earlier (Theodore of Mopsuestia, John Chrysostom, and the fifth-century poet Narsai), similarly describe baptism as a renovation of humanity's original image and a return to paradise. Narsai's hymn for Epiphany (quoted above) echoes these themes in a metrical sermon, in which he speaks of the divine image as having been tarnished by sin but cleaned and refreshed in spiritual colors through baptism, with features redrawn and engraved on the tablet of the human body.[26]

The Jordan River, the Rivers of Paradise, and the Fountain

As discussed in chapter 1, the story of the Israelites' safe crossing of the Red Sea is a figure of the cleansing aspect of baptism.[27] To enter the promised land, however, the people had to follow Joshua across the Jordan River (Josh. 3:14–17). That river, ever after, became the metaphorical boundary between sin and salvation (i.e., death and resurrection). Its crossing came to symbolize a safe arrival in heaven. On the other side, milk and honey waited—items that, in antiquity, were offered to the newly baptized after they joined the community for their first Eucharist.[28]

Origen may have been the first to interpret this story as a baptismal type. He comments that priests carrying the ark of the covenant led the people across the river. When they began to cross, the water rose up and stood still to let them pass on dry ground. This prodigy, Origen explains, has a counterpart during baptism. Those who enter the font symbolically cross the Jordan, although theirs is an even better or more mystical crossing, although not on dry ground, but as if through air (cf. Paul's mystic ascent in 1 Thess. 4:17).[29]

25. Ephrem, *Epiph.* 6.9–10; Finn, *Early Christian Baptism*, 2:167–68.
26. Narsai, *Hom. Epiph.* 375–79.
27. See chap. 1, under the heading "The Red Sea Crossing."
28. See chap. 3, under the heading "Milk and Honey."
29. Origen, *Hom. Jos.* 4.1.

In his *Oration on the Baptism of Christ* (given on the Feast of Epiphany), Gregory of Nyssa also recalls the story of the children of Israel crossing the Jordan. He points out that they did not arrive at that place until they had wandered a long time and suffered much. He refers to Joshua as their guide and thus sees Joshua as the figure of his namesake, Jesus (Yeshua). The twelve stones that Joshua set up prefigured the twelve disciples, whom Gregory identifies as "ministers of baptism." A little further along in the treatise, after he has discussed Naaman's healing in the river, he describes the Jordan as uniquely bearing in itself the first fruits of sanctification and blessing, and through its type—the baptismal font—able to convey salvation to the whole world. Going on, he compares John the Baptist to Elijah, both of whom consecrated the Jordan for the purpose of regeneration.[30]

In a different oration, an exhortation to catechumens who have deferred their baptism, Gregory elaborates the same theme. Here he calls the Jordan the "river of grace." Unlike its earthly manifestation, the Jordan (River of Grace) does not simply rise in Palestine to disappear into the Dead Sea. Against the outward flow of Eden's four rivers (Gen. 2:10–14), which waft sweet aromas and fertilize the land outside the garden, the Jordan carries people, generated from the Holy Spirit, back into paradise. Gregory then urges that everyone should imitate Joshua and carry the gospel (as he carried the ark of the covenant) across the river. They should leave their wilderness behind and hasten to cross over to the promised land.[31] Thus just as the Jordan was compared with the four rivers flowing from Eden at the beginning of the Bible, the image of the Jordan was also likened to the river of life that is described in its finale. The book of Revelation states, "The angel showed me the river of the water of life, bright as crystal, flowing from the throne of God and of the Lamb through the middle of the street of the city. On either side of the river is the tree of life" (22:1–2).

The Jordan not only was the prototypical "river of life" but also a special witness to a divine epiphany. Ambrose notes that this river alone turns back upon itself, so that one who descends into it would be brought back to God, the source of all life.[32] For his part, Cyril of Jerusalem, explaining why water is the fundamental element of life, recalls that the world began with water and that the Jordan witnesses the beginning of the Gospels.[33] In modern times baptismal fonts are sometimes even called "Jordans," thus making a link between a believer's baptism and its archetype (the baptism of Jesus), but also allowing the river itself to be evoked as a witness to the ritual.

For these reasons, in early Christian imagery all baptismal waters—and all baptismal fonts—are symbolic Jordans. Each is a boundary between the

30. Gregory of Nyssa, *Diem lum.*
31. Gregory of Nyssa, *Bapt.* (PG 46 [420d]).
32. Ambrose, *Psal.* 61.32; see also Cyril of Jerusalem, *Myst.* 3.1.
33. Cyril of Jerusalem, *Cat.* 3.5.

Figure 5.1. Preaching of John the Baptist and baptism of Jesus. Ivory panel, Werden Casket, Milan. Now in the Victoria and Albert Museum, London. Early fifth century. (Photo by author with permission from the Victoria and Albert Museum.)

wilderness and the promised land. The Jordan often appears as a flowing stream along the base of early Christian apse mosaics (fig. 2.10), but it also turns up in a personified form, an anthropomorphic figure much like the river deities of classical art. This figure, either reclining on the bank and holding a jug (the source of the water, fig. 2.1) or (more often) partially submerged, represents the Jordan itself as a participant in, and witness to, Jesus's baptism by John (fig. 5.1). The two different types of Jordan (submerged and reclining) are clearly illustrated in the two famous baptisteries of Ravenna (the Orthodox and the Arian).[34]

Like the Jordan, the four rivers that flowed out of Eden (they are listed in Gen. 2: Pishon, Gihon, Tigris, and Euphrates) were also part of a popular motif in Christian iconography, appearing often as springing from a rock on which Christ or the Lamb stands (figs. 2.10, 5.2). Paulinus of Nola describes such a scene in the vault decoration of the basilica of Felix. The composition was intended to depict the Trinity. The Father was represented as a hand coming from the sky, the Holy Spirit as a dove, and Christ as a lamb standing on a rock that signified the church. Four fountains flow from this rock. These fountains represent the four evangelists: the living streams of Christ.[35] Although Paulinus does not name those rivers, an inscription found in Ostia, at the entrance to what may have been an early Christian baptistery, reads: "In Christ, take of the fountains of Christians: Geon, Fison, Tigris, and Euphrata."[36]

A visual depiction of deer coming to drink at a stream frequently decorated early Christian baptisteries (fig. 5.3). A typical composition showed two deer facing each other to drink from a pool, a large vase (*cantharus*), a fountain, or a stream. The image recalls the first line of Psalm 42: "As a deer longs

34. The figure still appears in most Orthodox icons of the baptism. On the personified Jordan in the images of baptism, see Jensen, "What Are Pagan River Gods Doing?"; Ristow, "Zur Personifikation des Jordans."

35. Paulinus of Nola, *Ep.* 32.10. Paulinus actually says that the Father is represented as a voice, which seems most likely to have been depicted visually as a hand.

36. See Calza, "Una basilica."

for flowing streams, so my soul longs for you, O God." The baptismal significance of these streams and fountains is evident from their inclusion in baptistery décor. For example, the line from Psalm 42 is inscribed in Latin on a mosaic pavement at the entrance to a sixth-century baptistery at Salona: SICUT CERVUS DESIDERAT AD FONTES AQUARUM ITA DESIDERAT ANIMA MEA AD TE DEUS.[37]

According to the *Liber Pontificalis*, Constantine presented the Lateran Baptistery with a sculptural version of this motif: seven silver stags were designed to pour water.[38] A similar gift, a marble deer that spouted water from its mouth, is recorded by the donor, a sixth-century Carthaginian grammarian, Calbulus, who recounts the words

Figure 5.2. Lamb on rock with four rivers. Sarcophagus (end view), Sant' Apollinare Nuovo, Ravenna. Fifth century. (Photo by author.)

said by the bishop as candidates entered the chamber, descended into the font, ascended, and then faced the bishop. Calbulus also includes a dedication, presumably intended to be inscribed on the circumference of the font, "Calbulus, in supplication, remembering the spring in which he was reborn, presents a beautiful thing of marble: the form of a deer whose mouth is the source of the water."[39]

Scenes of deer drinking at fountains usually include all kinds of blooming plants, vines, birds, and baskets of fruit. These images depict the delights of paradise awaiting those who have been reborn in the font.[40] For example, in addition to sea creatures, candles, and flowers, the sixth-century font at Kélibia (fig. 5.4) contains images of four fruit-bearing trees representing the four seasons: a date palm (spring), an olive (winter), a fig (summer),

37. On this baptistery, see Dyggve, *History of Salonitan Christianity*, 49–63; see also Davies, "Arian and Orthodox Baptisteries at Salona."

38. *Lib. Pont.* 34 (Sylvester).

39. *Ant. Lat.* 378, trans. author. Published in Buecheler and Riese, *Anthologia Latina*, 290–91, trans. author.

40. On the symbolism of the four rivers, see Bruyne, "La décoration des baptistères paléochrétiens"; and Stern, "Le décor des pavements." The four rivers appear in other contexts as well, especially in images of Jesus or the Lamb, standing on a rocky mound (from which the rivers flow), as in the apse mosaic of Rome's Basilica of Ss. Cosmas and Damian.

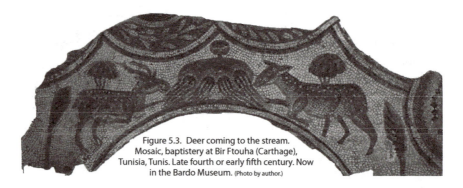

Figure 5.3. Deer coming to the stream.
Mosaic, baptistery at Bir Ftouha (Carthage),
Tunisia, Tunis. Late fourth or early fifth century. Now
in the Bardo Museum. (Photo by author.)

and an apple (autumn).[41] The Orthodox Baptistery at Ravenna is filled with
lush paradisiacal images such as vines and birds, flowers and trees. This
tradition presents Eden (or paradise) as a garden rather than a utopian city
bisected by a river of life (cf. Rev. 21–22). One of Cyprian's epistles has a
passage relevant to this kind of Edenic iconography: "The church is like
Paradise; within her walls she encloses on the inside fruit-bearing trees. Of
those trees, any which do not produce good fruit are cut out and cast onto
the fire. And those trees she waters by means of fours—that is by the four
Gospels; by them she generously spreads in a saving and heavenly flood the
graces of baptism."[42]

A similar text, showing the continuity of North African imagery, comes
from Augustine's *City of God*. In this work, Augustine acknowledges his
conscious use of allegory to describe paradise, in which all the fruit-bearing
plants represent pious habits; the trees, all useful knowledge; and the four
rivers, the cardinal virtues as well as the writings of the four evangelists:
"Paradise, most certainly, is the Church, as it is identified in the Canticle of
Canticles; the four rivers of Paradise are the four evangelists, the fruit trees
are the saints, and the fruits themselves are their good works. The tree of life
is the holy of holies, Christ himself."[43]

Thus, spaces for baptism were filled with images that reinforced the symbolism of paradise, perhaps in order to become an actual, physical re-creation
of that past and future home. The water of the font becomes the sacred river
that flows back to Eden, against the current of the other four rivers, which
bring thirst-quenching water (the story of salvation as contained in the four
Gospels) out to the world.

41. On the four trees as symbols of the four seasons, see Perler, "Die Taufsymbolik."
42. Cyprian, *Ep.* 73.10.3, trans. Clarke, *Letters of Cyprian*, 4:59. See also Cyprian, *Ep.* 69.2.1.
43. Augustine, *Civ.* 13.21.23–28 (CCSL 47:404), trans. author. See also Ambrose, *Myst.* 9.56,
which describes the fruit trees in the garden as dipping their roots into the water of the sacred
spring; or *Sacr.* 3.14, in which the newly baptized is a tree that had lost its sap but now has
recovered and will be fruitful.

Figure 5.4. Baptismal font from Kélibia. Now in the Bardo Museum, Tunis. Sixth century. (Photo by author.)

Water from the Rock

Early exegetes also read the story of Moses's striking the rock in the wilderness to cause it to gush forth water as a type of baptism (Exod. 17:1–7; Num. 20:2–13; cf. Isa. 48:21). This interpretation first occurs in Paul's First Epistle to the Corinthians, which says that the Israelites ("our ancestors") were baptized into Moses in the cloud and the sea, all eating the same spiritual food and drinking the same spiritual drink. The drink was from the rock that followed them, and that rock was Christ (1 Cor. 10:1–4). Paul's addition to the Exodus story (that the rock followed the Israelites through the wilderness) was drawn from a preexisting Jewish interpretation of the water-gushing rock as a messianic figure.[44]

Despite Paul's figurative interpretation, extant early Christian literature has very little evidence of the rock-striking narrative being widely interpreted as a baptismal type. The crossing of the Red Sea was far more popular as a symbol of baptismal cleansing.[45] Nevertheless, some early writers listed the rock-striking story with other types of baptism. These included Tertullian, who (like Paul) identifies Christ as the rock, and Cyprian, who cites the Isaiah passage (48:21) as pointing to Christ split open when the sword pierced his side.[46] Basil of Caesarea refers to Moses's rock-striking as the figurative baptism of Israel, when the people drank from the spiritual rock and ate the bread of angels (Ps. 78:25).[47]

44. See Murray, *Symbols of the Church and Kingdom*, 205–11.
45. See chap. 1, under the heading "The Red Sea Crossing."
46. Tertullian, *Bapt.* 9.3; Cyprian, *Ep.* 63.8.2. Other brief references to this passage as a baptismal figure are in Basil of Caesarea, *Bapt.* 2; Aphrahat, *Dem.* 12.8.
47. Basil of Caesarea, *Bapt.* 2; see also *Spir. Sanct.* 32–33.

Ambrose mentions the story of the rock several times in his catechetical or mystagogical lectures, but in each instance he cites it to explain why water is mixed with wine at the Eucharist. For example, in his fifth homily on the sacraments, he refers to the Exodus text, and, following Paul (1 Cor. 10:4), he explains that the rock that gushed water was not only Christ but also a "very mobile" rock that followed the people as they traveled. Exhorting his audience to drink so that Christ can follow them as well, Cyprian then joins this idea to a line of Jesus's dialogue with the Samaritan woman: "Consider this mystery. Moses, that is, as a prophet, touched the rock with his staff, that is, with the word of God; as a priest he touched the rock with the word of God, and water flowed forth, and the people of God drank. The priest, therefore, touches the chalice, water flows into the chalice, and it 'wells up to eternal life,' and the people of God who have received his grace drink from it."[48]

The image of Moses striking the rock with a staff to produce a spring of water for the thirsty Israelites occurred with moderate frequency in pre-Constantinian Christian iconography (cf. fig. 4.4). Despite a lack of decisive textual evidence, scholars have long assumed this scene to be a baptismal typology just as the image of the woman at the well was.[49] In the fourth century, however, the composition of the scene was radically transformed; rather than Moses, it showed the apostle Peter as the rock-striking, staff-wielding wonder-worker. Viewers may easily identify Peter from his unique portrait type (a low forehead, square jaw, short beard, and bushy hair) and from the common juxtaposition of scenes of his denial (designated by a rooster) and arrest. The Israelites reaching up to drink have become Roman soldiers, identified by their short military tunics, capes, and fur caps. This popular composition appears on catacomb walls, sarcophagus reliefs, gold leaf decoration on glass, and ivories (figs. 1.9, 5.5).

This transformation of the iconography to show Peter, rather than Moses, striking the rock has two possible explanations. First, it may reflect an anti-Jewish polemic. Moses was punished by God for his lack of trust (demonstrated when he struck the rock) and prevented from going with the Israelites into the promised land (Num. 20:12). By replacing Moses with Peter, the image suggests that God has preferred the apostle who leads a new Israel into the land of promise. Moses represents the "Old Law" that has passed away, and Peter the "New Law" that has replaced it. This explanation accounts for the images' Roman context, in the sphere of a church that revered Peter as its first bishop and one of its founding apostles. Since Peter's name literally means "rock" (Matt. 16:18), he is the obvious one to be charged to strike the rock

48. Ambrose, *Sacr.* 5.2, trans. Yarnold, *Awe-Inspiring Rites of Initiation*, 141. See also Ambrose, *Myst.* 8.48 and 8.51.

49. See, e.g., Becker, *Das Quellenwunder des Moses.*

Figure 5.5. Peter striking the rock, his arrest, and his denial of Christ. Sarchophagus, Museo Pio Cristiano, Vatican. Mid-fourth century. (Photo by author with the permission from the Vatican Museum.)

that is Christ (1 Cor. 10:4), and he also is charged to bring "living water" to the people.

A second explanation assumes an early form of a sixth-century narrative, in which Peter actually strikes a rock to produce a miraculous spring of water in order to baptize some converts to the faith. The extant narrative, a late insertion into the second-century *Acts of Peter* purportedly from the records of Pope Linus (d. 76), recounts the story of Peter baptizing his Roman guards, Proclus and Martinus, while he was in jail awaiting execution.[50] Although the surviving document is too late to be a direct source for the iconography, the legend could have circulated in an earlier textual or oral form. The juxtaposition of this scene of Peter striking the rock with scenes of Peter being arrested and restrained by two Roman soldiers (figs. 1.9, 5.5) makes this interpretation of the iconography particularly persuasive. Furthermore, the images of Moses striking the rock show only one (if any) Israelite receiving the water, whereas the images of Peter striking the rock consistently depict two Roman soldiers, apparently the same two also shown arresting Peter, stretching forth to drink from the fountain.

The Fountain as a Baptismal Figure

Baptisteries frequently were decorated with images of deer on either side of a brimming vase (*cantharus*) or a bubbling spring. The deer often appear within a lush garden setting, filled with all kinds of blooming plants, fruit-bearing trees, birds, and baskets of flowers. Sea creatures of every sort also appear in

50. On this document, see Nordström, "Water Miracles of Moses."

fonts and on surrounding pavements.[51] Carolingian illuminated Bibles with images of an enclosed fountain surrounded by columns and covered with a canopy are related to this rich Edenic imagery.[52] The enclosure represents the church; the fountain is the font. Such an image has a textual parallel in the Lateran Baptistery inscription (perhaps composed by Leo I and quoted above in chapter 4), which refers to the font as "the fountain of life that cleanses the whole world."[53]

Leo's inscription, however, goes on to identify the source of the fountain as the water that flowed with the blood from the wound of Christ (John 19:34) rather than the aboriginal Edenic stream. This idea is very characteristic of Leo's writing; for example, in his letter exhorting the Sicilian bishops to administer baptism at Easter, he reiterates the paschal dimension of the rite and observes that the water from Christ's wound signifies the water of baptism.[54] In another letter, Leo refers to the text of 1 John 5:6–8: "This is he that came by water and blood, Jesus Christ: not by water only, but by water and blood. . . . There are three that bear witness, the Spirit, the water, and the blood, and the three are one."[55] In a third letter, Leo explains that when Christ's side was pierced, the water that sprang forth intimated the water of baptism, while the blood was the cup shared in the eucharistic meal, thus uniting in one sign the mysteries of both regeneration and redemption.[56]

Receiving a shower from a baptismal fountain may have been an actual experience for some candidates in Milan. According to a short poem by Bishop Ennodius of Pavia (511–521), when Bishop Eustorgius rebuilt the baptistery of San Stefano, he equipped it with a marvelous water feature.[57] Apparently, a machine allowed water to fall into and fill the font from above, likely from the underside of a stone canopy. This simulation of rain may have been intended to suggest fresh, living water:

Behold, it rains without a cloud under the canopy,
a rain shower in a clear sky.

51. On fish in the decoration of baptisteries and fonts, see above, chap. 2, under the heading "Fish."

52. On the Carolingian iconography (and its earlier parallels), see Underwood, "Fountain of Life."

53. See translation of the entire inscription at the beginning of chap. 2.

54. Leo I, *Ep.* 16.6. See discussion of this letter, chap. 4, "Baptism at Easter." It is also clear in *Ep.* 28.5.

55. Leo I, *Ep.* 28.5, *NPNF²*, 12:42.

56. Leo I, *Ep.* 59.4. These texts may remind some readers of the nineteenth-century hymn by William Cowper, "There Is a Fountain Filled with Blood," or the gospel classic by Elisha Hoffman, "Are You Washed in the Blood (of the Lamb)?"

57. Ennodius, *Carm.* 2.149 (titled "On the Baptismal Font of St. Stephen and the Water Which Falls from Its Columns") (CSEL 6:607).

The clear face [form] of heaven provides the water;
flowing rivers run down over sacred marble blocks.
See again, see! The stone brings forth water.
Truly the dry canopy poured forth pure springs
and the celestial wave has come to renew birth.
Sacred water flows through the air from the vault
built while Eustorgius was bishop.[58]

The canopy mentioned here would not have been unusual in itself. Most ancient baptismal fonts were covered by ciboria, supported by four, six, or eight columns, although it is unlikely that many (if any others) had rain-making mechanisms.

The Samaritan Woman at the Well as a Baptismal Figure

In the story of the Samaritan woman at the well, Jesus asks a stranger for a drink and, in return, offers her "living water" (John 4:4–42). When she questions what he means, he answers: "Those who drink of the water that I will give them will never be thirsty. The water that I will give will become in them a spring of water gushing up to eternal life" (v. 14). This passage is echoed a few chapters later at the Feast of Tabernacles when Jesus stands up to proclaim: "Let anyone who is thirsty come to me, and let the one who believes in me drink. As the scripture has said: 'Out of the believer's heart shall flow rivers of living water'" (7:37–38).

This text has obvious baptismal significance, which was recognized by many early Christian writers. Among the earliest of these was Irenaeus, who compares baptism to making bread, with water from heaven to moisten the dough. In this description he also brings up the story of the Samaritan woman:

For as a compacted lump of dough cannot be formed of dry wheat without fluid matter, nor can a loaf possess unity, so in like manner neither could we, being many, be made one in Christ Jesus without the water from heaven, for our bodies have received unity among themselves by means of that laver which leads to incorruption; but our souls by means of the Spirit. Wherefore both are necessary, since both contribute toward the life of God. Our Lord showed compassion to that erring Samaritan women, who did not remain with one husband but committed fornication by contracting many marriages. He did so by pointing out and promising to her living water, so that she should thirst no

---

58. Trans. author: "En sine nube pluit sub tectis imbre sereno, Et cadi fades pura ministrat aquas. Proflua marmoribus decurrunt flumina sacris, Atque iterum rorem parturit ecce lapis. Arida nam liquidos effundit pergula fontes, Et rursus natis unda superna venit. Sancta per aetherios emanat limpha recessus, Eustorgi vatis ducta ministerio."

more, nor occupy herself in acquiring the refreshing water obtained by labor, having in herself water spring up to eternal life.[59]

The story appears most often as a straightforward baptismal typology. Tertullian simply includes it in his list of baptismal figures.[60] Cyprian defines Jesus's living water as baptismal water and associates it with the eucharistic cup, maintaining that while one never needs repeating (it is eternally thirst-quenching), the faithful constantly thirst for the other.[61] Elsewhere, Cyprian quotes the text from John 7 to refer to the church's pure, unsullied baptismal water (in contrast to schismatic or heretical sects): "The Lord proclaims that whoever thirsts should come and drink from the rivers of living water which flowed out of his belly."[62] Optatus of Milevis bids his audience to hear in the story what Christ has promised for the salvation of humanity.[63]

In his oration *On Baptism*, Gregory of Nazianzus draws this story into dialogue with a passage from Isaiah (55:1): "Ho, everyone who thirsts, come to the waters." In his sermon, Gregory explains that God's graciousness is so vast that desire for the water of baptism is all that is needed, that God deems the desire itself as the great price, that "he thirsts to be thirsted for; he gives drink to all who desire to drink; he takes it as a kindness to be asked for kindness; he is ready and liberal." Gregory then cites the Samaritan woman as an example for all Christians: "Blessed is the one from whom Christ asks a drink . . . and to whom he gives a 'fountain of water springing up to eternal life.'"[64]

Augustine offers a much fuller interpretation of the Samaritan woman's story as a type of coming to faith. In his *Homilies on the Gospel of John*, he takes up the story and, elaborating at length, argues that the well water signifies vain and worldly pleasures while Christ's thirst-quenching water represents spiritual nurture. Yet, he does not actually equate the water of life with baptism as such.[65]

The woman at the well appears in the iconographic decoration of two surviving baptisteries: one from the mid-third century at Dura Europos (fig. 5.6), the other from the baptistery of San Giovanni in Fonte in Naples (fig. 5.8). However, her identification in the Dura baptistery is somewhat controversial; according to some scholars she might be any number of biblical women who are associated with wells, including Mary at the annunciation, according to the apocryphal

59. Irenaeus, *Haer.* 3.17.2, ANF 1.444–45.

60. Tertullian, *Bapt.* 9.4. "When engaged in conversation he invites the thirsty to come to his eternal water."

61. Cyprian, *Ep.* 63.8.4.

62. Cyprian, *Ep.* 73.11 (CCSL 3C:541), trans. author.

63. Optatus of Milevis, *Parm.* 5.5.

64. Gregory of Nazianzus, *Or.* 27, trans. Harrison, *Festal Orations*, 123.

65. Augustine, *Tract Ev. Jo.* 15.5–31. See also Augustine, *Div. Quaest.* 64.

Protevangelium of James (11.1).[66] More-over, it is possible to see any (or all) biblical wells as an allusion to baptism. Gregory of Nyssa, for example, claims a number of wells from Scripture as types of baptism. Among these he lists Hagar's well, shown to her by an angel (Gen. 21:19).[67]

A similar list of wells appears in Je-rome's letter to a Roman nobleman named Oceanus regarding the remarriage of a bishop whose first marriage was contracted before he had been baptized. In this letter, Jerome emphasizes the life-altering efficacy of baptismal water and then offers a re-flection on the symbolism of water, gener-ally, in the Bible. He particularly notes the many times wells appear in sacred text, recalling that both Abraham and Isaac dug wells (Gen. 26:15, 18–19), both Rebekah and Rachel were discovered at wells (Gen. 24:15–16; 29:10–11), and at a well Jesus bid the Samaritan woman to quench her thirst with "living water."[68]

Figure 5.6. Woman at the well. Painting from the Dura Europos baptistery. Mid-third cen-tury. (Photo from Marsyas/Wikimedia Commons.)

Based on these many instances of women at wells in the Bible, interpret-ers might reasonably identify the Dura painting of a woman standing by a well as showing one of any number of biblical women who were associated with wells. Yet the frequency of the Samaritan woman elsewhere in early Christian art and her particular and explicit assocation with "living water" make her an appropriate—and likely—figure for the décor of this baptistery (e.g., fig. 5.7).

Supporting this identification is the Samaritan woman's appearance in the ceiling mosaic of the baptistery at Naples. Here she holds out a jug of water to Christ (whose figure is partially missing) (fig. 5.8). No doubt can be raised about her identity here; the Johannine narrative is clearly the source for the iconography, since the Cana miracle is juxtaposed with it. The double scene, in fact, emphasizes the sacramental significance of both stories, since the one (the Samaritan woman) should be understood as a baptismal reference, while the other (the Cana miracle) alludes to the Eucharist.

---

66. See discussion of this identity confusion in Serra, "Baptistery of Dura-Europos"; and Peppard, "New Testament Imagery."

67. Gregory of Nyssa, *Diem lum.*

68. Jerome, *Ep.* 69.6. See the parallels in Origen, *Hom. Gen.* 10.5, which may show the influence of Origen on Jerome.

Figure 5.7. Samaritan woman with Christ. Painting. Via Latina Catacomb, Rome. Fourth century. (Photo © Estelle Brettman, The International Catacomb Society.)

Most early Christian representations of the Samaritan woman depict the well in the center, between Jesus and the woman (cf. figs. 5.7 and 5.8). In one exception on the sixth-century ivory throne of Maximian in Ravenna, Jesus stands on the same side of the well as the woman and holds a cross, perhaps to indicate the source of his living water.

The common inclusion of the Samaritan woman in early Christian funerary art makes the same sense as the representations of Adam and Eve. The latter intimates the restoration of innocence, achieved in the ritual, while the former alludes to the promise of eternal life through the living water itself. Together they offer a summary of the economy of salvation: the fall, the state of sin, the grace of salvation, and the transcendence of death.

Bridal Motifs in Baptismal Catecheses

Early Christian writings on baptism are filled with nuptial symbolism. Among the Scriptures that inspired them, the Song of Songs was the most influential. Ambrose, for example, refers to the first communion of the neophytes by giving the bridegroom's words to Christ who, feeding his church with the sacrament of the Eucharist, says to her: "How comely are thy breasts, my sister, my spouse, how comely they are made by wine, and the smell of thy garments is above all spices."[69]

As here, when incorporated into baptismal lessons or homilies, the bride is not the church but an individual soul joined to Christ, the bridegroom. This draws on Paul's letter to the Christians in Corinth: "I promised you in marriage to one husband, to present you as a chaste virgin to Christ" (2 Cor. 11:2). Paul's comparison of the believer to a bride has a parallel in the Epistle to the Ephesians, which compares "the washing of water by the word" to the bride's prenuptial bath (5:26). In baptism, the bride's spiritual chastity is restored in the baptismal font; male or female, the newly baptized become a virginal bride.

Figure 5.8. Samaritan woman at the well; Cana miracle. Mosaic, Baptistery of Sta. Restituta, San Giovanni in Fonte, Naples. Late fourth century. (Photo by author.)

Another scriptural source is the hymn for the wedding of the Lamb in the book of Revelation: "For the marriage of the Lamb has come, and his bride has made herself ready; to her it has been granted to be clothed with fine linen, bright and pure" (19:7–8). The hymn closes with an instruction from the angel, in words that would become the invitation to the eucharistic table: "Blessed are those who are invited to the marriage supper of the Lamb" (19:9). This text provides a basis for describing the baptismal rite as a mystical marriage, although one that would produce spiritual (rather than earthly) progeny. Tertullian was one of the first to articulate this idea, although he saw the Holy Spirit as the bridegroom rather than the Lamb. In his treatise *On the Soul*, he explains that when the soul embraces the faith and is renewed through baptism, it is married to the Holy Spirit. The flesh, joined to the bride-soul, is wholly part of this nuptial union, which will be fully realized in the resurrection.[70]

The idea of baptism as a form of spiritual marriage is a common motif in apocryphal and gnostic documents. For example, the *Acts of Thomas* relates the baptism of Mygdonia, who deserts an earthly husband for Christ,

69. Ambrose, *Myst.* 9.55; see also 6.30; 7.35, 37–41; 9.35–41, 55–59. References to the Song are also found in Theodore of Mopsuestia, *Bapt. hom.* 2.8; and Cyril of Jerusalem, *Myst.* 2.2; *Cat.* 3.7.

70. Tertullian, *An.* 41.4. In *Res.* 63 he insists that the flesh is as much the bride of the Spirit as the soul, which is why they will rise together.

a "true husband."[71] After her baptism, she explains to her furious and griev-
ing (earthly) spouse:

> You have seen the wedding, which passed over, and remains here. This wedding
> remains in eternity. That communion was of destruction; this is of eternal life.
> Those groomsmen and bridesmaids are temporary men and women; but these
> now remain to the end. That wedding . . . passes away, but this remains forever.
> That bed was covered with mantles, but this with charity and faith. You are a
> bridegroom who passes away and are destroyed, but Jesus is the true bridegroom,
> remaining immortal in eternity. That bridal gift was treasures and garments that
> grow old; this, however, is living words, which never pass away.[72]

The *Gospel of Philip* actually refers to a ritual involving a bridal chamber.
This ceremony appears to be a completion of both baptism and postbaptismal anointing, and one of five rituals of the community (baptism, chrism,
Eucharist, redemption, and bridal chamber). The rite reunites the two sexes,
repairing their essential distinctions that are, according to this document,
the source of their mortality. Those who are united to the bridegroom in the
bridal chamber overcome death and gain eternal rest. This text describes the
neophytes' act of going down into the water (of baptism), not as descending
into death, but rather for receiving the Holy Spirit. In its final lines the *Gospel*
asserts, "If anyone becomes a son of the bridal chamber, he will receive the
light. If anyone does not receive it while he is in these places, he will not be
able to receive it in the other place."[73] Thus the baptismal font is the scene of
a divine marriage: not between the water and the Spirit (as Paulinus describes
it), or between the neophyte and the Spirit (as in Tertullian), but between the
neophyte and Christ.[74]

This imagery was very popular with the fourth-century catechists. Cyril
of Jerusalem opens his prebaptismal lectures by addressing his candidates as
brides. They have arrived at the threshold of the king's palace, where they will
celebrate their mystical marriage with sweet-scented garlands crowning their
heads. Even now, he says, they hold the nuptial candles in their hands.[75] Cyril
then reminds his listeners that the Gospels compare the kingdom of heaven
to a wedding banquet organized by a king for his son (Matt. 22:2). In this
story, one of the guests arrived inappropriately dressed and was thrown into

---

71. *Acts Thom.* 82–133. See discussion of this text in chap. 3 under the heading "Baptism
in the Acts of Thomas."

72. *Acts Thom.* 124, *ANT*, 495.

73. *Gos. Phil.*, 86, *NHL*, 151. See chap. 3, under the heading "Valentinian Baptism"; and
DeConick, "True Mysteries." See also the work of Pagoulatos, *Tracing the Bridegroom in Dura*,
which traces the evidence for an early Christian marriage ritual in the *Acts of Thomas*, the
Gospel of Philip, and the *Symposium* of Methodius of Olympus.

74. Paulinus of Nola, *Ep.* 32.5.

75. Cyril of Jerusalem, *Procat.* 1.

the outer darkness. Cyril, identifying the appropriate wedding garb as a white robe, explains that it is the symbol of purity. He warns the catechumens that they need to take care that Jesus, the bridegroom, not see them in their sullied garments. They should go home, visit the laundry, and then return wearing the right clothes for the occasion: their bright gowns of chastity. He assures them that the forty-day Lenten fast is their advance notice of the bridegroom's arrival, so they have plenty of time to get dressed and ready. Then, on the eve of the wedding itself (i.e., the night before their baptism), he tells them that they must put aside other concerns and be entirely focused on preparations for the marriage feast.[76] In a different lecture, Cyril promises his candidates that when they come to baptism, they will be like the brides at the wedding feast (cf. Matt. 22:9, 10). The king will bring them to his chambers and they will exult and rejoice in love for him (cf. Song 1:3). He then quotes Isaiah 61:10: "He has clothed me with the garments of salvation, he has covered me with the robe of righteousness, as a bridegroom decks himself with a garland, and as a bride adorns herself with jewels."[77]

Similarly, two Cappadocians, Gregory of Nazianzus and Gregory of Nyssa, employ bridal and wedding metaphors in their exhortations to catechumens. Gregory of Nazianzus assures his audience that when they come from the font and stand before the altar platform in the church (*bēma*), they will experience a foretaste of future glory. The psalms that they will hear there are a prelude to the heavenly hymns; the lights that they carry are like the ones they will bring when they go, with virginal souls, to meet the bridegroom. He urges them to be like the wise maidens who came prepared with enough oil to keep their lamps burning while they awaited that bridegroom (Matt. 25:1–13). He admonishes them to be alert and not distracted when the bridegroom arrives, to avoid missing the wedding altogether (Luke 14:16–24). Finally, he exhorts them to be dressed in proper attire (Matt. 22:11–13).[78]

Gregory of Nyssa concludes his sermon on Epiphany with a hymn of joy based on Isaiah 41: "Let my soul be joyful in the Lord; for he has clothed me with a garment of salvation and has put upon me a robe of gladness: as on a bridegroom he has set a mitre upon me, and as a bride he has adorned me with fair array. And truly, the adorner of the bride is Christ, who is, and was, and shall be, blessed now and forever more."[79]

Among other fourth-century catechetical sermons, those of John Chrysostom are perhaps the most richly illustrated with wedding imagery. Chrysostom calls baptism a "spiritual marriage" and a "great mystery." He compares it

---

76. Cyril of Jerusalem, *Procat.* 3–4, 6. On the white baptismal garments, see chap. 4, under the heading "Reclothing with White Garments."

77. Cyril of Jerusalem, *Cat.* 3.2.

78. Gregory of Nazianzus, *Or.* 46. Basil of Caesarea also cites the story of the wise and foolish maidens, *Bapt.* 7.

79. Gregory of Nyssa, *Diem lum.*

to earthly marriage, which, he insists, can be true only if the bride leaves her past life behind and gives herself entirely—body and soul—to her husband so that they might become one flesh (Gen. 2:24; Eph. 5:31). He also claims that a worldly bridegroom would never accept a bride who lacked beauty and wealth. In this, the spiritual marriage of baptism, however, the bridegroom overlooks the fact that the bride is ugly or poor and, despite her flaws, hurries to save her and raise her up. All the bridegroom asks is that the bride forget her past and commit herself to the future. No mortal man, Chrysostom insists, would ever do this much for his bride: to pour out his own blood for her in order to sanctify and cleanse her by the bath of baptism. He does this so that he might present her to himself as gloriously spotless and worthy.[80]

In another lesson, Chrysostom revisits this theme and reiterates that baptism is a ritual that amounts to a spiritual marriage. He exhorts his hearers to keep their nuptial robes spotless, and he compares the traditional seven-day bridal feast to the octave of baptism. Each day the newlyweds arrive at the table (the Eucharist). The seven days also mystically signify the gradual perfection of the espoused: "And why do I say seven days? If you are willing to live soberly and to keep vigilant, this banquet is prolonged for you through all time, provided you keep your bridal robe inviolate and intact. For in this way you will draw the bridegroom to a fuller love and you yourselves will shine forth with increasing radiance and luster as time goes on, because grace increases more and more with the good deeds we do."[81]

The Wise and Foolish Virgins

At the conclusion of his preparatory lectures, Chrysostom gives his candidates their final warning and cites the parable of the wise and foolish virgins (Matt. 25:1–13): "I have come as the last to tell you that after two days the bridegroom is coming. Arise, kindle your lamps, and by their shining light receive the King of Heaven. Arise and keep watch. For not during the day but in the middle of the night the bridegroom comes to you. This is the custom for the bridal procession—to give over the brides to their bridegrooms late in the evening."[82] Chrysostom finally reminds them of another bridal custom that is mirrored in baptism. Whereas in the world the bride goes to the house of the bridegroom, in baptism the bridegroom comes to the bride. The vast differences in their rank or wealth do not matter. Suddenly a beggar or an outcast is transformed into a queen, and beaming with indescribable beauty, she is worthy to stand beside the king.[83]

80. John Chrysostom, *Catech.* 1.11–17 (Stav. 1).
81. John Chrysostom, *Catech.* 6.23–24 (Stav. 6), trans. Harkins, *St. John Chrysostom*, 102–3.
82. John Chrysostom, *Catech.* 11.1 (Pk. 3), trans. Harkins, *St. John Chrysostom*, 161.
83. John Chrysostom, *Catech.* 11.1–10 (Pk. 3).

A visual representation of the parable of the wise and foolish virgins arguably appears in one prominent baptismal context, the Dura Europos baptistery. The dominant image shows several women approaching a building (or tent) with a gabled roof that has two comets, one at its right and another at its left side (fig. 3.6). This scene appears on the northern wall, just before it joins the font area on the west. Thus it is sited directly around the corner from the font. Only two of the figures are still fully visible, although the left arm and part of the torso of a third are evident. They wear veils and white garments, carry torches in their right hands, and hold some kind of vessel in their left hands. Trace remains of other figures suggest that the three visible figures were joined by two others, and perhaps even five additional women to form two groups of five.

Many historians have identified these three figures as the three women coming to Jesus's tomb on Easter morning (cf. Mark 16:1–2).[84] Their vessels might be unguent bowls, containing spices for anointing the body, and the torches could be used to light their way in the predawn darkness. The comets may have symbolized the resurrection that had taken place in the night.[85] However, other scholars have identified these women as a party of five and, thus, as the five wise maidens who come to the tent of the bridegroom (Matt. 25:1–13), rather than as the three mourning women arriving at Jesus's tomb.[86] This alternative identification is strengthened by the extant remains of five pairs of female feet on the adjacent eastern wall, perhaps belonging to the group of foolish maidens. In this case, the three women's torches should be read, instead, as burning lamps and their vessels as supplies of extra oil. As noted above, this story of the wise and foolish brides was sometimes elaborated as a figure of baptism, with the maidens as symbols of steadfast candidates coming to meet Christ, their bridegroom. The solution to the problem of identification may be unanswerable. Yet both possibilities—that the scene alludes to Christ's resurrection (and therefore the general promise of resurrection given in baptism) or that it illustrates the parable of the five maidens—are appropriate for a baptismal chamber.

84. See chap. 3, under the heading "Candles, Torches, and Fire."

85. The comets may be compared with the comet that appeared at the games to honor Julius Caesar after his death. See Suetonius, *Jul.* 88; Plutarch, *Caes.* 69.3; Pliny the Elder, *Nat.* 2.93.

86. Kraeling is the most frequently cited interpreter of the image as one of the three women coming to the tomb; see his "Christian Building." But that group also includes Grabar, "La fresque des saintes femmes." Those who argue that the image is of the five wise maidens include Pijoan, "Parable of the Virgins," and—more recently—Mathews, *Clash of the Gods*, 153; Serra, "Baptistery at Dura-Europos," who argues that this is a scene of the annunciation to Mary at the well, based on the *Protoevangelium of James*; Peppard, "New Testament Imagery"; Pagoulatos, *Tracing the Bridegroom in Dura*; and Dieter Korol, *Neues zu den alt- und neutestamentlichen Darstellungen im Baptisterium Von Dura-Europos.* See also Wharton, *Refiguring the Post-Classical City*, 53–54; and Cartlidge and Elliott, *Art and the Christian Apocrypha*, 36, who argue that the image depicts virgins escorting Mary to the temple.

The Wedding at Cana

The story of Jesus arriving at a marriage feast and turning water into wine is the first miracle in the Gospel of John and a key, initial event of Christ's epiphany: "Jesus did this, the first of his signs, in Cana of Galilee, and revealed his glory; and his disciples believed in him" (John 2:11). Most early Christian writers saw this story as having eucharistic, rather than baptismal, symbolism. For example, Irenaeus claims that Mary had urged her son to perform the miracle because she desired to drink from the emblematic cup.[87] Cyprian, referring to the mixing of wine and water in the eucharistic cup, interprets the water as representing God's people and the wine the blood of Christ. Once intermingled the wine and water cannot be separated. This symbolizes the marriage bond between Christ and his church and, for Cyprian, explains why Jesus chose a wedding for this demonstration.[88]

Cyril of Jerusalem's mystagogical (postbaptismal) lecture on the Eucharist is unequivocal. The Cana miracle prefigures the Eucharist: "Once, at Cana in Galilee, he changed water into wine by his sovereign will. Is it not credible, then, that he changed wine into blood? If as a guest at an earthly marriage, he performed this stupendous miracle, shall he not far more readily have bestowed on his friends (the friends of the true bridegroom) the fruit of his own body?"[89] Tertullian, however, includes the Cana miracle in a list of figures of baptism, and Jerome argues the sacred properties of water for baptism, because Jesus made it the matter of his first miracle.[90]

By the late fourth century, much of the Christian world celebrated three different events on the Feast of Epiphany: the arrival of the magi, the baptism of Christ, and the miracle at the Cana wedding.[91] Although this complicated feast developed partly in order to coordinate different dates for the celebration of Christ's nativity, the triple commemoration was a liturgical assertion of the different ways Christ was manifest, first to the gentile magi, then at his baptism, and finally at the wedding where he performed his first sign. In those regions where Epiphany was also a baptismal day, the story of the Cana miracle could not have been far from peoples' minds. In a sermon for the Feast of the Epiphany, Peter Chrysologus comments on the overlapping significance of the three events:

This, brothers and sisters, is the feast, which was conceived on different occasions and bore three characteristic signs of the Divinity. Through the Epiphany

87. Irenaeus, *Haer.* 3.16.7.

88. Cyprian, *Ep.* 63.12.2–13.3.

89. Cyril of Jerusalem, *Myst.* 4.2, trans. McCauley and Stephenson, *Works of Saint Cyril of Jerusalem*, 2:181.

90. Tertullian, *Bapt.* 9; Jerome, *Ep.* 69.9.

91. The parallel traditions of the Feast of the Nativity and the Feast of Epiphany are too complicated to explain here. One useful source on this matter is Talley, *Origins of the Liturgical Year*, 117–55.

the Magi acknowledge Christ as God with mystical gifts. . . . During Epiphany Christ at the wedding gave water the taste of wine, so that it was on account of power and not pleasure that Christ attended the wedding. . . . During Epiphany Christ entered the basin of the Jordan to consecrate our baptism, in order that those whom he had assumed by being born on earth, he would raise up to heaven by being reborn. . . . Thus it was that Christ was recognized as God at different times, but on one and the same day, by the Magi's gifts, by the transformation of the water, and by the voice of the Father as a threefold testimony, and that from the triple revelation of Christ the one hallowed feast of Epiphany was established.[92]

Depictions of the Cana miracle are well represented in the Christian catacombs and on sarcophagus reliefs, as well as on other, smaller objects such as ivories and gold glasses. One of the earliest examples is in the Catacomb of Peter and Marcellinus, in a lunette painting that also shows a funeral meal. Here Jesus touches his staff to the jars to produce wine for the banquet. It appears a second time in a slightly later painting in the same catacomb. More frequently, however, it appears on sarcophagus friezes from the early fourth century, often adjacent to other Johannine scenes (e.g., the raising of Lazarus and the healing of the man born blind) or with depictions of Adam and Eve, the resurrection of the dead, and Peter striking the rock (cf. fig. 1.9). The scene also appears on the late fourth-century mosaic vault of the Naples baptistery, where it is juxtaposed with the figure of the Samaritan woman at the well (fig. 5.8). It is also one of the scenes carved onto the early fifth-century wooden doors of the Basilica of Sta. Sabina in Rome, and it appears among the panel carvings on the sixth-century ivory throne of the archbishop Maximian in Ravenna.

The iconography has notable consistency. In all these examples, Jesus points a staff at the stone jars. Their numbers vary, even though the text specifies that there are six. Onlookers often appear and are probably meant to be disciples. In the earliest depictions, the mother of Jesus is oddly missing, as is the wedding party.[93] Later on, Jesus's coming to this wedding would be used to confirm his sacramental institution of marriage, and medieval and Renaissance iconography would emphasize the bridal pair and give pride of place to Jesus's mother. Here, however, the emphasis is not on the wedding at all; rather, the large stone jars brimming with water-turned-wine are the primary subject. In a funerary context, it likely indicated the eschatological banquet or simply the abundance of mercy shown by God to those who trust in his promises.

92. Peter Chrysologus, *Serm.* 157, trans. Palardy, *St. Peter Chrysologus*, 3:267–71. See also Peter Chrysologus, *Serm.* 160 for a parallel explication of the feast.

93. Jesus's mother appears on the Andrews Diptych in the Victoria and Albert Museum, an object whose date is much disputed (either fourth or ninth century).

The *Ogdoad* as a Figure of the Resurrection

The mystical significance of the number eight (the *ogdoad*) has a place in both the theology and the physical context of baptism, particularly as a symbol pointing to the eschatological regeneration of creation. In early Christian numerology, the number eight generally refers to the eighth day, which is the first day of the new creation, the day on which Jesus was resurrected from the dead, and the day on which the world will be renewed.

The earliest known expression of this idea occurs within the millennialist text the *Epistle of Barnabas* which presents God as saying, "After I have set everything at rest, I will create the beginning of an eighth day, which is the beginning of another world." This is why, the *Epistle* explains, Christians celebrate on the eighth day, the day on which Jesus rose from the dead and, later, ascended into heaven.[94]

This numerological symbolism may account for the emphasis given in 1 Peter 3:20–21 to the eight persons who were saved through water in the story of Noah, a point reiterated in 2 Peter 2:5. The author interprets their number—as well as their watery rescue—as a symbol of Christian baptism. In his *Dialogue with Trypho*, Justin Martyr elaborates on this text, claiming that these rescued eight symbolized the eighth day, the day of Christ's resurrection. As noted above, Justin also draws a connection between Noah's ark and the cross, noting that both are made of wood and are figures of salvation.[95]

This numerological significance had a venerable pre-Christian history. In Greco-Roman philosophy the number eight symbolized perfection, eternity, and repose. It had cosmic associations too, as ancients claimed that eight spheres circled the earth. According to the first-century Greek philosopher and mathematician Theon of Smyrna, the number eight symbolizes both eternity and the time when God's rule will prevail in the universe.[96]

Eight was valued because it is mathematically unique. It is the first cube after one (i.e., 2 x 2 x 2) and constitutes the number of corners in a geometrical cube (the perfect shape of the New Jerusalem in Rev. 21:15–17). In the late fourth or early fifth century, the neoplatonist Macrobius elaborated on the geometrical perfection of the number eight, insisting that it had a special right to be called "full" because of its intimate association with the harmony of the spheres. He further notes that ancient Pythagoreans gave it the name "justice" because it was the product of equal, even numbers and could be equally divided into both halves and thirds.[97]

---

94. *Barn.* 15.8–9, trans. Holmes, *Apostolic Fathers*, 429.
95. Justin Martyr, *Dial.* 138. On the symbolism of the ark, see above, chap. 1, under the heading "Noah and the Flood."
96. Theon of Smyrna, *Exp. math.* 105.
97. Macrobius, *Som. Scip.* 1.5.3–18; 2.2.10.

Philo, apparently influenced by Pythagorean and middle Platonic numerological speculation, identifies the number eight with God's command to circumcise on the eighth day (Gen. 17:12). He expounds upon the beautiful properties of the number, claiming that the soul is composed of eight divisions and that the number eight indicates the beginning of the second hebdomad (a second seven-day creation that included the covenant between God and the chosen people).[98] Justin Martyr borrows this idea and, in his refutation of Judaism, transfers the covenantal sign to Christians: "The command of circumcision, again, bidding [the Jews] always to circumcise their children on the eighth day, was a type of the true circumcision, by which we are circumcised from deceit and iniquity through him who rose from the dead on the first day after the Sabbath, namely our Lord Jesus Christ. For the first day after the Sabbath, remaining the first of all the days, is called, however, the eighth, according to the number of all the days of the cycle, and yet remains the first."[99]

In certain gnostic cosmologies, the chief archon was enthroned in the eighth heaven, the fixed sphere and the point of the soul's release from the lower spheres. Arriving at this place meant achieving eternal unity with the Divine. These ideas are expounded in writings of the church fathers against certain gnostic teachers. They also occur in documents that may have been written within gnostic circles. For example, according to Clement of Alexandria, Basilides taught that Righteousness and her daughter, Peace, dwelled in that eighth sphere.[100] Irenaeus, while refuting various gnostic teachings, discusses the different "primary *ogdoads*" of Valentinus, Secundus, and the followers of Ptolemy and Colorbasus.[101] From the other side comes confirming evidence, including the so-called Valentinian "Hymn of the Revelation" from the *Apocryphal Acts of John,* which describes the eightfold power (the *ogdoad*) as "singing with us."[102] One of the fragments from Theodotus, a Valentinian teacher in Alexandria, contrasts the death-bound one who was born of an earthly mother with the one who is transferred by the regeneration of Christ into life in the *ogdoad.*[103]

Clement of Alexandria agrees that the number eight mystically refers to the new creation. He argues that this was even prophetically incorporated into Plato's *Republic* (10:616B), which describes souls arising from seven days of rest in a meadow to set out on their journey again on the eighth. According to Clement, the meadow signifies the fixed sphere—the realm of the pious

---

98. Philo, *QG* 1.75; 3.49. For an analysis of the latter issue, see Staehle, *Die Zahlenmystik bei Philo.*

99. Justin Martyr, *Dial.* 41.1, *ANF,* 1:215, slightly adapted by author. See also a similar text taken from Asterius of Amasea, quoted in Daniélou, *Bible and the Liturgy,* 65–66.

100. Clement of Alexandria, *Strom.* 4.25.

101. Irenaeus, *Haer.* 1.11–12.

102. *Acts of John* 95, *ANT,* 319.

103. Theodotus, *Excerpt.* 80.

ones—and the seven days represent the motion of the seven planets. Time, he says, comes to an end on the eighth day, when the journey to heaven begins.[104]

Augustine equates the number eight with the number one as a symbol of rebirth, which explains why Easter is always celebrated on a Sunday (it is both the eighth and the first day of the week). He points out that the prophets and patriarchs knew the mystery of this eighth day. This is made evident by their observation of circumcision on the eighth day. Augustine also insists that the full meaning of this sign had been hidden until Christ's resurrection on the eighth day.[105]

In a sermon for the octave of Easter, Augustine returns to the symbolism of the eight persons in Noah's ark, as presented by 1 and 2 Peter. He reminds the newly baptized that the flood that once purged the earth of its iniquity is a figure of baptism, and the ark is thus the symbol of the church. Then he calls their attention to the importance of the eight days since their baptism and assures them that the parallels are far from coincidental. Because the Genesis story mentions eight persons and the neophytes have had their octave, the numbers are profoundly connected:

> And so what is prefigured by the number eight is everything that belongs to the age to come, where nothing either advances or falls away with the unrolling of times and seasons, but everything persists in a steady state of blessedness. And since the times of this age slip by with the repetition, round and round, of the number of seven days, it's only right that that should be called the eighth, which the saints will reach after their labors in time. . . . Once they have passed through this sevenfold course of time, there is an eighth and eternal felicity.[106]

In the last chapter of his *City of God*, Augustine again describes the perpetual Sabbath as the eternal repose, a kind of time outside time. Counting each of the ages as one day, he claims that the sixth age, which is coming to an end, will usher in the time of blessing and leisure before the beginning of the new, eternal day: the unending eighth day of the Lord, which will grant rest to both body and soul.[107] This calculation was echoed in some manuscripts of the *Gregorian Sacramentary*, where the number six is said to stand for the present age, the number seven for the age of rest, and the number eight for the time of the general resurrection.[108]

Many early Christian freestanding baptisteries and baptismal fonts were octagonally shaped (fig. 5.9). This is especially characteristic of early Christian baptisteries in Italy and France, where the octagonal design was widespread (e.g.,

---

104. Clement of Alexandria, *Strom.* 5.

105. Augustine, *Ep.* 55.13.23. See Staats, "Ogdoas als ein Symbol."

106. Augustine, *Serm.* 260C.2–3, trans. Hill, *Works of Saint Augustine*, 3/7:195. See also Augustine, *Serm.* 260A.4.

107. Augustine, *Civ.* 22.30.

108. See Wilson, *Gregorian Sacramentary*, 304; also cited in Underwood, "Fountain of Life," 83n161.

Figure 5.9. Baptistery, Lateran Basilica, Rome. (Photo by author.)

the baptisteries of Ravenna and Milan). The earliest baptistery at the Lateran Basilica in Rome was probably originally octagonal in shape, although that is a fairly recent theory.[109] In any case, the *Liber Pontificalis* states that Sixtus had eight porphyry columns erected on spurs projecting from the font's outer edge to create an inner octagonal colonnade. These columns were ones that Constantine had originally imported from Egypt and set against the inside walls of the building.[110] They supported an octagonal marble architrave that, in turn, supported another octagonal colonnade (a second story), an upper clerestory with eight windows, and a small dome.

In at least one case, the octagonal design inspired an allegorical interpretation. This is evident in the inscription composed for the octagonal baptistery built for the second Milan cathedral. The inscription, which scholars generally attribute to Ambrose, is a poem of eight couplets, transcribed in the eighth century and now preserved in the Vatican Library. This poem asserts that an eight-sided building and font serve and, in their shape, reflect a sacred purpose. Either originally inscribed on the baptistery's dome or on the perimeter of the

109. See Brandt and Guidobaldi, "Il Battistero Lateranense"; and Castelfranchi, "L'edificio battesimale." The archaeological questions, architecture, and function of this monument have most recently been summarized by Brandenburg, *Ancient Churches of Rome*, 37–54.

110. *Lib. Pont.* 46 (Sixtus III). 7. The text here describes Sixtus providing decorations that had not previously been there, collecting and setting Constantine's eight porphyry columns and adorning them (or the architrave) with verses.

font, the eight stanzas confirm the theological significance of the octagonal structure of the baptistery:

> The eight-sided temple has risen for sacred purposes.
> The eight-sided font is worthy for this task.
> It is seemly that the baptismal hall arises in this number
> by which true health has returned to people
> by the light of the resurrected Christ, who loosens the bonds of death
> and revives the lifeless from the tombs.
> Absolving those who have confessed from their sordid crime,
> he washes them in the flow of the purifying font.
> Let whoever wishes to shed their shameful lives' transgressions
> wash their hearts here; let them show their breasts clean.
> Let that one come here quickly; however darkened by sin,
> let that one dare to approach, and then depart whiter than snow.
> Let the holy ones make haste to this place; no holy person is unac-
>   quainted with
> these waters. In them is the rule and counsel of God.
> O glory of justice! For what is there more divine,
> than that the people's guilt be abrogated in only a moment?[111]

Here the emphasis lies not only on the symbolism of the octagonal design of the building but also on the understanding of baptism as a death and rebirth. It reiterates the belief that baptism restores health, washes and absolves sin, and brings life out of death.

That Milanese fourth-century octagonal baptistery may have been among the first of its type. It was once presumed to have been the model for subsequent octagonal baptistery structures, including the baptisteries of Ravenna.[112] From the fifth century to the Middle Ages and beyond, the octagon continued to be one of the most popular shapes for a baptistery or font in the West. Added to octagonal fonts are other instances of eight-sidedness in architectural design, including an eight-columned ciborium (canopy) over the font (e.g., the Lateran Baptistery) and the eight mosaic panels radiating from the dome medallion in Naples. Whether or not all these octagonal features were specifically built to reflect the numerological significance of the *ogdoad*, they subsequently could

---

111. Translation by author. Ambrose's authorship of these lines is controversial, but parallels to themes can be found in many of his catechetical and mystagogical sermons. On this point, see Perler, "L'inscription du baptistère"; Dölger, "Zur Symbolik des altchristlichen Taufhauses"; and Underwood, "Fountain of Life," 81–82. The text is in the Vatican Library, *Palatino Latin Codex* 833, transcribed by an unknown author of the ninth or early tenth century. It has been published in several epigraphical collections, e.g., *CIL* 5.617.2 and *ICUR* 2.1, 161n2, and recently discussed in the Banterle et al., *Opera omnia di sant'Ambrogio*, 145–66.

112. See discussion of the presumed influence on the Ravenna baptisteries in Kostof, *Orthodox Baptistery of Ravenna*, 49–54.

have been interpreted as doing so.[113] The persistence of the design is evident in the continued popularity of octagonal baptismal fonts.

Ritual Acts Signifying the Restoration of Eden

Many of the liturgical actions discussed above as signifying cleansing, incorporation, illumination, or regeneration also symbolize the restoration of humans along with paradise itself. Among these are the candidates' stripping before going into the font and re-robing in white on leaving it. Another is the direction of their movements, as they renounce Satan while turning toward the west and proclaim their adherence to Christ while turning toward the east. A final example of a liturgical act that instantiates the restoration of the newly baptized to Eden as well as an affirmation of God's intention to renew all creation is the likelihood that catechumens came to the baptismal font chanting the Forty-Second Psalm.

Stripping and Re-robing in White Garments

As noted in chapter 4, stripping before entering the font expresses the idea of removing the old self.[114] And as discussed earlier in this chapter, baptismal nudity is a return to the state of Adam and Eve before they sinned and realized that they were naked.[115] Thus, both Theodore of Mopsuestia and Cyril of Jerusalem assure the candidates that they need not feel shame about their nakedness. Theodore, in fact, insists that those about to be baptized must take off their clothes as a sign of their desire to be born again and in anticipation of their immortality: "For they [clothes] are proof of mortality, convincing evidence of the humiliating sentence that made us to need clothes."[116] For his part, Cyril asks his candidates to remember the bride in the Song of Songs, who had removed her garment and wondered how she should ever put it on again (5:3). He exclaims: "Marvelous! You were naked in the sight of all and not ashamed! Truly you bore the image of the first-formed Adam, who was naked in the garden and was not ashamed."[117] In the same way, the donning

113. Not all scholars believe the octagonal shape was intentionally or definitively symbolic. See De Blaauw, "Kultegebäude," 340, for example. De Blaauw argues that the baptistery's octagonal shape was meant primarily to enhance liturgical movement within the space. Nevertheless, baptismal fonts are still octagonal in many modern churches, although most worshipers are unaware of the shape's symbolism.

114. See above, chap. 1, under the heading "Stripping and Preliminary Anointing," and also chap. 4, under the heading "Stripping and Nude Immersion."

115. See above, under the heading "Adam and Eve's Nudity as Symbolizing Innocence."

116. Theodore of Mopsuestia, *Bapt. hom.* 3.8, trans. Yarnold, *Awe-Inspiring Rites of Initiation*, 184–85.

117. Cyril of Jerusalem, *Myst.* 2.2, trans. McCauley and Stephenson, *Works of Saint Cyril of Jerusalem*, 2:162.

of new white garments is a sign not only of rebirth but also of innocence re-stored.[118] The robes of the saints are white (Rev. 6:11; 7:9, 14), and so are wed-ding garments, according to John the Deacon: "They wear the white raiment so that though the ragged dress of ancient error has darkened the infancy of their first birth, the costume of their second birth should display the raiment of glory; so that clad in a wedding garment the one baptized may approach the table of the heavenly bridegroom as a new person."[119]

But the color was not always as important as the general idea that the new Adam and Eve would at last exchange their garments of skins (Gen. 3:21) for garments of glory. Leo I, in an emphatic letter addressed to the clergy and people of Constantinople, explained that the sacrament of baptism typifies the union of the two natures of Christ. He recalls the story of the fall of Adam and Eve and asserts the consequent transmission of their sin to all their descendants. Christ must share in that mortal nature (the veil of flesh) in order to overcome its inherited sin through his righteousness. Leo insists that anyone who is ashamed of that or rejects it as unworthy neither recognizes the bridegroom nor can have any place at the wedding banquet. At the cruci-fixion, the bridegroom's flesh poured forth the elements of redemption and regeneration: blood and water. These are the elements that the faithful receive in the sacraments (Eucharist and baptism). However, Leo insists, baptism is more than a washing with water; it constitutes an exchange of old flesh for new, the garments of skin exchanged for garments of glory. Thus the clothes of the bride are the renewed flesh of the restored Adam.[120]

Turning toward the East

The candidates' turning toward the east in their affirmation of faith in Christ moved them toward Eden as well as to the rising sun. Cyril of Jerusalem com-ments on the importance of this turning in one of his mystagogical lectures: "When you renounce Satan, trampling underfoot every covenant with him, then you annul that ancient league with Hell and God's paradise opens up before you, that Eden, planted in the east, from which for his transgression our first parent was banished. Symbolic of this is your facing about from the west to the east, the place of light. It was at this point that you were told to say: 'I believe in the Father, and in the Son, and in the Holy Spirit, and in one baptism of repentance.'"[121]

118. See discussion of the white garment above, chap. 4, under the heading "Reclothing with White Garments."
119. John the Deacon, *Ep. Sen.* 6, trans. author. Text in Wilmart, *Analecta reginensia*, 174–75. See also Cyril of Jerusalem, *Procat.* 3—the wedding party is dressed in white; or Ambrose, *Sacr.* 3.14.
120. Leo I, *Ep.* 59.4.
121. Cyril of Jerusalem, *Myst.* 1.9, trans. McCauley and Stephenson, *Works of Saint Cyril of Jerusalem*, 2:158–59.

The meaning of a similar turning is explained in the *Apostolic Constitutions*, which instructs the congregation to rise and turn toward the east for a prayer after the penitents and catechumens have been excused from the liturgy. The reason for this, it adds, is twofold: Jesus ascended to heaven in the east, and the original Eden lies to the east.[122]

Ambrose explains this orientational importance in his synopsis of the baptismal rite. Observing that west is the direction of darkness, he instructs the candidates to turn that way in order to renounce Satan, that they should look toward the west to renounce the source of shadows.[123] Once they have completed that action, they must turn toward the east, toward Eden, from which Adam and Eve were expelled. This redirection, from west to east, he explains, symbolizes their change of allegiance.[124] The turning obviously indicates their conversion, but the compass points have additional significance. The east is the direction of the light and the dawn. Early Christians borrowed the imagery of Apollo and Sol Invictus for some of the iconography of Christ, a transference that makes perfect sense insofar as Christ is understood as the light emerging from darkness (John 1:5).[125] Ambrose insists that when the one who renounces Satan turns toward the east, he or she beholds Christ face-to-face.[126]

The practice of turning from west to east is reinforced by the symbolic orientation of churches and directing prayer toward the east. Clement of Alexandria gives the reason for praying while facing east:

> And since the dawn is an image of the day of birth and from that point the light which has shone forth at first from the darkness increases, there has also dawned on those involved in darkness a day of the knowledge in truth. In correspondence with the manner of the sun's rising, prayers are made looking toward the sunrise in the east. Whence also the most ancient temples looked toward the west, that people might be taught to turn to the east when facing the images.[127]

Evoking the tradition that Eden lay to the east, Basil of Caesarea explains, "We all look to the east at our prayers, but few of us know that, in doing so, we seek our own old country, Paradise, which God planted in Eden, in the east."[128]

---

122. *Apos. const.* 2.57. See also Basil of Caesarea, *Spir. Sanct.* 27; and Gregory of Nyssa, who claims that paradise is in the east, *Orat.* 5 (PG 44:1184).

123. Ambrose, *Sacr.* 1.4.

124. Ambrose, *Sacr.* 1.8.

125. The most famous example of this may be the image of Christ with a radiate halo, riding a chariot to bring light to the world, located in the Mausoleum of the Julii underneath St. Peter's in Rome.

126. Ambrose, *Myst.* 2.7

127. Clement of Alexandria, *Strom.* 7.7, ANF, 2:525. On the antiquity of the tradition, see also Tertullian, *Idol.* 16, where he notes that the practice of turning toward the east led some non-Christians to assume that his community worshiped the sun.

128. Basil of Caesarea, *Spir. Sanct.* 27.66, NPNF[2], 8:42.

Chanting the Forty-Second Psalm

Certain documents indicate that candidates may have chanted the Forty-Second Psalm as they processed to the baptistery for their initiation. The imagery in this psalm coincides with the iconography of deer coming to drink at flowing streams, and it reflects the desire of the candidates to drink from (or bathe in) the water of life. In his commentary on the psalm, Augustine acknowledges that while it urges all Christians to run like deer to the fountain of understanding, it has particular meaning for those who are approaching baptism. As they process to the font, they chant this text to express their longing for the fountain that remits sins in the same way that the deer longs for springs of water. That is why, he says, "we traditionally sing this psalm, to arouse in them a longing for the fountain of forgiveness of their sins, like the deer longs for the springs of water."[129]

The *Gelasian Sacramentary* (composed sometime between the sixth and the eighth centuries) instructs that candidates sing Psalm 42 on their way to the font during the Easter vigil. It adds the following prayer: "Almighty and ever-living God, look with favor on the devotion of your people at their second birth, who are like the deer drawn to the fountain of water, grant that in baptism their thirst for faith may sanctify their souls and bodies."[130]

In conclusion, the ritual of baptism reconstructs creation's mythical, primordial beginning and interrupts the ordinary cycle of birth and death. Baptism is not only a bath that cleanses or heals individuals from their sins, a ritual initiation into a new community, the imparting of the Holy Spirit and its gifts, and the regeneration of an individual. Baptism is also the restoration of the lost paradise. It is, in essence, an eschatological event that is comprised of rebirth, re-creation, and restoration. In the meantime, the new brides, the descendants of Adam and Eve, anticipate their wedding banquet in paradise, knowing that their initiation has given them a mere glimpse of its beauties and blessings. This idea is beautifully expressed by Paulinus of Nola in a prayer, written for the Feast of St. Felix at Nola:

> Let me now continue as an earthly Adam, but be born of the virgin earth, fashioned as a new form after putting off the old self. May I be led forth from my land and be untrue to my race. May I hasten to the honeyed streams of the Promised Land and be preserved from the fire of the Chaldean furnace. May I be like Lot, hospitable with door ever open, so that I may be delivered from

---

129. Augustine, *Enarrat. Ps.* 41.1 (CCSL 38:460), trans. author.
130. *Gel. Sac.* 87–88, trans. author. See also Underwood, "Fountain of Life," esp. 51–53.

Sodom. May I refrain from looking back so that I may not turn into a pillar of salt through lack of salt in my heart. May I be offered like the young Isaac as a living victim to God, carry my own wood, and follow my kindly father beneath the cross. May I discover wells, but I pray that the jealous Amalek, who impedes the course of living water, may not fill them in. . . . May I obtain a safe departure from Egypt, and journey under the guidance of the Law through the divided waters of my storm-tossed heart; so I may escape the Red Sea's billows and, when Pharaoh is drowned, sing of the Lord's triumph.[131]

Understanding baptism as the restoration of individuals is not limited to the renewal of humanity's divine image but is extended to all creation. This is made visible in the use of rich nature imagery in the décor of baptisteries: birds, animals, flowers, fruit-bearing trees, fish, flowing rivers, and splashing fountains. Then, as the newly baptized emerge from the water, receive the seal of the Spirit, are dressed in their white robes, and join the rest of the congregation, they obviously realize that they have been allowed only a glimpse of paradise and given a promise that this is their future and not their present reality. Even so, they have received this promise in their bodies as well as in their hearts and minds. They possess the joyous certainty of cosmic renewal at the dawn of the eighth day. This expectation is one of the most encompassing benefits of baptism in the early church.

Such expectation requires both imagination and hope. It depends on accepting that signs and symbols are reliable indicators of truths that may not be seen by others or that transcend their earthly forms. In the meantime, of course, the mundane things of the world do not pass away. Their continued existence is, in one sense, a scandal and, in another sense, the proof that the journey is not yet over, that baptism is only the beginning step toward a final, happy ending. Yet that beginning was not a simple step over a low threshold. It was a dramatic realignment of identity: an identity that meant living in two parallel worlds, one world in which everything is subject to death, the other in which every living thing is capable of eternal life. Such life may begin, again, as it did in the beginning, with a breath of God sweeping over water and the creation of a new morning.

---

131. Paulinus of Nola, *Carm.* 27.607, trans. Walsh, *Poems of St. Paulinus of Nola*, 292–93.

Bibliography

Amundsen, Darrell W. *Medicine, Society, and Faith in the Ancient and Medieval Worlds.* Baltimore: Johns Hopkins University Press, 1996.

Bamberger, Bernard. *Proselytism in the Talmudic Period.* New York: KTAV, 1968.

Banterle, Gabriele, et al., eds. *Opera omnia di sant' Ambrogio: Inni, Iscrizioni, Frammenti.* Milan: Biblioteca Ambrosiana, 1994.

Beasley-Murray, G. R. *Baptism in the New Testament.* Grand Rapids: Eerdmans, 1973.

Beatrice, Pier Franco. *La lavanda dei piedi: Contributo alla storia della antiche liturgie cristiane.* Rome: CLV Edizioni liturgiche, 1983.

Becker, Erich. *Das Quellenwunder des Moses in der altchristlichen Kunst.* Strassburg: J. H. Ed. Heitz, 1909.

Bedard, Walter. *The Symbolism of the Baptismal Font in Early Christian Thought.* Washington, DC: Catholic University of America Press, 1951.

Blaauw, Sible de. "Kultegebäude," *RAC* 20 (2008): 227–393.

Botte, B. "La sputation, antique rite baptismal?" In *Mélanges offerts à Mademoiselle Christine Mohrmann,* 196–201. Utrecht: Spectrum, 1963.

———. "Sacramentum catechumenorum." *Questions liturgiques* 43 (1963): 322–30.

Boulding, Maria, trans. *Works of Saint Augustine.* Pt. 3, *Sermons,* vol. 16: *Exposition of the Psalms.* Hyde Park, NY: New City Press, 2000.

Bowie, Angus. "Oil in Ancient Greece and Rome." In *Oil of Gladness: Anointing in the Christian Tradition,* edited by Martin Dudley and Geoffrey Rowell, 26–34. London: SPCK, 1993.

Bowman, John. "Exorcism and Baptism." In *A Tribute to Arthur Vööbus: Studies in Early Christian Literature and Its Environment, Primarily in the Syrian East,* edited by Robert H. Fisher, 249–63. Chicago: Lutheran School of Theology, 1977.

Bradshaw, Paul. "Baptismal Practice in the Alexandrian Tradition: Eastern or Western." In *Essays in Early Eastern Initiation,* edited by P. Bradshaw, 5–10. Nottingham, UK: Alcuin, 1988.

———. "*Diem baptismo sollemniorem*: Initiation and Easter in Christian Antiquity." In *Living Water, Sealing Spirit: Readings on Christian Initiation*, edited by Maxwell Johnson, 137–47. Collegeville, MN: Liturgical Press, 1995.

Bradshaw, Paul, Maxwell Johnson, and L. Edward Phillips. *The Apostolic Tradition: A Commentary*. Minneapolis: Fortress Press, 2002.

Brandenburg, Hugo. *Ancient Churches of Rome*. Turnhout, Belgium: Brepols, 2004.

Brandt, Olof. "Deer, Lambs, and Water in the Lateran Baptistery." *RivAC* 81 (2005): 131–56.

———. "Ipotesi sulla struttura del Battistero Lateranense tra Costantino e Sisto III." In *Ecclesiae urbis: Atti del congresso internazionale di studi sulle chiese di Roma (IV–X secolo)*, edited by Federico Guidobaldi and Alessandra Guiglia Guidobaldi, 2:923–32. Vatican City: Pontificio istituto di archeologia cristiana, 2002.

———. "Strutture del IV secolo per la lavanda dei piedi in due battisteri romani." *AM* 2 (2003): 137–44.

Brandt, Olof, and Federico Guidobaldi. "Il Battistero Lateranense: Nuove interpretazioni delle fasi strutturali." *RivAC* 84 (2008): 189–282.

Brock, Sebastian. *The Harp of the Spirit: Eighteen Poems of Saint Ephrem*. 2nd ed. San Bernardino, CA: Borgo Press, 1984.

———. "St. Ephrem on Christ as Light in Mary and in the Jordan: Hymni de Ecclesia 36." *ECR* 7 (1975): 137–44.

———. "The Transition to a Post-Baptismal Anointing in the Antiochene Rite." In *The Sacrifice of Praise*, edited by Bryan Spinks, 215–25. Rome: Edizioni Liturgiche, 1981.

Broek, R. van den. *The Myth of the Phoenix, according to Classical and Early Christian Traditions*. Translated by I. Seeger. Leiden: Brill, 1972.

Bruyne, Lucien de. "La décoration des baptistères paléochrétiens." *ACIAC* 5 (1957): 341–69.

———. "L'imposition des mains dans l'art chrétien ancien." *RivAC* 20 (1943): 173–85.

Buchinger, Harald. "Towards the Origins of Paschal Baptism: The Contribution of Origen." *StLit* 35 (2005): 12–31.

Buecheler, Franciscus, and Alexander Riese, eds. *Anthologia Latina*. Leipzig: Ver. Adolf M. Hakkert, 1973.

Buell, Denise Kimber. "Race and Universalism in Early Christianity." *JECS* 10 (2002): 429–68.

———. *Why This New Race: Ethnic Reasoning in Christianity*. New York: Columbia University Press, 2005.

Bunt, Annewies van de. "Milk and Honey in the Theology of Clement of Alexandria." In *Fides Sacramenti, Sacramentum Fidei: Studies in Honour of Pieter Smulders*, edited by Hans Jörg Auf der Maur et al., 27–39. Assen, NL: Van Gorcum, 1981.

Cabié, Robert. *La Pentecôte: L'évolution de la Cinquantaine pascale au cours des cinq premiers siècles*. Tournai, Belgium: Desclée, 1965.

Calza, G. "Una basilica di età Constantiniana scoperta ad Ostia." *Atti della Pontificia Accademia Romana di Archeologia*, ser. 3, recond. 16 (1940): fasc. 1–2, 63–88; and recond. 18 (1941–42): fasc. 3–4, 135–48.

Cansdale, Lena. *Qumran and the Essenes: A Re-evaluation of the Evidence.* Tübingen: J. C. B. Mohr, 1997.

Cartlidge, David, and Keith Elliott. *Art and the Christian Apocrypha.* London: Routledge, 2001.

Castelfranchi, Marina Falla. "L'edificio battesimale in Italia nel periodo paleocristiano." *ACIAC* 8 (2001): 267–301.

Christman, Angela Russell. "Origen's Prayer to Jesus the Footwasher." In *Prayer from Alexander to Constantine*, edited by Mark Kiley et al., 304–8. London: Routledge, 1997.

Clarke, Graeme, trans. *The Letters of Cyprian.* Vol. 4. New York: Newman Press, 1989.

Cobier, Mireille. "Divorce and Adoption as Roman Familial Strategies." In *Marriage, Divorce, and Children in Ancient Rome*, edited by Beryl Rawson, 47–78. Oxford: Clarendon, 1991.

Cohen, Shaye J. D. "Is Proselyte Baptism Mentioned in the Mishnah? The Interpretation of m. Pesahim 8.8 (= m. Eduyot 5.2)." In *Pursuing the Text: Studies in Honor of Ben Zion Wacholder*, edited by John C. Reeves and John Kampen, 278–92. Sheffield: JSOT Press, 1994.

Collins, Adela Yarbro. "The Origins of Christian Baptism." StLit 19 (1989): 28–46.

Collins, J. J. "Sibylline Oracles." In *The Old Testament Pseudepigrapha*, edited by John H. Charlesworth, 1:423–24. Garden City, NY: Doubleday, 1983.

Connolly, Richard H. *The Liturgical Homilies of Narsai: Texts and Studies.* Vol. 8. Cambridge: Cambridge University Press, 1909.

Cook, James I. "The Concept of Adoption in the Theology of Paul." In *Saved by Hope: Essays in Honor of Richard C. Oudersluys*, edited by James I. Cook, 133–44. Grand Rapids: Eerdmans, 1978.

Cullman, Oscar. *Baptism in the New Testament.* Translated by J. K. S. Reid. London: SCM, 1950.

Daniélou, Jean. *The Bible and the Liturgy.* Notre Dame, IN: University of Notre Dame Press, 1956.

———. *From Shadows to Reality: Studies in the Biblical Typology of the Fathers.* London: Burns & Oates, 1960.

Dassmann, Ernst. *Sündenvergebung durch Taufe, Busse, und Martyrerfürbitte in den Zeugnissen frühchristlicher Frömmigkeit und Kunst.* Münster: Aschendorff, 1973.

Davies, John G. *The Architectural Setting of Baptism.* London: Barrie & Rockliff, 1962.

———. "The Arian and Orthodox Baptisteries at Salona." *Antiquity* 33 (1959): 57–60.

DeConick, April. "The True Mysteries: Sacramentalism in the *Gospel of Philip*." VC 55 (2001): 225–61.

Deichmann, Friedrich. *Ravenna: Haupstadt des spätantiken Abendlandes.* Wiesbaden: Franz Steiner, 1969–89.

De Latte, R. "Saint Augustin et le baptême." *Questions Liturgiques* 56 (1975): 181–91.

Dirven, Lucinda. "Paradise Lost, Paradise Regained: The Meaning of Adam and Eve in the Baptistery of Dura Europos." *ECA* 5 (2008): 43–57.

Dix, Gregory, ed. *The Treatise on the Apostolic Tradition of St. Hippolytus of Rome.* London: SPCK, 1937.

Dixon, Suzanne. *The Roman Family.* Baltimore: Johns Hopkins University Press, 1992.

Dölger, Franz J. "Der Durchzug durch das Rote Meer als Sinnbild der christlichen Taufe." *AC* 2 (1930): 63–69.

———. "Die Inschrift im Baptisterium S. Giovanni in Fonte der Lateranensischen Basilika aus der Zeit Xystus III (432–440) und die Symbolik des Taufbrunnens bei Leo dem Grossen." *JAC* 2 (1930): 252–57.

———. "Heidnische Begrüssung und christliche Verhöhnung der Heidentempel: *Despuere* und *exsufflare* in der Dämonenbeschwörung." *AC* 2 (1932): 192–203.

———. "Sacramentum militae." *AC* 2 (1930): 268–80.

———. "Zur Symbolik des altchristlichen Taufhauses." *AC* 4 (1934): 153–87.

Dyggve, Ejnar. *History of Salonitan Christianity.* Oslo: H. Aschehoug, 1951.

Echle, Harry A. "Baptism of the Apostles." *Traditio* 3 (1945): 365–86.

Edwards, Mark. *Optatus: Against the Donatists.* Liverpool: Liverpool University Press, 1997.

Engemann, Josef. *Die Huldigung der Apostel im Mosaik des ravennatischen Orthodoxenbaptisteriums.* Mainz: P. von Zabern, 1989.

Ewald, Marie Ligouri, trans. *The Homilies of St. Jerome.* Washington, DC: Catholic University of America Press, 1963.

Fausone, Alfonse. *Die Taufe in der frühchristlicher Sepulkralkunst.* Vatican City: Pontificio Istituto di archeologia Cristiana, 1982.

Ferguson, Everett. *Baptism in the Early Church.* Grand Rapids: Eerdmans, 2008.

———. *Demonology of the Early Christian World.* Lewiston, NY: Edwin Mellen Press, 1984.

———. "Preaching at Epiphany: Gregory of Nyssa and John Chrysostom on Baptism and the Church." *CH* 66 (1997): 1–17.

Finn, Thomas. *Early Christian Baptism and the Catechumenate.* 2 vols. Collegeville, MN: Liturgical Press, 1992.

———. *From Death to Rebirth: Ritual and Conversion in Antiquity.* Mahwah, NJ: Paulist Press, 1997.

Finney, Paul Corby. "Do You Think God Is a Magician?" In *Akten des Symposiums "Frühchristliche Sarkophage," Deutches Archäologisches Institut,* 1999, 99–108. Mainz: P. von Zabern, 2002.

———. "Images on Finger Rings and Early Christian Art." *DOP* 41 (1987): 181–86.

Franke, Peter. "Bemerkungen zur frühchristlichen Noe-ikonographie." *RivAC* 49 (1973): 171–82.

Fuchs, Linda. "The 'Jonah Sarcophagus' and Origen on Peter's Journey to Emmaus." Paper delivered at the 2006 Byzantine Studies Conference, St. Louis, MO, November 10–12, 2006.

Gavin, Frank. *The Jewish Antecedents of the Christian Sacraments.* London: SPCK, 1928.

Goodenough, Erwin. *Jewish Symbols in the Greco-Roman Period*, vol. 8: *Pagan Symbols in Judaism*. New York: Pantheon Books, 1965.

Grabar, André. "La fresque des saintes femmes au tombeau à Dura." *CahArch* 8 (1956): 9–26.

Graffin, F., ed. *Narsai's Metrical Homilies on the Nativity, Epiphany, Passion, Resurrection, and Ascension*. Translated by Frederick G. McLeod. Turnhout, Belgium: Brepols, 1979.

Green, Deborah. "Sweet Spices in the Tomb." In *Commemorating the Dead: Texts and Artifacts in Context*, edited by Laurie Brink and Deborah Green, 145–73. Berlin: de Gruyter, 2008.

Griffiths, Gwyn, ed. and trans. *The Isis-Book (Metamorphoses, Book XI) of Apuleius of Madauros*. Études préliminaires aux religions orientales dans l'empire romain 11. Leiden: Brill, 1975.

Guy, Laurie. "'Naked' Baptism in the Early Church: The Rhetoric and the Reality." *JRH* 27, no. 2 (2003): 133–42.

Hallett, Christopher. *The Roman Nude: Heroic Portrait Statuary 200 BC–AD 300*. Oxford: Oxford University Press, 2005.

Hamman, A.-G. *Baptism: Ancient Liturgies and Patristic Texts*. Translated by Thomas P. Halton. Staten Island, NY: Alba House, 1967.

Harkins, Paul W., trans. *St. John Chrysostom: Baptismal Instructions*. ACW 31. New York: Newman Press, 1963.

Harrison, Nonna Verna, trans. *Festal Orations: St. Gregory of Nazianzus*. Crestwood, NY: St. Vladimir's Seminary Press, 2008.

Harvey, Susan Ashbrook. *Scenting Salvation: Ancient Christianity and the Olfactory Imagination*. Berkeley: University of California Press, 2006.

Heine, Ronald. *Origen: Homilies on Genesis and Exodus*. FC 71. Washington, DC: Catholic University of America Press, 1982.

Helgeland, John. "Christians and the Roman Army from Marcus Aurelius to Constantine." *ANRW* 2:23.1 (1979), 724–44.

Hermann, A. "Cilicium." *RAC* 2 (1957): 127–36.

Hill, Edmund, trans. *The Works of Saint Augustine*. Pt. 3, *Sermons*, vol. 6. Brooklyn, NY: New City Press, 1992.

Himmelmann, Nikolaus. *Über Hirten-genre in der antiken Kunst*. Opladen: Westdeutscher, 1980.

Hoek, Annewies van den. "Hymn of the Holy Clement to Christ the Saviour: Clement of Alexandria, *Pedagogue* 3.12.101.4." In *Prayer from Alexander to Constantine*, edited by M. Kiley, 296–303. New York: Routledge, 1997.

Holmes, Michael. *The Apostolic Fathers*. 3rd ed. Grand Rapids: Baker Academic, 2006.

Hooyman, R. P. J. "Die Noe-Darstellung in der frühchristlichen Kunst." *VC* 12 (1958): 113–15.

Israeli, Yael, and David Mevorah, eds. *Cradle of Christianity: Treasures from the Holy Land*. Beachwood, OH: Maltz Museum of Jewish Heritage; Jerusalem: Israel Museum, 2000. Exhibition catalog.

Jefferson, Lee M. "The Image of Christ the Miracle Worker in Early Christian Art." PhD dissertation. Vanderbilt University, 2008.

Jensen, Robin M. "Baptism *ad Sanctos*?" In *Studies on Patristic Texts and Archaeology*, edited by George Kalantzis and Thomas Martin, 93–110. Lewistown, NY: Edwin Mellen Press, 2009.

———. "Baptismal Practices at North African Martyrs' Shrines." In *Ablution, Initiation, and Baptism: Late Antiquity, Early Judaism, and Early Christianity*, edited by David Hellholm, Tor Vegge, Øyvind Norderval, and Christer Hellholm, 1673–95. Berlin: de Gruyter, 2011.

———. "Earliest Christian Images and Exegesis." In *Picturing the Bible: The Earliest Christian Art*, edited by Jeffrey Spier, 65–85. New Haven: Yale University Press, 2007.

———. "Inscriptions in Early Roman Baptisteries." Forthcoming.

———. "*Mater Ecclesia* and *Fons Aeterna*: The Church and Her Womb in Ancient Christian Tradition." In *A Feminist Companion to Patristic Literature*, edited by Amy-Jill Levine and M. M. Robbins, 137–55. London: T&T Clark, 2008.

———. "Poetry of the Font: Inscriptions in Early Christian Baptisteries." In *Acta ad archaeologiam et artium historiam pertinentia* 24, no. 101 (2011): 65–83.

———. *Understanding Early Christian Art*. New York: Routledge, 2000.

———. "What Are Pagan River Gods Doing in Scenes of Jesus' Baptism?" *BRev* 9 (1993): 34–41.

———. "With Pomp, Apparatus, Novelty, and Avarice: Alternative Baptismal Practices in North Africa." StPatr 44 (2010): 77–83.

John, Jeffrey. "Anointing in the New Testament." In *Oil of Gladness*, edited by Martin Dudley and Geoffrey Rowell, 46–76. London: SPCK, 1993.

Johnson, Maxwell. *Rites of Christian Initiation*. Collegeville, MN: Liturgical Press, 2007.

———. "Tertullian's '*Diem Baptismo Sollemniorem*' Revisited: A Tentative Hypothesis on Baptism at Pentecost." In *Studia Liturgica Diversa: Essays in Honor of Paul F. Bradshaw*, edited by Maxwell Johnson and L. E. Phillips, 31–43. Portland, OR: Pastoral Press, 2004.

Kantorowicz, Ernst. "Baptism of the Apostles." *DOP* 9 (1956): 203–51.

Karras, Valerie. "Sex/Gender in Gregory of Nyssa's Eschatology: Irrelevant or Non-existent?" StPatr 41 (2003): 363–68.

Kavanagh, Aidan. *The Shape of Baptism: The Rites of Christian Initiation*. New York: Pueblo Press, 1978.

Klauser, Theodor. "Studien zur Entstehungsgeschichte." JAC 1 (1958): 20–51; JAC 3 (1960): 112–33; JAC 8–9 (1965–66): 126–70.

Kolping, Adolf. *Sacramentum Tertullianeum*. Vol. 1. Münster: Regensburgsche Verlag, 1948.

Korol, Dieter. "Neues zu den alt- und neutest amentlichen Darstellungen im Baptisterium von Dura-Europos." In *Ablution, Initiation, and Baptism: Late Antiquity, Early Judaism, and Early Christianity*, edited by David Hellholm, Tor Vegge, Øyvind Norderval, and Christer Hellholm, 1611–72. Berlin: de Gruyter, 2011.

Kostof, Spiro. *The Orthodox Baptistery of Ravenna*. New Haven: Yale University Press, 1965.

Kraeling, Carl. "The Christian Building." In *The Excavations at Dura Europos, Final Report 8*, pt. 2. New Haven: Dura-Europos Publications, 1967.

Krautheimer, Richard. "Introduction to an Iconography of Medieval Architecture." *JWCI* 5 (1942): 135–36.

Lampe, G. W. H. *The Seal of the Spirit*. London: Longmans, Green, 1951.

LaPiana, G. "Foreign Groups in Rome during the First Centuries of the Empire." *HTR* 20, no. 4 (1927): 183–403.

Lawrence, Marion. "Three Pagan Themes in Christian Art." In *De Artibus Opuscula* 40, edited by Millard Meiss, 323–24. New York: New York University Press, 1961.

Layton, Bentley. *The Gnostic Scriptures*. Garden City, NY: Doubleday, 1987.

Leclercq, H. "Nu dans l'art chrétien." In *DACL* 12.2 (1936): 1782–808.

———. "Nudité baptismale." In *DACL* 12.2 (1936): 543–70.

Lienhard, Joseph. *Origen: Homilies on Luke, Fragments on Luke*. FC 94. Washington, DC: Catholic University of America Press, 1996.

Lundberg, Per. *La typologie baptismale dans l'ancienne église*. Leipzig: A. Lorentz, 1942.

MacMullan, Ramsay. *Roman Social Relations, 50 B.C. to A.D. 284*. New Haven: Yale University Press, 1974.

Malherbe, Abraham, and Everett Ferguson. *Gregory of Nyssa: The Life of Moses*. New York: Paulist Press, 1978.

Mango, Cyril. *The Art of the Byzantine Empire, 312–1453: Sources and Documents*. Toronto: University of Toronto Press, 1986.

Markus, Robert. *Christianity in the Roman World*. London: Thames & Hudson, 1974.

Masseron, Alexandra. *Saint Jean Baptiste dans l'art*. Paris: Arthaud, 1957.

Mathews, Thomas. *The Clash of the Gods*. Princeton, NJ: Princeton University Press, 1993.

———. "La nudità nel cristianesimo." In *Aurea Roma: Dalla città pagana alla città cristiana*, edited by Eugenio La Rocca, 396–98. Rome: L'Erma di Bretschneider, 2000.

McCauley, Leo, and Anthony Stephenson. *The Works of Saint Cyril of Jerusalem*. FC 64. Washington, DC: Catholic University of America Press, 1969–70.

McCready, Wayne O. "*Ekklēsia* and Voluntary Associations." In *Voluntary Associations in the Graeco-Roman World*, edited by J. S. Kloppenborg and S. G. Wilson, 59–73. London: Routledge, 1996.

McDonnell, Kilian. *The Baptism of Jesus in the River Jordan*. Collegeville, MN: Liturgical Press, 1996.

McDonnell, Kilian, and George Montague. *Christian Initiation and Baptism in the Holy Spirit*. Collegeville, MN: Liturgical Press, 1994.

McGowan, Andrew. *Ascetic Eucharists: Food and Drink in Early Christian Ritual Meals*. New York: Oxford University Press, 1999.

McLeod, Frederick G., trans. *Narsai's Metrical Homilies on the Nativity, Epiphany, Passion, Resurrection, and Ascension*. PO 40/1. Turnhout, Belgium: Brepols, 1979.

Meeks, Wayne A. "The Image of the Androgyne: Some Uses of a Symbol in Earliest Christianity." *HR* 13 (1974): 165–208.

Meyer, R. T. *Palladius: The Lausiac History.* ACW 34. New York: Longmans, Green, 1965.

Mingana, A., trans. *Commentary of Theodore of Mopsuestia on the Lord's Prayer and on the Sacraments of Baptism and the Eucharist.* Woodbrooke Studies 6. Cambridge: W. Heffer & Sons, 1933.

Mitchell, Leonel L. *Baptismal Anointing.* London: SPCK, 1966.

Mitchell, Margaret M. "Looking for Abercius: Reimagining Contexts of Interpretation of the 'Earliest Christian Inscription.'" In *Commemorating the Dead: Texts and Artifacts in Context*, edited by Laurie Brink and Deborah Green, 303–35. Berlin: de Gruyter, 2008.

Mohrmann, Christine. "Sacramentum dans les plus anciens textes chrétiens." *HTR* 47 (1954): 141–52.

Morey, C. R. "The Origin of the Fish Symbol, Part 4." *PTR* 9 (1911): 282–83.

Murray, Robert. *Symbols of the Church and Kingdom: A Study in Syriac Tradition.* London: Cambridge University Press, 1975.

Mylonas, George. *Eleusis and the Eleusinian Mysteries.* Princeton, NJ: Princeton University Press, 1962.

Nordström, C. O. "The Water Miracles of Moses in Jewish Legend and Byzantine Art." *Orientalia Suecana* 7 (1958): 78–109.

Ofrasio, Timoteo José M., SJ. "The Baptismal Font: A Study of Patristic and Liturgical Texts." PhD diss. Rome: Pontificio Istituto Liturgico, 1990.

Ouspensky, Leonid, and Vladimir Lossky. *The Meaning of Icons.* Crestwood, NY: St. Vladimir's Seminary Press, 1989.

Pagoulatos, Gerasimo. *Tracing the Bridegroom in Dura.* Piscataway, NJ: Gorgias Press, 2008.

Palardy, William B., trans. *St. Peter Chrysologus: Selected Sermons.* Vol. 3. Washington, DC: Catholic University Press, 2005.

Penn, Michael. *Kissing Christians: Ritual and Community in the Late Ancient Church.* Philadelphia: University of Pennsylvania Press, 2005.

———. "Performing Family: Ritual Kissing and the Construction of Early Christian Kinship." *JECS* 10, no. 2 (2002): 151–74.

Peper, Bradley. "Augustine's Baptismal Analogy of the *Nota Militaris.*" *AugStud* 28 (2007): 353–63.

Peppard, Michael. "New Testament Imagery in the Earliest Christian Baptistery." In *Dura Europos: Crossroads of Antiquity*, edited by Lisa Brody and Gail Hoffman, 103–21. Boston: McMillan Museum of Art, 2011.

———. *The Son of God in the Roman World: Divine Sonship in Its Social and Political Context.* New York: Oxford University Press, 2011.

Perler, O. "Die Taufsymbolik der vier Jahreszeiten im Baptisterium bei Kelibia." In *Mullus: Festschrift Theodor Klauser*, edited by Alfred Stuiber and Alfred Hermann, JAC S1, 282–90. Münster Westfalen: Aschendorff, 1964.

———. "L'inscription du baptistère de Sainte-Thècle à Milan et le 'De sacramentis' de Saint Ambroise." *RivAC* 27 (1951): 145–66.

Phillips, Edward. *Ritual Kiss in Early Christian Worship.* Nottingham, UK: Grove Books, 1996.

Pijoan, Joseph. "The Parable of the Virgins from Dura-Europos." *Art Bulletin* 9 (1937): 592–95.

Plumpe, Joseph C. *Mater Ecclesia: An Inquiry into the Concept of the Church as Mother in Early Christianity.* Washington, DC: Catholic University of America Press, 1943.

Porter, Joshua R. "Oil in the Old Testament." In *Oil of Gladness,* edited by Martin Dudley and Geoffrey Rowell, 35–45. London: SPCK, 1993.

Porton, Gary. *The Stranger within Your Gates: Converts and Conversion in Rabbinic Literature.* Chicago: University of Chicago Press, 1994.

Pryke, J. "John the Baptist and the Qumran Community." *Restoration Quarterly* 4 (1964): 483–96.

Quasten, Johannes. "Das Bild des Guten Hirten in den altchristlichen Baptisterien und in den Taufliturgien des Ostens und Westens." In *Pisciculi,* edited by F. J. Dölger, AC S1, 220–44. Münster Westfalen: Aschendorff, 1939.

———. *Patrology.* 3 vols. Utrecht: Spectrum; Westminster, MD: Newman Press, 1960–75.

———. "Theodore of Mopsuestia on the Exorcism of the Cilicium." *HTR* 35 (1942): 209–19.

Riley, Hugh. *Christian Initiation.* Washington, DC: Catholic University of America Press, 1974.

Ristow, Gunter. "Zur Personifikation des Jordans in Taufdarstellungen der frühen christlichen Kunst." In *Aus der Byzantinischen Arbeit der Deutschen Demokratischen Republik,* edited by J. Irmscher, 120–26. Vol. 2, Berliner Byzantinische Arbeiten 6. Berlin: Akademie, 1957.

Robinson, J. A. T. "The Baptism of John and the Qumran Community." *HTR* 50 (1957): 175–92.

Rordorf, Willy. "Tertullians Beurteilung des Soldatenstandes." *VC* 23 (1969): 105–41.

Saller, Richard. *Patriarchy, Property, and Death in the Roman Family.* Cambridge: Cambridge University Press, 1994.

Schumacher, W. N. *Hirt und "Guter Hirt."* Römische Quartalschrift Supplementheft 34. Freiburg im Breisgau: Herder, 1977.

Scott, James M. *Adoption as Sons of God: An Exegetical Investigation into the Background of the Pauline Corpus.* Tübingen: J. C. B. Mohr, 1992.

Serra, Dominic. "The Baptistery at Dura-Europos: The Wall Paintings in the Context of Syrian Baptismal Theology." *EphLit* 120 (2006): 67–78.

Smith, Christine. "Pope Damasus' Baptistery in St. Peter's Reconsidered." *RivAC* 64 (1988): 257–86.

Smith, Jonathan Z. "The Garments of Shame." *HR* 5 (1966): 217–38. Reprinted in *Map Is Not Territory,* 1–23. Leiden: Brill, 1978.

Spinks, Bryan. "Baptismal Patterns in Early Syria: Another Reading." In *Studia Liturgica Diversa: Essays in Honor of Paul F. Bradshaw*, edited by Maxwell Johnson and L. Edward Phillips, 45–52. Portland, OR: Pastoral Press, 2004.

———. *Early and Medieval Rituals and Theologies of Baptism*. Aldershot, UK: Ashgate, 2006.

Staats, Reinhart. "Ogdoas als ein Symbol für die Auferstehung." *VC* 26 (1972): 29–53.

Staehle, Karl. *Die Zahlenmystik bei Philo von Alexandreia*. Leipzig: B. G. Teubner, 1931.

Stauffer, Anita. *On Baptismal Fonts: Ancient and Modern*. Bramcote, UK: Grove Books, 1964.

Stern, Henri. "Le décor des pavements et des cuves dans les baptistères paléochrétiens." In *Actes du Ve Congrès International d'Archéologie Chrétienne: Aix-en-Provence, 13–19 septembre 1954*, 381–90. Vatican City: Pontificio Istituto di Archeologia Cristiana; Paris: Les Belles Lettres, 1957.

Stroumsa, Guy. "The Early Fish Symbol Reconsidered." In *Messiah and Christos: Studies in the Jewish Origins of Christianity*, edited by Ithamar Gruenwald, Shaul Shaked, and Gedaliahu G. Stroumsa, 199–200. Tübingen: Mohr Siebeck, 1992.

Stryzgowsky, Josef. *Iconographie der Taufe Christi: Ein Beitrag zur Entwicklungsgeschichte der christlichen Kunst*. Münster: Verlag von Theodor Riedel, 1885.

Styger, Paul. "Nymphäaen, Mausoleen, Baptisterien." *Architectura* 1 (1933): 50–54.

Sühling, Friedrich. "Die Taube als religiöses Symbol im christlicher Altertum." *RQ Supplementheft* 24 (1930): 150–54.

———. "Taube und Orante: Ein Beitrag zum Orantenproblem." *RQ* 83 (1930): 333–54.

Swift, E. H. *Roman Sources of Christian Art*. New York: Columbia University Press, 1951.

Tabbernee, William. "Revelation 21 and the Montanist New Jerusalem." *ABR* 37 (1989): 52–60.

Talley, Thomas. "The Origin of Lent at Alexandria." *StPatr* 17 (1982): 594–612.

———. *The Origins of the Liturgical Year*. New York: Pueblo, 1986.

Teske, R., trans. *Works of Saint Augustine*. Pt. 1, vol. 25. Hyde Park, NY: New City Press, 1999.

Thiering, B. E. "Inner and Outer Cleansing at Qumran as a Background to New Testament Baptism." *NTS* 26 (1980): 206–77; *NTS* 27 (1981): 266–67.

Tronzo, William. *The Via Latina Catacomb: Imitation and Discontinuity in Fourth-Century Roman Painting*. University Park: Pennsylvania State University Press, 1986.

Underwood, P. "The Fountain of Life and the Manuscripts of the Gospels." *DOP* 5 (1950): 43–138.

Valantasis, Richard. "The Question of Christian Identity in the Early Period: Three Strategies Exploring a Third Genos." In *The Feminist Companion to the New Testament Apocrypha*, edited by Amy-Jill Levine and M. M. Robbins, 60–76. Cleveland: Pilgrim Press, 2006.

Van Roo, William A. *The Christian Sacrament*. Rome: Editrice Pontificia Università Gregoriana, 1992.

Vigne, Daniel. *Christ au Jourdain: Le Baptême de Jésus dans la tradition judéo-chrétienne.* Paris: Librarie Lecoffre, 1992.

Walsh, P. G., trans. *The Poems of St. Paulinus of Nola.* ACW 40. New York: Newman Press, 1975.

Weitzmann, Kurt, ed. *Age of Spirituality.* New York: Metropolitan Museum of Art, 1979.

Werblowsky, Raphael Jehuda Zwi. "On the Baptismal Rite according to St. Hippolytus." StPatr 2 (1957): 93–105.

Wharton, Annabel. *Refiguring the Post-Classical City.* Cambridge: Cambridge University Press, 1995.

Whitaker, E. C. *The Baptismal Liturgy.* London: SPCK, 1981.

Wilken, Robert. *The Christians as the Romans Saw Them.* New Haven: Yale University Press, 1984.

———. "The Interpretation of the Baptism of Jesus in the Later Fathers." StPatr 11 (1972): 268–77.

Williams, Michael A. *The Immovable Race: A Gnostic Designation and the Theme of Stability in Late Antiquity.* NHS 29. Leiden: Brill, 1985.

Wilmart, André. *Analecta reginensia: Extraits des manusrits latins de la reine Christine conservés au Vatican.* Studi e Testi 59. Vatican City: Vatican Library, 1933.

Wilson, Henry A. *The Gregorian Sacramentary under Charles the Great.* London: Henry Bradshaw Society, 1915.

Winkler, Gabriele. "The Appearance of the Light at the Baptism of Jesus and the Origins of the Feast of the Epiphany." Translated by D. Maxwell. In *Between Memory and Hope: Readings on the Liturgical Year,* edited by Maxwell Johnson, 291–347. Collegeville, MN: Liturgical Press, 2000.

———. "The Original Meaning of the Prebaptismal Anointing and Its Implications." In *Living Water, Sealing Spirit,* edited by Maxwell Johnson, 58–81. Collegeville, MN: Liturgical Press, 1995.

———. "The Syriac Prebaptismal Anointing in Light of Armenian Sources." In *Symposium Syriacum 1976,* 317–24. Rome: Pontificium Institutum Orientalium Studium, 1978.

Wischmeyer, W. "Die Aberkiosinschrift als Grabepigramm." StPatr 17, no. 2 (1987): 777–81.

Yarnold, Edward. *The Awe-Inspiring Rites of Initiation.* Collegeville, MN: Liturgical Press, 1994.

———. "Baptism and the Pagan Mysteries in the Fourth Century." *Heythrop Journal* 13 (1972): 247–67.

Yegül, F. *Baths and Bathing in Classical Antiquity.* New York: Architectural History Foundation; Cambridge, MA: MIT Press, 1992.

———. "Baths and Bathing in Roman Antioch." In *Antioch: The Lost Ancient City,* edited by C. Kondoleon, 146–51. Princeton, NJ: Princeton University Press, 2000.

Ancient Writings Index

Subject Index